The Privilege of Being a Physicist

Victor F. Weisskopf

The Privilege of Being a Physicist

W. H. Freeman and Company
New York

Library of Congress Cataloging in Publication Data
Weisskopf, Victor Frederick, 1908–
  The privilege of being a physicist.
  Sequel to: Physics in the twentieth century.
  Includes index.
  1. Physics. I. Title.
QC71.W443 1988 530 88-24532
ISBN 0-7167-1982-7

Printed in the United States of America

1 2 3 4 5 6 7 8 9 0 VB 6 5 4 3 2 1 0 8 9 8

To my children,
Thomas and Karen

Contents

III   Ideas in Physics
67

IV   Two Physicists
155

V   Science and Society
175

Preface

This book presents some of my essays, written over the last fifteen years. It is a sequel to my earlier book, *Physics in the Twentieth Century* (MIT Press, 1972), which contained essays written in the previous fifteen years. These collections reflect my principle interests: natural science, mainly physics; the expression of human creativity, such as in technology, philosophy, and art; and the burning problems of contemporary society, especially the crisis in education, the impact that our modern lifestyles have on the environment, and first and foremost, the mortal threat of confrontation between the superpowers—the nuclear arms race.

In all these fields, great changes and new developments took place during the last fifteen years. I noticed them when I went through the preparation of my essays for republication in this book. Many of my former statements are no longer appropriate. New discoveries in science have occurred; new attitudes toward political situations have developed. I had to change and amend some parts, adding remarks and explanations to adapt these essays to the spirit of the times in which the book is published.

Fewer amendments were called for when my first collection of essays appeared in 1972. The recent past witnessed faster development in science and in human relations. I consider this a desirable change. Science has become more lively and innovative, and the political tensions of the period covered by the first volume were so threatening that recent turns for the better are a welcome change.

This collection is accessible to most readers, whether or not they have a knowledge of physics. The most technically difficult essays are found in Part III, Ideas in Physics. The reader can follow the flow of the concepts in these essays though without mastering the vocabulary.

The lasting influence of Niels Bohr on my thinking is more visible in this volume than in the previous one, particularly in the essays, "Art and Science," "The Frontiers and Limits of Science," and "The Double-Edged Sword Called Technology." Bohr's concept of complementarity plays an essential part.

I would like to express my gratitude to my friends, David Hawkins, Philip Morrison, and Cyril Smith for many revealing discussions about the topics in these essays. I also thank Robert Ubell for his invaluable help in arranging the book and in making the essays more readable and understandable and Elaine Cacciarelli for her assistance with the manuscript.

I

The Life
of a Scientist

1

The Privilege
of Being a Physicist

A physicist enjoys certain obvious privileges in our society. He is reasonably paid; he is given instruments, laboratories, complicated and expensive machines, and he is asked not to make money with these tools, like most other people, but to spend money. Furthermore he is supposed to do what he himself finds most interesting, and he accounts for what he spends to the money givers in the form of progress reports and scientific papers that are much too specialized to be understood or evaluated by those who give the money—the federal authorities and, in the last analysis, the taxpayer. Still, we believe that the pursuit of science by the physicist is important and should be supported by the public. In order to prove this point, we will have to look deeper into the question of the relevance of science to society as a whole. We will not restrict ourselves to physics only; we will consider the relevance of all the natural sciences, but we will focus our attention on basic sciences, that is to those scientific activities that are performed without a clear practical application in mind.

The question of the relevance of scientific research is particularly important today, when society is confronted with a number of immediate, urgent problems. The world is facing threats of nuclear war, the dangers of overpopulation and famine, mounting social and racial conflicts, and the destruction of our natural environment by the by-products of ever-increasing applications of technology. Can we afford to continue scientific research in view of these problems?

I will try to answer this question affirmatively. My comments will emphasize the diversity in the relations between science and society; there are many sides and many aspects, each of different character, but of equal importance. We can divide these aspects into two distinct groups. Science is important, on the one hand, in shaping our *physical* environment; on the other, in shaping our *mental* environment. The first refers to the influence of science on technology, the second to the influence on philosophy, on our way of thinking.

Technology

The importance of science as a basis of technology is commonplace. Obviously, knowledge about the way nature works can be used to obtain power over nature. Knowledge acquired by basic science yielded a vast technical return. There is not a single industry today that does not make use of the results of atomic physics or modern chemistry. The vastness of the return is illustrated by the fact that the total cost of all basic research, from Archimedes to the present, is less than the value of ten days of the world's present industrial production.

Perhaps the most beneficial effects of basic science are in the medical applications. Many diseases have been eliminated; the average age of humans has doubled; infant mortality has been reduced to a small fraction of what it was in past centuries; the amount of pain and suffering has been drastically reduced.

We are very much aware today of some of the detrimental effects of the ever increasing pace of technological development. These effects begin to encroach upon us in environmental pollution of all kinds, in mounting social tensions caused by the stresses and dislocations of a fast-changing way of life, and, last but not least, in the use of modern technology to invent and construct more and more powerful weapons of destruction.

In many instances, scientific knowledge has been and should continue to be applied to counteract these effects. Certainly, physics and chemistry are useful to combat many forms of pollution and to improve public transportation. Biological research could and must be used to find more effective means of birth control and new methods to increase our food resources. It has been pointed out many times that our exploitation of the sea for food gathering is still in the hunting stage; we have not yet reached the neolithic age of agriculture and animal breeding in relation to the oceans.

Many of the problems that technology has created cannot be solved by natural science. They are social and political problems dealing with the behavior of man in complicated and rapidly evolving situations. In particular, the questions arise: "What technical possibilities should or should not be realized? How far should they be developed?" A systematic investigation of the positive and negative social effects of technical innovations is necessary. But it is only partly a problem for natural sciences; to a greater extent, it is a problem of human behavior and human reaction. I am thinking here of the supersonic transport, of space travel, of the effects of the steadily increasing automobile traffic, and again, last but not least, of the effects of the development of weapons of mass destruction.

Physical Environment

What role does basic science have in shaping our physical environment? It is often said that modern basic physical science is so advanced that its problems have little to do with our terrestrial environment. It is interested in nuclear and subnuclear phenomena and in the physics of extreme temperatures. These are objectives relating to cosmic environments, far away from our own lives. Hence, the problems are not relevant for society; they are too far removed; they are studied for pure curiosity only. We will return later to the value of pure curiosity.

Let us first discuss how human environment is defined. Ten thousand years ago, metals were not part of human environment; pure metals are found only very rarely on earth. When man started to produce them, they were first considered to be esoteric and irrelevant materials and for thousands of years were only used for decorative purposes. Now they are an essential part of our environment. Electricity went through the same development, only much faster. It is observed naturally only in a few freak phenomena, such as lightning or friction electricity, but today it is an essential feature of our lives.

This shift from periphery to center was most dramatically exhibited in nuclear physics. Nuclear phenomena are certainly far removed from our terrestrial world. Their place in nature is found rather in the center of stars or of exploding supernovae, apart from a few naturally radioactive materials, which are the last embers of the cosmic explosion in which terrestrial matter was formed. This is why Ernest Rutherford remarked in 1927, "Anyone who expects a source of power from transformations of atoms is talking moonshine." It is indeed a remarkable feat to recreate cosmic phenomena on earth, as we do with our accelerators and reactors, a fact often overlooked by the layman, who is more impressed by rocket trips to the moon. That these cosmic processes can be used for destructive as well as constructive purposes is more proof of their relevance in our environment.

Even phenomena as far removed from daily life as those discovered by high-energy physicists may some day be of technical significance. Mesons and hyperons are odd and short-lived particles, but they have interactions with ordinary matter. Who knows what these interactions may be used for at the end of this century? Scientific research not only investigates our natural environment, but also creates new artificial environments, which play an ever-increasing role in our lives.

Mental Environment

The second and most important aspect of the relevance of science is its influence on our thinking, its shaping of our mental environment. One frequently hears the following views about the effect of science on our thought: "Science is materialistic; it reduces all human experience to material processes; it undermines moral, ethical, and aesthetic values, failing to recognize them because they cannot be expressed in numbers. The world of nature is dehumanized as it is relativized; there are no absolutes any more; nature is regarded as an abstract formula; things and objects are nothing but vibrations of an abstract mathematical concept." (Science is accused at the same time of being materialistic and of negating matter.)

Actually science gives us a unified, rational view of nature; it is an eminently successful search for fundamental laws with universal validity; it is an unfolding of the basic processes and principles from which all natural happenings are derived, a search for the absolutes, for the invariants that govern natural processes. It finds law and order—if I am permitted to use that expression in this context—in a seemingly arbitrary flow of events. There is a great fascination in recognizing the essential features of nature's structure, and a great intellectual beauty in the compact and all-embracing formulation of a physical law. Science is a search for meaning in what is going on in the natural world, in the history of the universe, its beginnings and its possible future.

Public Awareness

These growing insights into the workings of nature are not only open to the scientific expert, they are also relevant to the nonscientist. Science did create an awareness among people of all ways of life that universal natural laws exist, that the universe is not run by magic, that we are not at the mercy of a capricious universe, that the structure of matter is largely known, that life has developed slowly from inorganic matter by evolution in a period of several thousand million years, and that this evolution is a unique experiment of nature here on Earth, which leaves us humans with a responsibility not to spoil it. Certainly the ideas of cosmology, biology, paleontology, and anthropology changed the ideas of the average man in respect to future and past. The concept of an unchanging world or a world subject to arbitrary cycles of changes is replaced by a world that continuously develops from more primitive to more sophisticated organization.

Although there is a general awareness of the public in all these aspects of science, much more could be and must be done to bring the fundamental ideas nearer to the intelligent layman. Popularization of science should be one of the prime duties of a scientist and not a secondary one as it is now. A much closer collaboration of scientists and science writers is necessary. Seminars, summer schools, direct participation in research should be the rule for science writers, in order to obtain a free and informal contact of minds between science reporters and scientists on an equal level, instead of an undirected flow of undigested information.

Education

Science also shapes our thinking by means of its role in education. The study of open scientific frontiers where unsolved fundamental problems are faced is, and should be, a part of higher education. It fosters a spirit of inquiry; it lets the student participate in the joy of a new insight, in the inspiration of new understanding. The questioning of routine methods and the search for new and untried ways to accomplish things are important elements to bring to any problem, whether scientific or not. Basic research must be an essential part of higher education. In elementary education, too, science should and does play an increasing role. Intelligent play with simple, natural phenomena and the joys of discovery of unexpected experiences are much better ways of learning to think than any teaching by rote.

A Universal Language

The international aspect of science should not be forgotten as an important part of its influence on our mental environment. Science is a truly human concern; its concepts and its language are the same for all human beings. It transcends any cultural and political boundaries.

Scientists understand each other immediately when they talk about their scientific problems; it is therefore easier for them to speak to each other on political or cultural questions and problems about which they may have divergent opinions. The scientific community serves as a bridge across boundaries, as a spearhead of international understanding.

As an example, we quote the Pugwash meetings, where scientists from the East and West met and tried to clarify some of the divergences regarding political questions that are connected with science and technology. These meetings have contributed to a few steps toward peace, such as the stopping of bomb tests above ground, and they prepared the way for more rational discussions of arms control. Another example is the western European laboratory for nuclear research in Geneva—CERN—in which thirteen nations collaborate successfully in running a most active center for fundamental research. They have created a working model of the "United States of Europe" as far as high-energy physics is concerned. It is significant that this laboratory has very close ties with the laboratories in the eastern European countries; CERN is also equipping and participating in experiments carried out together with Russian physicists at the giant accelerator in Serpukhov near Moscow.

The influence of science on our thinking is not always favorable. There are dangers stemming from an uncritical application of a method of thinking, so incredibly successful in natural science, to problems for which this method is inadequate. The great success of the quantitative approach in the exploration of nature may well lead to an overstressing of this method for other problems. It neglects the irrational and the affective in human behavior, the realm of the emotional, the instinctive world. There are aspects of human experience to which the methods of natural science are not applicable. Seen within the framework of that science, these phenomena exhibit a degree of instability, a multidimensionality for which our present scientific thinking is inadequate and, if applied, may become dangerously misleading.

Deep Involvement, Deep Concern

The foregoing should have served to illustrate the multilateral character of science in its relation to society. The numerous and widely differing aspects of relevance emphasize the central position of science in our civilization. Here we find a real privilege of being a scientist.

He is in the midst of things; his work is deeply involved in what happens in our time. This is why it is also his duty to be deeply concerned with the involvement of science in the events of the day.

In most instances he cannot avoid being drawn in one form or another into the decision-making process regarding the applications of science, be it on the military or on the industrial scene. He may have to help, to advise or to protest, whatever the case may be. There are different ways in which the scientist will get involved in public affairs; he may address himself to the public when he feels that science has been misused or falsely applied; he may work with his government on the manner of application of scientific results to social and military problems.

Scientists face an urgent problem today in regard to the application of scientific research for military purposes. It is questionable whether the present rapid development of new and better weapons improves the security of the nation or leads to an arms race ending with catastrophe. Furthermore, weapons development attracts many of our best scientists because military research makes ample means available, and some of those research problems have undeniable intrinsic technical interest. Civilian technology suffers by this "brain drain," which has seriously reduced our ability to compete with other nations in world markets.

In all these activities the scientist will be involved with controversies that are not purely scientific but political. In facing such problems and dilemmas, he will miss the sense of agreement that prevails in scientific discussions, where there is an unspoken understanding of the criteria of truth and falsehood, even in the most heated controversies. Mistakes in science can easily be corrected; mistakes in public life are much harder to undo because of the highly unstable and nonlinear character of human relations.

How Much Emphasis?

Let us return to the different aspects of relevance in science. In times past, the emphasis has often shifted from one aspect to the other. For example, at the end of the last century there was a strong overemphasis on the practical application of science in the United States. Henry A. Rowland, who was the first president of the American Physical Society, fought very hard against the underemphasis of science, as is seen in the following quotation from his address to the American Association for the Advancement of Science in 1883:

American science is a thing of the future, and not of the present or past; and the proper course of one in my position is to consider what must be done to create a science of physics in this country, rather than to call telegraphs, electric lights, and such conveniences by the name of science. I do not wish to underrate the value of all these things; the progress of the world depends on them, and he is to be honored who cultivates them successfully. So also the cook, who invents a new and palatable dish for the table, benefits the world to a certain degree; yet we do not signify him by the name of a chemist. And yet it is not an uncommon thing, especially in American newspapers, to have the applications of science confounded with pure science; and some obscure character who steals the ideas of some great mind of the past, and enriches himself by the application of the same to domestic uses, is often lauded above the great originator of the idea, who might have worked out hundreds of such applications, had his mind possessed the necessary element of vulgarity.

Rowland did succeed in his aim, although posthumously. He should have lived to see the United States as the leading country in basic science for the last four decades. His statement—notwithstanding its forceful prose—appears to us today inordinately strong in its contempt of the applied physicists. The great success of this country in basic science derives to a large extent from the close cooperation of basic science with applied science. This close relation—often within the same person—provided tools of high quality, without which many fundamental discoveries could not have been made. There was a healthy equilibrium between basic and applied science during the last decades and thus also between the different aspects of the relevance of science.

Lately, however, the emphasis is changing again. There is a trend among the public, and also among scientists, away from basic science toward the application of science to immediate problems and technological shortcomings, revealed by the crisis of the day. Basic science is considered to be a luxury by the public; many students and researchers feel restless in pursuing science for its own sake.

Perspective

The feeling that something should be done about pressing social needs is very healthy. "We are in the midst of things," and scientists must face their responsibilities by using their knowledge and influence to rectify the detrimental effects of the misuse of science and technology. But we must not lose our perspective in respect to other aspects of science. We have built this great edifice of knowledge; let us not neglect it during a time of crisis. The scientist who today devotes his time to the solution of our social and environmental problems does an important job. But so does his colleague who goes on in the pursuit of basic science. We need basic science not only for the solution of practical problems but also to keep alive the spirit of this great human endeavor. If our students are no longer attracted by the sheer interest and excitement of the subject, we were delinquent in our duty as teachers. We must make this world into a decent and livable world, but we also must create values and ideas for people to live and to strive for. Arts and sciences must not be neglected in times of crisis; on the contrary, more weight should be given to the creation of aims and values. It is a great human value to study the world in which we live and to broaden the horizon of knowledge.

These are the privileges scientists enjoy: we are participating in a most exhilarating enterprise right at the center of our culture. What we do is essential in shaping our physical and mental environment. We therefore carry a responsibility to take part in the improvement of the human lot and to be concerned about the consequences of our ideas and their applications. This burden makes our lives difficult and complicated and puts us in the midst of social and political life and strife.

But there are compensations. We are all working for a common and well defined aim: to get more insight into the workings of nature. It is a constructive endeavor, where we build upon the achievements of the past; we improve but never destroy the ideas of our predecessors.

This is why we are perhaps less prone to the feeling of aimlessness and instability that is observed in so many segments of our society. The growing insight into nature is not only a source of satisfaction for us, but also gives our lives a deeper meaning.

2

Threats and Promises

My own commencement took place fifty-two years ago at the University of Goettingen. Since then, I have devoted my life to the science of physics. Much has happened in these fifty-odd years: The destruction of two oppressive regimes in World War II, the subsequent confrontation of two opposing superpowers in the East and in the West, and many—all too many—bloody battles between smaller nations around the globe.

But not everything was negative during this period. Let me turn to the impressive development of science during my lifetime. I spent my first years as a scientist during the birth of quantum mechanics—the key discovery for understanding the material structures we see around us and the properties of solids, liquids, and gases. Only a few years later, physics penetrated the atomic nucleus, the key to understanding the source of solar and stellar energy and the processes of radioactivity. And twenty years later, physics went even deeper into nuclear constituents, discovering a new world of natural phenomena—subnuclear, or particle, physics—the key to understanding the origin of the universe, what happened at the primal bang.

During the same period, molecular biologists succeeded in delving into the innermost processes of the living cell, revealing how nature regulates the development of living entities and how heredity works. Great new discoveries were also made in astronomy and materials science, and new forms of matter were discovered. New celestial phenomena were found—quasars, pulsars, and a pervading radiation that fills space and is probably optical reverberations from the primal bang.

Science provides insight into the way nature works. It is one of the noblest forms of intellectual activity. But its technological applications also provide power over nature. As such, it is both a great boon and a great danger. As we know, the positive effects of the application of science have enabled us to treat many previously incurable diseases. The average life span has almost doubled. Food production has vastly increased. Communication and transportation have made our lives more interesting and exciting. It could be possible for everybody on earth to live a better, more-fulfilled life today if progress were for the benefit of all and not accompanied by an increase in the power of the few.

The application of science to technology has also brought about serious threats. The most critical one is from nuclear science because progress in this area has led to the development of nuclear explosives. Nuclear weapons have changed the human situation at least as much as all other applications of science. At the time of my graduation, war between the great powers was still possible. Indeed, World War II came about because one could imagine containing Hitler and the Japanese aggressors by force, albeit through destruction and at great cost of lives.

Today, it is no longer so. Whatever we may think about the Soviet regime, the time is past when a government that is considered to be objectionable can be removed by force. Nuclear weapons have changed the meaning of war. A war between nuclear powers is no longer acceptable. Hundreds of millions of people would be killed and the earth would be made uninhabitable.

Although the imagination balks at the prospect of a world war, today we witness an ever-escalating nuclear arms race between the superpowers. Only a few hundred bombs are needed to destroy the world. But the opposing superpowers have deployed ten thousands of them and increase their efficiency every year. This is the craziest arms race the world has ever seen: the opponents know very well that the use of even a fraction of their nuclear resources would annihilate both sides.

The other threats of science come from the ever-growing influence of science-based industry in our environment. In the past, the effects of human action on our environment were negligible or sometimes even benign because destructive effects were localized, nature could recover; today, these effects can be overwhelming. The production of carbon dioxide by combustion will change the world's climate. The destruction of the ozone layer by industrial wastes is detrimental to humans, animals, and plants. Our forests are dying from chemical pollutants.

Are there ways to prevent these negative effects? Although scientific research finds more and more effective means of avoiding these threats, not much is done to alleviate the situation because the means are too expensive and many of them would diminish the productivity of our present industry. But, if nothing is done today, it will be too late to save our environment later on.

What can we do against this ever-increasing danger of nuclear war and of pollution? Fourteen years ago, the youth of America helped to end the Vietnam War. Young people forced the government to change its policy. Today you have a much more important task: you can begin to save yourself, your children, and the whole world from nuclear annihilation and devastation of the ecosystem by standing up and joining groups active here and abroad against pollution and the senseless arms race. The arms race is the result of fear. We fear that the Soviets want to spread their power over the world, and they fear our encirclement and our intent to free the world from Communism. But these fears are irrational. Neither side can annihilate the other and take over, because neither side can win a nuclear war.

So stand up and ask for a sensible, rational policy—not unilateral disarmament. Ask for mutual reduction of the numbers to a reasonable limit, enough to deter the other side from a wanton attack. But this is not enough. Even such lower numbers would destroy the world if they were deployed. Stand up and ask for a policy that reduces mutual fear. We have no choice but to share the world with a regime that we dislike in some ways. We cannot change it; we can only hope that it may slowly improve when mutual fear subsides and repressive ideologies decay. So replace confrontation with cooperation. Let us have interdependence so that both partners are interested in peaceful relations. Let us not compete with them in military matters, where they can do the same as we do, but cooperate with them in economic and social actions, helping the poor nations of the world to better their lot by peaceful means. Let us collaborate with them in cleaning up our environment.

Is there any hope the Soviets will follow suit? It will be in their interest. They have always served their interest. One thing is certain: they will not cooperate if we pursue relentless confrontation. We can stop the arms race and turn it around only by finding ways of dealing with the Soviets that are to our mutual advantage and that do not threaten their existence. If fear subsides, their policies will also change.

Stacks/RWK

Fear has always been a critical cause of aggression and internal oppression. Our common enemy, nuclear war and world pollution, may yet bring us together.

It is in your hands to initiate change. And we are already witnessing a beginning. Questions are asked that were not asked before. There is a strong and growing grass-roots movement in the United States and in Europe, including many professional groups and religious organizations. These efforts are directed against the escalating nuclear arms race and toward protecting the natural world. A change in the peoples' attitudes will produce a change in the governments' policies. Some change is already noticeable.

In the East, the process of change will take other forms. There, social and political change are different and take other forms rather than public pressure against their governments. Nevertheless, a shift from confrontation to cooperation on one side may induce similar shifts on the other. It has already begun in the Soviet Union.

Never be fatalistic about the inevitability of nuclear war or the destruction of our environment. There *are* ways to avoid the holocaust and to make the world a cleaner place. We must never cease to search for them. The fate of the world is in your hands. Use your knowledge, your power, and your enthusiasm for a saner policy.

What is needed is full dedication, on ethical and moral grounds, with the aim that nuclear war cannot, must not, and will not occur— dedication that is not always present among the superpower leaders. If we don't succeed, our century will be remembered by unfortunate survivors as the time of preparation for the great catastrophe, and science will be condemned as the main culprit. Our century ought to be remembered as the age in which humankind acquired its deepest insights into the universe and learned to control its martial impulses and its tendency to destroy nature. Let us hope, strive, and act so that it will.

II

Science and Culture

3

Is Physics Human?

There are many people who assert that physics is not "human"; in the view of these people, the methods of physical research and the results obtained from it do not touch on values, emotions, and sentiments that we associate with the word "human." Physics, they claim, has little to do with human relations, with experiences that are important in the world of feelings and emotions, with our being members of a family and a human society, or with any contacts of one human being with another.

There is one side of this alleged "inhumanity" of physics that I would like to exclude from this discussion: I will not discuss the inhumanities caused by the application of physics to technology; nor will I discuss the use of physics discoveries for the design of new weapons of destruction or the detrimental effects of modern science-based technology upon the natural and social environment in which we live. These concerns are in other essays in this book.

The Charges Against Physics

Why is physics as a science considered "inhuman" by so many people, including some of our own students? Let me divide the reasons into four groups, which roughly can be described by the following assertions:

1. Physics is removed from direct human experience.

2. Physics is quantitative and based on mathematics.

3. The basic concepts of physics are too abstract.

4. Much of modern physics deals with matter under conditions far removed from the human environment.

Let us start with the first point, which expresses the feeling that the approach to phenomena in physics does not correspond to our direct experience. What the physicist considers essential in a natural phenomenon is quite different from what the layman may consider so. The physicist tries to isolate certain processes from the flow of events because he is convinced that they contain the essential information he seeks. Those processes do not appear to be "natural" to the layman. I have often observed the astonishment of a layman entering a physics laboratory, where he sees the usual complicated mass of wires, electronics, and other instrumentation. "With these tricks you intend to get at the essentials of nature? It looks as if you torture it and destroy what you are seeking to find out!"

A hundred and fifty years ago, Goethe argued against Isaac Newton along these lines when he ridiculed Newton's method of decomposing white sunlight into colors. He wondered how one could obtain relevant information about bright sunlight by squeezing the light through a narrow slit in a dark room. Goethe's argument was that the methods of physics exclude some essential part of nature from being recognized.

Freunde, flieht die dunkle Kammer,
Wo man euch das Licht verzwickt
Und mit kümmerlichstem Jammer
Sich verschrobnen Bildern bückt.
Abergläubische Verehrer
Gab's die Jahre her genug,
In den Köpfen eurer Lehrer
Lasst Gespenst und Wahn und Trug.

Wenn der Blick an heitern Tagen
Sich zur Himmelsbläue lenkt,
Beim Sirok der Sonnenwagen
Purpurrot sich niedersenkt:
Da gebt der Natur die Ehre,
Froh, an Aug' und Herz gesund,

Und erkennt der Farbenlehre
Allgemeinen ewigen Grund.

—Johann Wolfgang Goethe,
Zahme Xenien.

Friends, escape the dark enclosure,
where they tear the light apart
and in wretched bleak exposure
twist, and cripple Nature's heart.
Superstitions and confusions
are with us since ancient times—
leave the specters and delusions
in the heads of narrow minds.

When you turn your eyes to heaven
skyward to the azure flow,
when at dusk the Sun is driven
down in crimson fireglow
There in Nature's deepest kernel
healthy, glad of heart and sight
you perceive the great eternal
essence of chromatic light.

—Translation by
Douglas Worth and the author.

The second point is based on the undeniable fact that a large part of the population is turned off even by simple mathematical expressions. I will not argue here whether this could be remedied by a better way of teaching mathematics or whether it is altogether unavoidable. In any case, the mathematical formulation of natural events is considered by many an inhuman way of talking about human experiences. It is true that the lack of appreciation for simple mathematics is a formidable obstacle to an appropriate understanding of natural events. I recognized this aspect in its full force one day when I tried to transmit to a person not versed in mathematics the intense joy and satisfaction we experience when we go through Newton's argument that the free fall on Earth of a pebble leads directly to the monthly revolution of the Moon around the Earth, solely on the basis of the natural assumption that the force decreases with the square of the distance. The person was a most sensitive human being, deeply interested in nature and thought, but I was not able to reach my aim because those simple mathematical steps appeared to him as an endlessly drawn out sequence of small logical steps in which all excitement is quenched. Let the poets speak once more—this time it is Walt Whitman:

> *When I heard the learn'd astronomer;*
> *When the proofs, the figures, were ranged in columns before me;*
> *When I was shown the charts and the diagrams, to add, divide,*
> *   and measure them,*
> *When I, sitting, heard the astronomer, where he lectured with much*
> *   applause in the lecture-room,*
> *How soon, unaccountable, I became tired and sick*
> *Till rising and gliding out, I wander'd off by myself,*
> *In the mystical night-air, and from time to time,*
> *Look'd up in perfect silence at the stars.*

A Bridge Between Nations

Recognition and enjoyment of even the most elementary insight in physics requires a knowledge of and a facility with a new language: mathematics. You cannot enjoy poetry in a language unknown to you. In this sense, every introductory physics course is like teaching a foreign language. Here, physics teachers are at a tremendous disadvantage, compared with teachers in the humanities. Compare a freshman course in physics with a freshman course in literature. The literature teacher is able to talk to the student on equal terms directly about the emotions and thoughts engendered by reading a particular work of art. The physics teacher cannot; he must teach the language first. In physics it is a one-sided affair: the teacher teaches, the student learns, whereas in literature, student and teacher are on the same level of approach—if not of sophistication. Elementary language courses always lack excitement until the student masters the new language to some extent and can begin to talk in it.

There is, however, a positive side to the fact that physics requires a new language. This language is international and independent of cultural, social, and political background. Once it is learned, it not only serves us in understanding nature, but it also serves as a bridge between nations and as a step towards a more united mankind.

We now come to the third point. The concepts that are most fundamental for a true insight into the workings of nature are abstract and far removed from our direct, intuitive understanding. There are many examples for this: let me mention concepts such as entropy, electromagnetic fields, relativity, and, last but not least, quantum mechanics, on which our modern physical understanding of the properties of matter is based. The difficulties encountered here are not necessarily mathematical: they are conceptual. Again, much training and experience is needed before we can grasp the significance of these concepts. In contrast to the familiarity culture bestows on concepts used in the humanities, there is little or no intuitive preparation or preformation of these concepts in the culture of today. This is why they appear "inhuman" to the uninitiated. Once assimilated, they will be recognized as an expression of the most significant relations between man and nature.

The fourth point concerns recent physics. Many of the processes that are at the center of interest today seem to be far removed from the ordinary human environment. I refer to nuclear or subnuclear phenomena, astrophysics, low-temperature physics, and plasma physics, to name a few. The interest of today's researchers is centered on matter under very unusual conditions, which are realized in nature only at far away places of the universe. In nuclear physics we study phenomena with interatomic energy exchanges of millions of electron volts; this happens in nature only in the centers of stars or during star explosions. In particle physics, the energy exchanges are at least a thousand times higher; apart from rare cosmic-ray events, such exchanges take place only in neutron stars or perhaps during the first few instants of the big bang. Plasma physics deals with phenomena at unusual pressures and temperatures and so does low-temperature physics. Naturally, astrophysics looks into phenomena far away from us. Why should we be interested in the behavior of matter under such "inhuman" conditions (apart from possible technological applications, a focus we excluded earlier)?

These four points should serve as examples and illustrations of why physics appears "inhuman" to many people. My answer to the question posed in the title of this essay is simply: Yes, physics is indeed human; it can and should be made to appear so in our teaching and writing. This is the first and foremost task of the physics teacher. Let us now go through these four points again with some remarks about how we may emphasize the human angle of our science.

The Case for the Defense

Back to point one. The history of physics shows that deeper insights into the nature of things are best achieved with distance from daily experience. A falling pebble on earth is direct experience. In order to establish a connection with the motion of the moon and the planets, it was necessary to introduce more abstract concepts, such as the force of gravity and its dependence on the distance. That was the way to celestial mechanics and the universality of the gravitational law. Daily experience with heat, boiling water, and steam had to be abstracted, or generalized, in order to achieve a comprehensive view of heat that can be applied to all concrete examples. Direct experience of temperature and change of the state of aggregation developed into thermodynamics, with its more abstract concepts of energy, entropy, and phase transitions. Most impressive was the development of direct experience of electricity in the form of lightning or of friction, to the sophisticated concepts of the electromagnetic field on which our knowledge of material structure rests.

Therefore one way of overcoming this difficulty is to take the historical approach in teaching physics. It may help to clarify the necessity and the importance of studying phenomena especially contrived to maintain "sterile" conditions of strict separation from other influences. It would show that such a seemingly "unnatural" approach to nature has indeed revealed the essential traits of nature and established a deeper relation between man and his environment. It is the great miracle of science that it was such a successful enterprise. As Albert Einstein said: "The most incomprehensible fact of nature is the fact that nature is comprehensible."

Another way to meet this problem is an early involvement of the student in experimental research. He or she will see how important all these wires, amplifiers, and gadgets are for penetrating the essential processes of nature and—if the student has not made a very bad choice of a team—will witness the deeply human enthusiasm with which most physicists try to get at these processes. The student will participate in the immense joy of finding something new, even if it is only a tiny bit of an essential insight.

I have little advice on how to remedy the situation described in point two. It is indeed impossible to transmit most physical insights without the aid of some mathematics. Nevertheless some ideas can be transmitted with a minimum of quantitative thinking. When teaching an introductory physics course, the teacher should make use of qualitative thinking whenever possible. He should be aware that he teaches a language and he should use that language as early as possible for some "poetry"—for the revelation of basic and unexpected connections in nature. The student should see and feel that quantitative relations do indeed reveal essential aspects of nature.

Pattern Into Structure

I have more to say about point three, which deals with the abstract nature of some of the fundamental concepts, but I will restrict myself to some remarks about quantum mechanics. Let me stress the fact that quantum mechanics has introduced the elements of form, shape, and symmetry into physics. Nature—from crystals to flowers—is full of ever-recurring characteristic shapes and symmetries. There must be a fundamental reason for the typical properties of materials and forms that we observe in the flow of natural events. This reason is found in quantum mechanics: the wave nature of electrons forces them into typical patterns, the shapes of standing waves in the spherically symmetric Coulomb field. These shapes are the fundamental patterns of nature and the basis of all the shapes we observe—the German language has a better expression: *die Urformen der Natur* (roughly translated, the primal forms of nature). This "morphic" character of quantum mechanics was pointed out to me by Laszlo Tisza of MIT, who emphasized the basic importance of this trait (see essay seven).

These forms exhibit not only the typical shapes of atoms but also a stability against changes and an ability to regenerate after having been perturbed by influences from their surroundings. Nature combines these patterns, puzzle-like, into molecular structures showing the ever recurring variety of substances that we find in our environment—from minerals to the macromolecules that are the basis of life.

The significance of quantum mechanics becomes clearer when we realize that only the wave–particle duality can give us the stable, regenerating patterns that form the basis of nature. Classical physics, with its atoms as planetary systems, is incapable of reproducing the most obvious facets of nature. Indeed quantum mechanics is a simpler explanation of the nuclear atom than is the classical theory. The quantization of electron orbits and the simple superposition laws make quantum mechanics a much easier theory for treating the motion of electrons under the influence of nuclei than classical mechanics. Unfortunately, the difficult classical problem is not merely an academic task; it occurs in plasma physics when high temperatures force electrons into highly excited orbits whose dynamics are the same as that of the classical motion. Plasma physics indeed poses almost intractable problems that are much more complicated than the quantum mechanics of atoms at low excitation.

The Physics of the Far Away

We now come to point four, which stresses the apparent remoteness from human interest of some of the topics in recent physics, such as particle physics or astrophysics. For astrophysics, strangely enough, no strong defense is needed against this accusation. Studies of the universe and its strange objects have always attracted the minds of the general public. Today the objectives of these fields have become even stranger—I am thinking of neutron stars, quasars, and black holes—and the history of the universe has become a subject of scientific research. Questions about the beginning and the end of everything are coming within the reach of science, and there appear to be even observations of some of the reverberations of the big bang with which everything began: a cool radiation filling the universe. These questions have a strong human appeal, although they are dealing with objects enormously far away in time and space from the human scene. Perhaps this is so because these questions are the same ones treated by the old mythological and religious traditions; there is an innate urge to know about the ultimate whence and whither.

The situation is different in nuclear and particle physics. Here we also deal with phenomena far removed from our terrestrial environment. Tremendous efforts are spent in building accelerators to produce the processes under investigation. The seeming lack of human appeal of these studies comes from the question of why one should be interested in processes that need such "inhuman" efforts to realize. Again I leave out the important problems and promises that nuclear technology has posed.

I think that there are direct answers to this question that show the fundamental relevance and importance of studying nuclear and subnuclear processes. Unfortunately, the scientists engaged in this work have not exerted enough efforts to communicate with the public and have not shown enough eloquence and persuasion to convince students and outsiders of the true significance of their work. It seems to be more difficult for them than for astronomers to do so, probably because the innate urge to know about the innermost structure of matter is not as strong as the urge to know about the cosmos at large.

There are many ways to argue against point four; I will mention only a few. First of all, it is probably correct to say that much more matter in the universe is found under conditions where nuclear processes are active than where molecular physics of the terrestrial kind (including life) is relevant. Indeed, nuclear processes are the source of stellar energy and therefore are the precondition for human existence.

In modern particle physics the situation may be different, because the necessary energy exchanges that produce the phenomena studied in that field are so large that even the interiors of stars are not hot enough to bring them forth. Perhaps only the particles within neutron stars get near such energy levels. Only during the first moments of the big bang were conditions possibly such that the processes produced with our big accelerators occurred abundantly. However, there is a certain spirit of romance and human adventure in the endeavor to produce processes of nature in our laboratory that reach back to the early times of our universe. We explore and excite new worlds of phenomena that, under ordinary conditions, lie dormant in the deepest confines of matter.

Molecular Architecture

Today we have a basis for understanding chemical processes: the quantum mechanics of the electric interaction between atomic nuclei and electrons. We understand the principle, if not the details, of why electrons and atomic nuclei form molecules of all sorts, including the macromolecules that are the basis of life. There is one essential feature that is basic for the structure of molecules: the large mass difference between nuclei and electrons. Nuclei are between a thousand and ten thousand times heavier than electrons. This ratio is responsible for the "architecture" of molecules, for structural properties such as the helical form of DNA. It makes it possible for nuclei to have well-defined positions in the molecule, whereas the electrons, with their low mass, act as the distributed glue to the structure. Without this large mass ratio there would be no molecular architecture.

Why are nuclei so heavy? They consist of protons and neutrons that are about 2000 times heavier than the electron, but the reasons for this weight are essentially unknown to us. We believe that this difference in mass may come from the fact that the nucleons—protons and neutrons—are the source of the nuclear force which is much stronger than the electric force emanating from the electron. The only way to get at the explanation of this mass difference is to study the internal structure and dynamics of the nucleon; this is the object of particle physics.

Another fundamental question bearing on the structure of matter is the nature of electric charge. Why does it occur only in multiples of e, the electronic charge? The reason for that value and no other is completely unknown. In particular, the fact that e^2 is 137 times smaller than the product hc of Planck's constant and the light velocity is of fundamental significance for the structure of matter. If e^2 and hc were equally large, the world as we know it could not exist! The study of this problem is also part of modern particle physics. By trying to solve these fundamental problems of human existence, physicists have been forced to penetrate deeper and deeper into the innermost regions of matter. A whole new world of mesons, hyperons, and quarks was opened up that demonstrates how nature is so much richer and multifaceted than the human mind could ever have conceived.

The Urge to Find Out

Let me come back to the question, Is physics human? I definitely would answer this question in the positive. It is human because it is nothing but a highly developed form of the urge to find out where we are in the environment into which we were born. This urge is common to all people, which explains why it is an activity in which human beings from all countries and cultures can and do participate equally.

This supernational character of the scientific community is an important element of the human side of science. Scientists, in particular physicists, often have contributed to better understanding among nations even in nonscientific issues. The Pugwash movement is an example of the ability of scientists to approach sensitive questions with greater ease and less danger of misunderstandings because of the supernational character of science. CERN, the high-energy research center in Geneva where the European nations have been able to achieve a degree of collaboration impossible to attain in other fields, is perhaps another example.

In this essay I have endeavored to show that physics is indeed a very human activity in that it expresses the relation between nature and man, a relation that becomes ever more intimate and involved because of the growing understanding of nature by human beings. This growth has been rather fast during this century. It has led to an ever more rapid growth of technical applications, with both beneficial and detrimental effects on our way of life.

This rapid growth has had effects of a more philosophic character. I believe that some of the aversions to physics and to science in general are connected with the rapid growth of science. It has led to the generally accepted claim that, in principle, science can and will find an explanation for every human experience.

I am not so sure that this claim is justified—but even if it were, the scientific explanation of a human experience does not necessarily touch all aspects of this experience. Indeed, in some cases it may not include the most relevant aspects. A simple example is the phenomenon of an artistic experience, say the enjoyment of a Beethoven sonata. It can be interpreted acoustically or neurophysiologically or even psychologically. However, there is something in that experience that is not covered by these scientific descriptions; yet that something is probably the most relevant part of it.

There are many other examples in the relations between human beings and between man and nature in which scientific interpretation may not cover all the aspects of human experience. This is particularly so for those aspects that are connected with concepts such as love, dignity, and ethics. Perhaps the recognition of the intrinsic value of physics could be enhanced if there were a greater awareness of the fact that science is only one way—albeit a very important one—of establishing a relation between mankind and its natural and social environment.

4

Teaching Science

We often hear about the crisis in education. While it may seem like an abstract concept, the crisis is all too real. In particular, our approach to science education needs to be improved. It is our real "window of vulnerability." Unfortunately, much less is done about it than about the imagined weapons vulnerability.

Many arguments designed to improve the situation have been presented. A popular one exhorts, "Improve science education to increase our competitive edge in the world market." This is a poor argument. The United States lost its competitive edge because most of its effort and ingenuity has gone into other things, especially the military. At best, reestablishing our competitive position will be a byproduct of quality education.

Another argument goes like this: "Science education permits people to understand our political, social, and technical environment." Certainly a better argument, but still that result should be a byproduct of education—not its principal purpose.

Perhaps the best formulation I have found is this: "Quality science education contributes to a more interesting and thoughtful life by instilling a deeper awareness of what we see around us." Yes, that is its true purpose. After all, science is part of our culture. It contributes to our pleasure in seeing, understanding, and admiring the world around us—something that I like to call the "joy of insight," a sense of wonder about nature.

Science does not provide answers to definite questions. It is not flat knowledge, formulae, names. Richard Feynman, in a wonderful essay, relates how he came to science through his father's guidance. He and his father once went for a walk in the woods and Richard asked, "What is the name of that bird?" His father replied, "Well, I can tell it to you, but what is the use? We have one name, the Chinese another. But names are not essential. The essential things are how the bird uses its wings to fly, how and what he eats, how he gets little ones, and how he came to be in the course of evolution. That is true science."

Science is curiosity, discovering things and asking why. Why is it so? Indeed, science is the opposite of knowledge. Science asks the why and how questions and therefore is the process of questioning, not the acquisition of information. We must always begin by asking questions, not by giving answers. We must create interest in things, phenomena, and processes.

Sometimes it's easy to draw attention to topical phenomena; for example, the tornados that ravage our country. One might show how tornados somehow are connected to vortices flowing out of the bathtub. How do these effects come about? We can also discuss different forms of energy encountered in daily life: kinetic, solar, and nuclear energy, heat, electricity, and gravity. Where do these forms of energy come from? How are they produced? How important are they to us? And we must never forget the social significance of it all.

A few weeks ago I had a discussion with a class of junior high school students about energy: What is good and what is bad about energy—kinetic energy, for example. The children supplied wonderful answers, some saying that it is good that we can quickly go from one place to another by car, plane, or train. But what's bad about it, I wondered? "Well," one student raised his hand and replied, "Shooting a gun. That's bad kinetic energy." A wonderful answer. Of course, the same can be said about other forms of energy. And when you finally come to nuclear energy as used in making atomic bombs, you are in the middle of the gravest problem we face and that our children ought to face too, optimistically, not with passive fatalism.

We must not overlook one fact: youngsters and adults cannot learn if information is pressed into their brains. You can teach only by creating interest, by creating an urge to know. Knowledge has to be sucked into the brain, not pushed into it. First, one must create a state of mind that craves knowledge, interest, and wonder. Indeed, that's largely our duty. Then we must help children find knowledge, by hinting, guiding, evoking questions. "Wrong" questions are often more instructive than "right" ones. And as much as possible, we must avoid frontal learning, with the teacher talking and students listening.

I know this is not easy. The first difficulty is the curriculum. Teachers must cover what is in the curriculum. The problem of the curriculum is an issue that teachers and scientists must confront seriously. At the start of a course, I frequently say to my students, "I will not cover the subject, I will try to uncover part of it." It is more important to understand a smaller part of your subject completely and in depth than to have a vague idea of the larger field. Only then can students become aware of what "understanding" means.

As teachers, you face principals, departmental tests, SATs, and the like. We must work together to reevaluate the whole question of what we mean by "necessary" knowledge. Actually, students don't need to know so much. "Oh, he doesn't even know the chemical formula for alcohol," some might say in despair. You don't need to know the details, if you know where to find them. Youngsters should be able to see what the essential question is: alcohol is made up of molecules and each molecule is made up of atoms. Which ones? Look it up in the chemistry book! Only then will they get the idea of what science *is*, not simply what it *says*, and then they will become eager to know more, not less.

Unfortunately, interest in science among our students is falling rapidly, and because teachers' salaries are inadequate, it is difficult to encourage gifted students to go into teaching. Only the most dedicated do, but there are not many who are prepared to sacrifice their own well being for a higher purpose.

There is also the question of recognition. High-school teaching is not appreciated as a great and important profession. In Europe, where I was raised, high-school teachers are called professors and given their due recognition. The degree of social status they achieve attracts bright students to the profession.

American teachers also lack the time to think, to prepare innovative teaching, and to encourage intellectual renewal. They are burdened with paperwork, custodial supervisory activities, lunchroom supervision, and other tasks unrelated to education. Financial support is required to permit teachers to be free of these burdens.

Moreover, teachers are handed a curriculum over which they have no influence, when they should be participating in creating their own curriculum, leaving enough freedom and time for them to choose their own subjects and ideas. Yet today the demand is for a still more comprehensive curriculum and for even more comprehensive tests. Educators say that students do not absorb enough science. And so the curriculum forces teachers to cover more subjects, instead of un-covering fewer.

To make matters worse, there are too few qualified teachers. Fifty percent of new science teachers in our high schools today are not really qualified. Many have never learned anything about science. Frequently, they must prepare assignments by quickly reading text-books before class.

We are faced with hard tasks. We need the active collaboration of teachers, principals, superintendents, industry, and the universities. And we need the understanding of the public and Congress. Industry is already beginning to see that it will suffer—if it has not already been harmed—by the lack of sufficient numbers of scientifically trained professionals. On average, American industry spends $750 per year per employee for educational development. IBM actually spends $1500 per employee.

Government and congress is about to change their attitudes toward education. So much can be done with funding from public and private sources. Schools and industry and high schools and colleges can offer exchanges. High-school teachers should be able to spend some time in universities or industrial laboratories, activities that will surely improve their social status. High-school teachers should be given sab-baticals to participate in the activities of other schools, to change their methods, to be challenged by new ideas.

Another approach is to create Chatauqualike courses, where teachers are paid to get together for at least a week during vacations to discuss better ways of teaching.

Most important of all, these activities must be in the hands of teachers themselves, who will plan and organize them. Otherwise, the material is pressed into their brains, rather than emerging from their own initiative.

Science is an important part of the humanities because it is based on an essential human trait: curiosity about the how and why in our environment. We must foster wonder, joy of insight. Such attitudes are crucial not only in the natural sciences but in human relations, social issues, politics, and art. We must be concerned, ask questions, and see things from different angles. There are no pat answers; there is no flat knowledge. Science can foster an open attitude, helpful in other human activities and culture. It can give us a much fuller, more meaningful life.

5

Art and Science

What could be more different than science and art? Science is considered a rational, objective, cool study of nature; art is often regarded as a subjective, irrational expression of feelings and emotions. But is that so? One can just as well consider scientific discoveries as the products of imagination, of sparks of sudden insight, whereas art could be viewed as the product of painstaking work, carefully adding one part to the other by rational thinking. Surely art and science have something in common: Both are ways to deal with experience and to lift our spirits from daily drudgery to universal values. But the roles of art and science in society certainly are very different. Science, unfortunately, is a closed book for most people outside the scientific community; its influence on society, however, is decisive in two ways. One is through science-based technologies that have fundamentally changed the social texture of society and our style of life. The other is by means of the philosophical implications of scientific insights, which, it is often asserted, support a materialistic, rationalistic view of the world around and within us. The role of art is not so easy to define. It does, or should, contribute to a deeper appreciation of our existence and should help us to endure and understand the human predicament. Unfortunately, much of contemporary art is also a closed book to many.

Let us start with the diversity of human experiences. There are outer and inner experiences, rational and irrational ones, social experiences between two or many human beings, and experiences with the non-human part of nature. Our reactions to these experiences are manifold and varied. We think and ponder about them. We are oppressed or elated by them. We feel sadness and joy, love and hate. We are urged to act, to communicate them to others. We try to relate them to patterns of living. We make use of them to improve our lives and to avoid material and emotional hardships. We also use them to influence people by rational or emotional arguments and, unfortunately, also by the application of brutal force.

All these experiences and the way we deal with them are the raw material of human creativity. What are its manifestations? The creative spirit shapes it into various forms of most diverse character: myths, religions, philosophies, diverse arts and literatures, architecture, sciences, medicine and technology, and social structures. These manifestations are directed toward many aims, practical and spiritual. Their actual effects upon humankind are sometimes positive and constructive, sometimes negative and destructive, and often with little relation to what the creators intended.

Space Is Blue

Most forms of human creativity have one aspect in common: the attempt to give some sense to the various impressions, emotions, experiences, and actions that fill our lives, and thereby to give some meaning and value to our existence. Meaning and sense are words difficult to define but easy to grasp. We cannot live without meaning—oh, yes, we can, but a meaningless life would seem empty and cold. The crisis of our time in the Western world is that the search for meaning has become meaningless for many of us.

Different forms of human creativity often seem to be incommensurable, mutually exclusive, or even contradictory. I believe, however, that a better word is *complementary,* a term that has acquired a more focused significance since its use by Niels Bohr. My main purpose here will be to point out the complementarity, in Bohr's sense, between the different avenues of human creativity—in particular between the arts and sciences. Even within physics itself, we deal with concepts and discourses that on the surface are contradictory and mutually exclusive but that on a deeper level are what Bohr aptly has called complementary. They represent different aspects of reality; one aspect excludes the other, yet each adds to our understanding of the phenomenon as a whole. The quantum state of an atom evanesces when it is observed by a sharp instrument designed to locate the electron.

The state is restituted when the atom is left alone and given enough time to return to its original state. Both aspects—quantum state and location—are complementary to each other; they are necessary concepts to provide a full insight into atomic reality.

Similar complementarities appear in all fields of human cognition, as Bohr often pointed out. They have to do with the question of relevance. In the atom, the wave picture (quantum state) is relevant for certain aspects of its reality, the particle picture for others. There are different ways of perceiving a situation, ways that may seem unconnected or even contradictory but that are necessary for understanding the situation in its totality. A simple example may suffice for the moment. A waterfall may be an object of scientific study, in which case the velocity distribution and the size of the droplets and their electric charge are relevant; it may be something to be technologically exploited as a source of water power, in which case the quantity of water, its height and smoothness of flow are relevant; ot it may be the object of a poem describing the beauty or the overwhelming force of the phenomenon; then very different properties become relevant. Consider that well-known conversation between Felix Bloch and Werner Heisenberg about the subject of space. Bloch was reporting to Heisenberg some new ideas about the relevance of certain mathematical structures in space when Heisenberg, his mind drifting into other avenues of experience, exclaimed, "Space is blue and birds are flying in it!"

The Holistic Approach

We face a world of many dimensions and infinitudes, of which the world of the natural sciences is only a subdivision. The separation of the natural world outside ourselves from the internal world of the mind is an ever-recurring problem of philosophy and subject to questions and doubts.

Natural science, of course, is built upon some kind of separation of the external from the internal world; it regards the objects of its study as distinct and independent from the emotions and psychologic reactions that they may evoke in the observer. Emotions and the inner self are not excluded as objects of scientific investigation. But such studies are performed in a detached way, either by studying what is going on in the human brain by the methods of neurophysiology or by systematically analyzing human emotions and reactions with the methods of psychology.

Science is a relatively new creation of the human intellect. Before its appearance, the approach to human experience was essentially holistic. Myths, religions, and philosophies try to derive the totality of human experience, external and internal, from one leading principle and thus to provide it with a well-defined meaning. Everything is connected and represents the will of one or many gods; every event, every phenomenon is an expression of a deeper meaning strongly felt but only partially revealed when the course of events is interpreted. That deeper meaning need be neither logical nor unidirectional; it was often regarded as the result of warring forces, such as good and evil.

Art has always played an essential part in this holistic approach. It was, to a large extent, a servant of myth, religion, and philosophy and was a most suitable instrument to transmit holistic thoughts and emotions, transforming them into concrete, visible, or audible entities. Think of Greek sculpture, Homer's poetry, the Gothic cathedrals, and Bach's Passions. There they stand, works of art, representing ideas and symbols immediately and directly, with all their spirit and power. They impose upon the beholder their meaning and their general validity, their grandeur, terror, or beauty—if the beholder is part of the human soil from which the myths or religions grew.

It is often said that another source of art exists: the immediate urge to embellish and decorate objects of special value and significance. There is not much difference between this and the intensification of symbols and ideas. The embellished objects are symbols that art renders significant; they acquire a meaning beyond their ordinary role through decoration and embellishment.

Whenever the mythologic and religious fervor begins to weaken, art tends to separate from these realms and acquire an independent role, replacing myth and religion to an increasing extent. It continues to create realizations of ideas and emotions that are important and significant in the culture of the time, although they may no longer be derived from a myth or a religion. Art serves as a powerful synthesizer of human experiences of the day, presenting to us messages of joy or sadness, greatness or meanness, beauty or terror, salvation or torture that cannot be transmitted in any other way. Two periods of separation between art and religion are well-known: one is that of Hellenistic-Roman art; the other is our own period, which started in the Renaissance and has resulted in an almost complete separation in modern times.

Art, just like myth and religion, is a holistic approach to human experience. Every true work of art transforms and molds a complex of many varied impressions, ideas, or emotions into a unique entity;

it compresses a great variety of internal or external perceptions into a single creation. It expresses a whole truth—if this word may be applied here—and not a partial one or an approximation of the truth. If it is a great work of art, it cannot be improved, changed, or redone in order to comply with new insights that were not taken into account in the first creation. It is an organic whole that says what it says in its own special way. At different epochs it may mean different things to the beholder or listener or reader; it will be interpreted in different ways: it may have more meaning at one period and less at another. It may mean different things to different groups of people, but it is valid and effective only in its original form. As R. M. Rilke said:

> Der Dichter einzig hat die Welt geeinigt
> Die weit in jedem auseinander fällt.
> Das Schöne hat er unerhört bescheinigt
> Und da er selbst noch feiert was ihn peinigt
> Hat er unendlich den Ruin gereinigt
> Und auch noch das Vernichtende wird Welt.

Here is a translation by Douglas Worth:

> Only the poet gathers what keeps falling
> Apart in each of us unformed and furled;
> In one hand beauty past belief enthralling
> The other full of darkness so appalling
> Yet sanctioned by his holy touch. Then balling
> The two together he remakes the world.

The Scientific World View

The holistic tradition, which stresses totality of human experience, suffered an important change with the birth of natural science. A new era began. Instead of reaching for the whole truth, people began to ask limited questions in regard to the natural world. They did not ask questions such as "What is matter?" "What is life?" "What is the nature of the universe?" Instead, they asked. "How does the water flow in a tube?" "How does a stone fall to earth?" "What makes the blood flow through the veins?" General questions were shunned in favor of investigating separable phenomena, where it was easier to get direct and unambiguous results.

Then the great miracle happened: from the systematic study of many detailed phenomena, whose relevance was not obvious at all at the start, some fundamental insights into the basic structure of nature emerged. The renunciation of immediate contact with absolute truth, the detour through the diversity of experience, paid off. The restraint was rewarded as the answers to limited questions became more and more general. The study of moving bodies led to celestial mechanics and an understanding of the universality of the gravitational law. The study of friction and of gases led to the general laws of thermodynamics. The study of the twists of frog muscles and of voltaic cells led to the laws of electricity that were found to be the basis of the structure of matter. Some sensible answers emerged to those holistic questions that were shunned at the beginning. The nonholistic approach led to holistic results.

The holistic character of scientific insights differs greatly in character from that of myth, religion, and art. First, it does not directly include what we commonly refer to as the human soul, our feelings of awe or desolation, our ambitions, our convictions of right or wrong. It includes only the physiological and psychological phenomena accompanying these realities. The holistic character refers to the unity of natural phenomena outside our "souls." Second, and equally characteristic, scientific insights are always tentative, open to improvement and change; they have a restricted validity, appearing as incomplete perceptions of parts of a greater truth hidden in the plenitude of phenomena, a truth that is slowly but steadily revealed to us. Every step toward more insight adds to the value of previous steps. Scientific creations do not stand, each by itself, as works of art; they cannot be regarded as separable entitites. They are parts of a single edifice that is collectively assembled by scientists and whose significance and power are based upon the totality of contributions. In German this is referred to by the untranslatable term *"Das 'Weltbild' der Naturwissenschaften."* Newton said, "I stand on the shoulders of giants." His work, like that of Einstein and other great scientists, comprises only a few stones of this edifice—albeit rather large ones at pivotal locations.

It must be said, however, that there is something like a collective edifice of achievement in the arts. There is tradition which develops from one period to the next; Mozart could not have written his music without Haydn and the development of baroque music since Bach and Handel; Schubert and Brahms would not have been without Beethoven. Michelangelo's art builds upon Greek art and that of the early Renaissance. We understand a work of art much better when it is considered with the cultural framework of its time. Art grows from a cultural soil fertilized by previous creations. In this sense the artist also "stands on the shoulders of giants."

Art Versus Science

The scientific culture differs from the artistic one in several respects. Here are a few important examples. There exists something that may be called scientific progress. We definitely know and understand more today than we did before. Einstein's theory of gravity is nearer to the "truth" than Newton's. If Newton were alive today he would freely, and probably enthusiastically, admit that Einstein's theory is an advance, compared with his own (a statement that is hard to prove; nevertheless it is convincing to every scientist). No such progress can be found in art. There is no reason why a Gothic sculpture should be considered better than a Romanesque one, or why Raphael represents an advance compared to early medieval art, or Mahler compared to Mozart. True enough, there is a tendency to increased sophistication in art as time proceeds. The means of expression become more manifold, varied, and intricate. Of course, a similar tendency exists in the sciences. In the latter case, however, it is connected with a genuine increase of insight into, and understanding of, nature. The increased sophistication of art may have led to a wider scope of subject matter and a greater variety of creative forms but hardly to a more powerful force of artistic expression.

Another characteristic difference between art and science concerns the role and significance of the original creation: the distinction between content and the form in which it is expressed. It is much harder to separate these two elements in art than in science. The way the content is expressed plays an essential role in art; indeed, it is what makes the difference between art and mere description or photography. Any change in the way of expression would change and weaken the content of a work of art. You cannot paraphrase or explain it without greatly diminishing its impact. I remember my literature teacher in high school who asked us to repeat a poem by Goethe "in our own words." What a ridiculous request! The same is true about translations. Evidently they are necessary to provide access to literature that would otherwise remain inaccessible. But a translated poem or novel cannot exert the same impact as the original does on somebody who is well-versed in the language. Nevertheless, commentaries or analyses are useful to deepen the impact of the original work, but they cannot replace it. The weakness of describing the content of a work of art is especially obvious in music, which seems so inappropriate to talk about in words but, after all, the theologians also talk about God.

In science, the situation is very different. The original creation of the scientist, his first publications of the idea, are read and appreciated by the bulk of scientists only for a few years. Later, they are of interest only to historians of science. The important part of the creation is its content, which in most cases is better brought to effect in later presentations, usually by other authors. In most instances, the original creator of a new insight was not fully aware of its significance and of its connection with other fields. It takes time to do so and it is done by scientists with different points of view. For example, any scientist who wants to become acquainted with and appreciate Einstein's work today would read books such as Steven Weinberg's *Gravitation and Cosmology,* instead of Einstein's original papers. Here, we face a major difference to the situation in the arts, where the original creation remains the most effective presentation of its content. It requires considerably higher standards from the artist. As Bertrand Russell said, "In art nothing worth doing can be done without a genius; in science even a moderate capacity can contribute to a supreme achievement." Perhaps we find a parallel with the situation in science when we consider dramatic arts and music, where the performance is an act of interpretation that may change the original significance of the work to the better or worse.

Another factor is the emotional impact of scientific and artistic creations. The work of art represents a personal entity which is transmitted to, and reexperienced by, other individuals as a personal experience. A scientific insight into the workings of nature is an impersonal entity, an abstraction from a multitude of specific direct or vicarious experiences and creative ideas of many individuals; it is understood by other individuals as an impersonal general intellectual entity. The work of art produces in the recipients very personal feelings of joy, sadness, spiritual elevation, or tragic dejection that are an essential part of the message. A scientific idea may also produce feelings and emotions, such as awe, joy of insight, satisfaction, and the like. But they are not an essential part of the message.

It is often said that the role of intuition is a common factor in art and science. Rarely is any advance made in science without an intuitive perception of some idea or of some hidden relations. In art, of course, intuition is the essential driving force of creativity. However, scientific and artistic intuition are not always of the same character. True enough, the first spark of an idea or the first glimpse of some grand unification may come to the scientist in a similar unexplainable flash of insight as an artistic revelation. But, more often than not, scientific intuition comes from an unconscious or half-conscious awareness of existing knowledge or of connections between concepts that have not yet been consciously realized. But any intuitive scientific insight must be rationally validated afterward before it can be incorporated into the scientific edifice. In contrast, artistic intuition is the main instrument of creation and does not require any additional validation; it reigns superior and is the highest instance of judgment over and above the mold of style and fashion.

The Complementarity of Art and Science

Both art and science give us deeper insights into our environment. But this environment is not at all the same. For science (only natural sciences are considered here) it is the natural world in which we live, including our own body and brain. For art, it also contains the natural world, albeit in a different way (remember Heisenberg's space), but it mostly consists of the vast realm of personal ideas, feelings, emotions, reactions, moods, attitudes, and relations between human beings. One might object to this and assert that all these elements are also subject to a scientific approach as phenomena within our brain. This certainly is true, but just as science approaches external natural events in a thoroughly different way than art, so does it approach the internal landscape of what we may call our souls.

This difference has very much in common with Niels Bohr's complementarity. There are several contradictory, mutually exclusive approaches to reality. The scientific approach to a phenomenon is complementary to the artistic approach. The artistic experience evanesces when the phenomena are scientifically explored, just as the quantum state is temporarily destroyed when the position of the particle is observed. We cannot at the same time experience the artistic content of a Beethoven sonata and also worry about the neurophysiological processes in our brains. But we can shift from one to the other.

Both aspects are necessary to get at the full reality of the phenomenon. We may admire the starry sky and the vastness of variety of star patterns, or we may contemplate the physical nature of the stars and star systems, their motions and their developments from the big bang to their present stage. We can be impressed by a clear sunset because of the beautiful blending of colors or because of some thoughts connected with this symbol of the end of a day in human life; however, we can also be impressed by the processes of refraction and scattering of light in the atmosphere by suspended particulate matter.

A similar complementarity characterizes science and religion or myth. Religious approaches to human experiences are contradictory to the scientific one only in a superficial way. The following anecdote may illustrate it. In a Jewish theological seminary, a discussion took place about the proofs of the existence of God. It lasted several hours. Finally, a rabbi got up and said: "God is so great, He doesn't even need to exist!" Existing is generally used as a scientific term; in this sense it obviously does not apply to religious concepts that have an "existence" in a complementary realm of human experience. Jean Hamburger expresses the complementary situation succinctly in his book, *La Raison et la Passion.* "We must accept the idea that man can acquire all kinds of truths. But let us not mix them up; we would risk that the mixture would dissolve them all."

The contrast between complementary approaches is not necessarily between rational thinking and emotional feeling; one can and does talk rationally about emotional impressions and about art, myths, and religion. Yet it is a very different type of discourse—lucid and concise within its own intrinsic scale of values, but fragile and indefinite when judged by the peculiar requirements of scientific intercourse. One view complements the other, and we must use all of them in order to get a full experience of life. Scientists in particular may become aware of this need because their professional life is one-sided: "In the morning I go from mystery to reality; in the evening from reality to mystery." But mystery is another form of reality. No wonder so many scientists are actively or passively interested in music, the most irrational of the arts.

Here again one may look at the situation in complementary ways. True enough, music is "irrational" in the sense that there is no "objective" way to prove what musical passage is right or wrong. But the structure of music is related to structure in science, especially in mathematics. I refer to symmetry, repetition of a passage in a different key, inversions of tunes, and many other topological features. No wonder scientists are attracted by the fugues of Bach.

The vast difference or complementarity of art and science ought to be so obvious that it should need no further comment. But there exists a subgroup of scientists who do not subscribe to this statement. Let us call them the "science chauvinists." They maintain that progress in neurophysiology and brain science will lead finally to an adequate scientific understanding of what is going on in our brain when we create or enjoy a work of art or when we are so spiritually elevated by art or religion that we sense a deeper meaning in it. Going one step further—now the subgroup becomes noticeably smaller—they maintain that we then may be able to create art or replace it scientifically by certain nerve stimulations, because we then would know its neurological function.

The notion of scientific insight into the essence of art is based on a number of fallacies. True, there is no imaginable limit to our understanding of brain action and of the identification of definite nerve processes with emotional, moral, or aesthetic thoughts or feelings. We may expect tremendous progress in this field of science within a few decades. But there are several reasons why there seems to be a definite limit to fundamental scientific understanding of such matters. One reason has to do with the fact that any scientific research is based upon reproducibility of results. Certain phenomena in our souls that are relevant to the arts are not reproducible. Every human being (except identical twins) not only has a different set of genes, but he or she has been subject to a different set of impressions. Some of these differences may be considered irrelevant in certain respects—for example, a medical doctor will treat a disease successfully by the same methods, whether the patient is an Einstein or a half-wit. But for the development of human cultures and traditions the differences become most relevant. Human culture is an amplifier for both the genetic differences and those acquired by experience. A nonrecurring unique combination of such differences makes the artist capable of creating a work of art. It also determines the unique way in which an individual experiences that work of art. How can such a process be scientifically analyzed when it occurs only once? Do we not face here a typical complementary situation between the structure of the nervous system on the one side and the creation and perception of art on the other? Indeed, does not the specific uniqueness of a work of art represent a fundamental obstacle to the application of scientific analysis to the creative and perceptive process?

The same problem also appears in the social sciences. Nonrecurring, unique events occur frequently in the minds of human beings; they have decisive influences on the social fabric of society because of the amplifier effect of human culture. This effect may turn out to be a serious impediment to reliable scientific predictions in the social sciences; it may also be a fundamental difficulty when animal sociobiology is applied to human societies.

I must confess that I may run into the same error that Niels Bohr committed when, some time ago, he argued that the processes of life are complementary to physics and chemistry. He based his conclusion on the fact that a strict chemical analysis of life processes requires the death of the investigated creature. Therefore, he considered it possible that living matter may represent a different state of matter, complementary to the nonliving state, an analogy to the atomic quantum state that is destroyed by an attempt to look at its detailed structure. He was wrong—as the discovery of DNA and all that followed have clearly shown. I do not think that I commit a similar error, but if I do I am in good company. I believe there are fundamental obstacles to a full scientific understanding of the creative processes in art that cannot be bridged over, just as no new physical theory will ever get rid of wave-particle complementarity.

Sense, Meaning, and Hope

Art and science have this in common: they provide meaning and sense to human experience. But the sense of the meaning is thoroughly different. If has been observed that art transforms general experiences into a single and unique form, whereas science transforms detailed single experiences into a general form. Either of the two transformations results in a holistic product: the work of art and scientific insight. But there are vast differences between the two. We have already mentioned the tentative, unfinished character of our scientific perception of nature. It represents only part of a truth that is developed step by step, whereas a work of art is finished and transmits its full message at all times, although the message may not be always interpreted in the same way.

In what sense does the universe make sense? In the sense you sense a sense. Every true scientist feels a sense, consciously or unconsciously. If he did not, he would not go ahead, with that fervor so common among scientists, in his search for something that he calls the truth. Surely a large dose of ambition is mixed into the fervor—acclaim, tenure, a Nobel Prize—but there is no denying that it exists. It is based upon a conviction that what the scientist does is worthwhile and will lead to an increase of insight, something that is great and valuable beyond any doubt, even if the fallibility of humankind makes the wrong use of it. Great insight leads to great power; great power always leads to great abuse.

The decay of a sense of meaning and the increase of cynicism in our culture have also contaminated natural scientists. These trends have shaken the conviction of some members of that community, but there is still a good deal of belief in the purpose and meaning of their collective work. I cannot help feeling that they represent a "happy breed of men" among so many others who grapple with the problems of meaning, sense, and purpose.

The emerging scientific *Weltbild* contains much to support the enthusiasm and fervor of its propagators. The great unifying principles that underlie the plenitude of events become clearer with every decade. An outline of a history of the universe from the big bang to the human brain is taking shape, and it becomes ever more convincing with the discoveries and insights that emerge from year to year. What is more startling and uncanny than the recent observation of the optical reverberation of the origin of the universe in the form of a cold radiation that fills all space? What is more impressive than the steady growth of our insights into the structure of matter, from molecules and atoms to nuclei, electrons, nucleons, and quarks, and our growing understanding of nature's fundamental forces? What is more overwhelming than the recognition of the chemical basis of life, in which the stability of the molecular quantum state emerges as the true basis of the fact that the same flowers appear again every spring?

Do we find a similar fervor and sense of purpose among other groups? Surely we do. We find it among those who are devoted to creative, artistic activities and among those who try to improve the social fabric of our times in many different ways. However, they face a much greater challenge. The problems of natural science are much less messy, much less interwoven with the complexity and fragility of the human mind. It is easier to perceive an underlying order in the flow of natural events if human behavior is excluded.

The decay of previously existing sources for meaning, sense, and purpose—such as myth and religion—has left a great void in our minds, a void that craves to be filled. Every human being craves meaning and sense to his existence. The answers to these cravings must, by necessity, be holistic. They must embrace the totality of human experience and endow it with luster and light. With the decay of myth and religion, all that was left was an autonomous art that has made itself independent of any prevalent religion, and a new, most vigorous intellectual development that is science. Can these two enterprises serve as providers of meaning and sense? Goethe said

> He who has Art and Science also has religion
> But those who do not have them better have religion.

Goethe's remark points out an important element common to both expressions of the human mind: their true significance is not easily accessible to a large part of humankind. Of course, there are many expressions of art, and some of science, that are indeed appreciated by large groups of people—such as folk art, popular science, and science fiction. Pop art, jazz, and rock music play an important role, arousing enthusiasm in large parts of the population. However, these manifestations are not the most effective providers of sense and meaning. The grandest creations and achievements of art and science serve as inspirational sources only to a small minority of humans; their values seem to be unsuitable for a wider spread. The large majority cannot get meaning, sense, and purpose from these sources. They crave some sort of religion, as Goethe says. Perhaps the greatest problem of our day is that this craving is no longer fulfilled by the conventional religions and that there is nothing to replace them.

The kind of meaning that science provides to its perpetrators has not proved satisfactory for this craving, even though everybody is fully aware that we live in an age dominated by science and technology. On the contrary, to a large extent this awareness is tied to practical applications, among which the military ones and the destructive effects of technology on the environment play an important role. The scientific insights into the greatness and unity of the universe, in the large and in the small, have not penetrated much into the minds of the people. This is probably the fault of scientists who do not try hard enough to transmit the elation they feel at the peak moments of their work. They are too much immersed in their narrow specialties and do not seek to express sufficiently the deep connections their insights have provided. It also is partly the fault of the artists and writers of today who neglect this task. Is it not the duty of art to remold all that is great and awe-inspiring in our culture and to lend it a form that stirs the souls of people? Perhaps the great ideas of science are not suitable to inspire outsiders with any true elation.

What is it, then, that contemporary art expresses? It reflects a frantic search for some kind of meaning by trying to go in many hitherto untried directions. We observe an outburst of new ways and forms of expression. From time to time, indeed, something really great and beautiful is created but, more often than not, what we see are the results of wild experimentation for the sake of being different from what has been done before. Perhaps this frantic search is a symptom of a lack of sense and meaning. Perhaps it is a method to arrive at a meaning.

Many creations of contemporary art, especially literature, deal with the tragedy and depth of our lack of purpose and meaning. In this effort our art is powerful, heart-rending, and deeply depressing. It acts as an amplifier of what is meant by the void in the mind; it follows the great tradition of art by elevating this to grand tragedy. Even cynicism has been ennobled by contemporary art. But in it we do not often enough find those ingredients that permeated art in past centuries—beauty and hope. This is perhaps the reason why the classical works of art have retained their power and significance. They seem today even more powerful and significant because they contain many of the ingredients missing in much of contemporary art.

Our material and spiritual world is in disorder and in danger of destruction. The great insights and elations of science, as well as of art, have not much impact on most of the people because these values cannot produce a ground swell of meaning capable of permeating the collective mind. Among the younger generation, however, there are many signs and portents of a craving for sense and purpose and for the dignity of the individual. This ground swell appears in various forms; some are constructive, some destructive. There are promising efforts to improve the social and spiritual climate; there are cults and semireligious sects. All too often some of these cults and sects have led to misconceived mysticism and to a concentration on the inner self, without the necessary relationship to society. There may come a day when scientific and artistic meaning will combine and help to bring forth that ground swell of meaning and value for which there is so great a need. The growing awareness of this need is in itself an important element that brings people together and creates common values and even elations. There is always hope—for hope.

6

The Frontiers and Limits of Science

Since the beginning of culture, man has been curious about the world in which he lives; he has continually sought explanations for his own existence and for the existence of the world—how it was created, how it developed and brought forth life and humankind, and how one day it will end. Early ideas on the subject were developed in mythological, religious, or philosophical frameworks. All these ideas have a common characteristic: they are directed to the totality of the phenomena; they want to account for everything that is. They intend to present the absolute truth by attempting to give immediate answers to the fundamental questions of existence: "Why is the world the way we find it? What is life? What is the beginning and the end of the universe?"

What is Science?

Several hundred years ago, human curiosity took a different turn: instead of reaching for the whole truth, people began to examine definable and clearly separable phenomena. They asked not "What *is* matter?" and "What *is* life?" but "What are the properties of matter?" and "How does blood flow in the blood vessels?"; not "How was the world created?" but "How do the planets move in the sky?" In other words, general questions were shunned in favor of limited ones for which it seemed easier to get direct and unambiguous answers.

By means of this detailed questioning, a framework was created for understanding the natural world. Thus, something like a scientific world view arose in the twentieth century, a synthesis of scientific insights gained over the previous five hundred years.

The world view of natural science differs in two important aspects from the religious, mythological, and philosophical ones. First, it does not directly contain concepts that are connected with the "human soul," such as faith, awe, desolation, happiness, good and evil, and so on. But it does contain these concepts in an indirect way. They appear as manifestations of certain neurophysical processes in the brain.

Second, the insights are "tentative"; they are considered as incomplete preceptions, as parts of a greater truth hidden in the plenitude of phenomena. The insights are not based upon dogmatic principles, revealed to us by divine inspiration, or by some internal sparks of full recognition. What is perceived as "scientific truth" is steadily revealed in partial steps, sometimes big ones, sometimes small ones, and sometimes even steps backward. Some recent knowledge will turn out to be mistaken. It was rare in the past that insights turned out to be outright wrong, but some of them became and will become too limited, not general enough, misconceived, or awkwardly formulated; some will appear irrelevant in view of future deeper insights.

Ten Steps in the Development of the Scientific World View

Here is a selective "al fresco" description of today's scientific world view. We may distinguish ten steps:

1. Unification of celestial and terrestrial mechanics

2. Existence of atomic species

3. Heat as atomic random motion

4. Electricity, magnetism, and optics having a common root: the electromagnetic field

5. Evolution of living species

6. Relativity

7. Quantum theory

8. Molecular biology

9. Quantum ladder

10. Universe

The first step put an end to the previous widespread belief that the heavens are governed by different laws than the earth. The second step, taken at the end of the eighteenth century, led to the recognition that the immense varieties of matter in different forms are the result of combining only ninety-two different species of atoms. The third step is one of the few examples in the history of physics where an important concept was found to be fundamentally wrong; it was the idea that heat is some substance different from ordinary matter, which was named "caloric." The fourth step was one of the great triumphs of nineteenth-century physics, when such seemingly disparate phenomena as electricity, magnetism, and light were found to be manifestations of the same agent. The fifth step, Darwin's theory of evolution, explains how purposeful and goal-directed events occur in a world governed by laws that are devoid of it.

We now come to the insights of the twentieth century. Einstein's theories of relativity imply the unity of time and space, mass and energy, inertia and gravity. A better term for his ideas would be "absolute theory," since they allow us to formulate the laws of nature independently of any system of reference; that is, in an absolute sense.

The seventh step is the most revolutionary of all. Quantum mechanics led to the recognition that there are limits in the atomic realm to the application of "classical" concepts such as location, energy, velocity, and momentum. These limits are codified by the famous uncertainty principle of Heisenberg. This principle acts as a signpost indicating how far classical concepts can be applied. Beyond these limits we encounter specific "quantum states," which are not describable by the classical system of concepts. The quantum states, however, are the basis of our understanding of the character of atomic systems, in particular of their stability and specificity, which are pervading features of our environment. It explains why atoms and molecules keep their identity, their shapes, and their patterns in spite of collisions and perturbations, why gold is gold wherever we find it, and in the last instance, why the same flowers bloom every spring. Heisenberg's principle, therefore, should be called "the limiting principle," because it limits the application of classical concepts to the microscopic world. This name, together with "absolute theory," could have prevented a lot of philosophical abuse.

The eighth step, molecular biology, has revealed the molecular processes that are responsible for the development and reproduction of living species. At present, this field is in the process of enormous expansion. The seminal idea was the recognition of the DNA macromolecule, which contains the code for the production of proteins, the substances that keep the life process going. We are still far from a complete understanding of the functioning and the development of living entities, but those ideas are being steadily expanded; almost every month we hear of some new insight into the chemistry of life.

The ninth point, the quantum ladder, deals with a hierarchy of material systems discovered since 1930. It stems from a typical consequence of quantum mechanics: the size-energy relation. In a somewhat simplified way, it says: the smaller the system, the higher is the threshold energy from the lowest quantum state to the next higher one, and the higher is the energy necessary to activate the system. For example, if we want to change the internal quantum state of an atomic nucleus, we must make use of much higher energies than those necessary to change the states of the atom. Only after the invention of cyclotrons and other particle accelerators that could deliver millions of electron volts was it possible to set nuclear processes into action. A new realm of phenomena was uncovered; nuclear transformations, radioactivity, fission, fusion, and so on. That realm remains dormant in an environment that cannot provide the required energies, such as the terrestrial one, except when man transcends these limits. It is active, however, in the center of the stars, where the temperature is high enough to overcome the nuclear threshold and to initiate nuclear reactions. These are the reactions that provide the power needed to keep the stars shining. A new force of nature makes its appearance, the nuclear force; it is the agent that keeps protons and neutrons together within the nucleus.

When even larger accelerators, providing billions of electron volts, were constructed, another realm of phenomena was discovered: the next higher rung of the quantum ladder. It revealed that the proton and the neutron are also composite systems; their constituents seem to be the "quarks," held together by a new type of force with the uninspiring name "strong force." Indeed, the above-mentioned nuclear force between neutrons and protons may turn out to be a weak effect of these "strong forces," just as the chemical forces that keep the atoms together in molecules and solids are a weak effect of the electronic force that holds the electrons tightly within the atoms.

The manifestations of the internal dynamics of the protons and neutrons include the existence of many excited quantum states of the proton and the neutron, new forms of radioactivity, new types of short-lived particles (the so-called mesons), and copious production and annihilation of antimatter. Antimatter is another form of matter consisting of antiparticles having opposite charges of ordinary particles. Antimatter can be created together with matter when sufficient energy is available. According to Einstein, the energy contained in an entity of mass m is mc^2, where c is the light velocity. Conversely, when matter and antimatter collide, they are both transformed into some other form of energy, for example, radiation.

The energies necessary to activate the phenomena of that highest realm are rarely available in the universe. That is why it is dormant even in the interior of ordinary stars. In all probability, it may play a role in some unusually hot stars, and did so during the first instances of the big bang.

We do not know whether this is the last rung of the quantum ladder; higher rungs may exist. The quarks, of which we already know five different types, may be composite systems, with an even higher threshold; there may exist an internal dynamics within the electron, dormant at currently available energies.

We now come to the last step in our description of the scientific world view, the universe. During this century, a number of discoveries widened our insights into the nature of the universe as a whole. One was the discovery of a steady expansion of the world at large, a fact from which one was led to conclude that there had been a beginning when matter was extremely hot and highly compressed. Perhaps the most uncanny discovery was the observation of a faint radiation seemingly filling the whole of space, with all the properties expected from an optical echo of this early beginning still reverberating through space.

Other discoveries in the depth of the universe revealed stars or star formations of a very uncommon character. The "neutron stars" seem to consist of matter billions of millions times denser than ordinary matter; the "quasars" seem to be galaxies emitting a billion times more energy than normal galaxies; the "black holes" seem to be extremely dense concentrations of matter around which the space is curved to such an extent that matter and light can get in but not out. In spite of the odd character of these objects, they probably can be understood on the basis of our present knowledge of the properties of matter and space.

The discovery of the optical reverberation of the primal bang must be regarded as an uncanny confirmation of the hypothesis that the universe began more than ten billion years ago. Perhaps it was a "new beginning," since, with our present knowledge, we cannot exclude the fact that the observed expansion may be followed by a subsequent contraction, ending with a hot concentration of matter, which would then be the beginning of a new expansion, repeating itself endlessly. The recognition of a beginning of this sort is the culmination of a development that has brought a historical aspect into the physical sciences. With the exception of geology, the physical sciences were for a long time nonhistoric; matter was studied in its present state and its history was not touched. Today, the history of matter is an important concern.

Our present ideas of that history are intimately connected with the hierarchies of material systems that represented the rungs of the quantum ladder. The ladder ranges from ordinary chunks of matter to molecules and atoms, then to nuclei, then to the constituents of nuclei and finally, as of today, to the quarks. The development of the universe went in the opposite direction, down the quantum ladder, as it were. It was a progression from the elementary to the composite, from the less complex to the more complex.

Far in the past, the primal bang occurred that created the elementary particles of matter in a hot state of high concentration and energy; quarks and electrons were formed; later on, in the process of expansion and cooling, the quarks combined into protons and neutrons; the latter ones and the electrons combined into atoms of hydrogen and helium; gravitational bunching of these atoms gave rise to the formation of stars and galaxies; in the center of stars, more complex atoms than hydrogen and helium emerged. Some stars were surrounded by planets where rocks, metals, and condensed matter of all kinds were formed. Under the benign influence of a nearby star like the sun, certain molecules combined into macromolecules on the surface of some planets; some of these macromolecules were able to reproduce themselves, which led to the development of cells, of multicellular species, and finally, of sentient beings.

Many steps in this history are still shrouded in ignorance and guesswork, such as the happenings immediately before or after the primal bang or the detailed steps of the development of life on our planet. This evolutionary history of the world, from the primal bang to the present universe, is a series of gradual steps from the simple to the complicated, from the unordered to the organized, from the hot, formless gas of elementary particles to the cooler structured atoms and molecules, and further, to the still more structured liquids and solids, and finally to the sophisticated, self-reproducing living organisms.

This development is by no means contradictory to the second law of thermodynamics, which requires a continuing decrease of order.

The increase of order and structure at certain restricted spots in the universe was more than compensated by the steady flow of radiative energy into the void during the process of cooling down. The dissipation of that radiation in the depths of space represents much more disorder, in the sense of the second law, than the established order, wherever matter assembled and formed organized structures, whether living or dead.

The Two Frontiers of Science

Natural science develops along two fronts. The first may be called the internal frontier. It is the study of the consequences of atomic interactions. The nature of these interactions is known in principle: electric interaction between atomic nuclei and electrons, regulated by quantum mechanics. The consequences, however, are so manifold and complex that their study was and continues to be the object of a widening frontier of research ever since these interactions have been understood.

There are good reasons for the complexity of the atomic world. Atomic structure permits a tremendous number of combinations and recombinations of atoms, by forming a large variety of specific structures and superstructures. The aptitude for combining is based on the specific patterns of electron quantum states; they allow for innumerable combinations and interlacings of atomic units.

The manifestations of atomic combinations range from the well-known properties of crystals, metals, liquids, and gases to new phenomena appearing only under special conditions, such as the superconductivity of metals and the superfluidity of liquids at very low temperatures, or the phenomenon of a special state of material aggregations called "plasma," which occurs at very high temperatures or very low pressures. The physics of surface films also belong to this category. More and more phenomena and material properties are found, explained, and exploited on that frontier, which comprises the largest part of modern physics and chemistry.

Today, even a good part of biology should be put into this category, in particular, molecular biology. The stability of DNA is based on the quantum states of its constituents. Thus, in principle, the mechanisms of heredity, the growth of living structures, and the evolution of different species are subject to the same laws that govern the relations between atoms and molecules.

All phenomena originating from the interaction of atoms are based on the quantum mechanics of electron motions under the influence of electric forces. We have no reason to doubt it. But this is only a statement of principle. In order to deal with the vast array of these phenomena, special concepts had to be introduced at every step, such as temperature, entropy, chemical bond, viscosity, gel, and many others. In particular, when we get nearer to the living world, the approaches and the modes of description are very far from those revealed by the underlying principles. We speak of genes, proteins, enzymes, hormones, and so on. When we come to the studies of the brain and its actions, the concepts and descriptions are even further removed from the basic structures of electronic quantum states.

Still, much has to be learned in order to get good insights into the complex and involved phenomena of the world of atoms, molecules, liquids, solids, plasmas, molecular chains, and living entities. We face problems of the relations between different aggregates of atoms or molecules, ordered and unordered, of the modes of transition from one structure to the other. Real understanding implies the distinction between the essential and the peripheral. Only when we reach such an understanding—when we are able to separate the relevant from the irrelevant—will the phenomena appear no longer complex but intellectually transparent.

We now come to the second frontier of natural science, which may be called the external frontier. It deals with the higher rungs of the quantum ladder, with the explorations of realms of nature that lie beyond currently understood principles. We know for sure that the atomic realm is based on the well-known electric forces between electrons and atomic nuclei. But the forces between protons and neutrons, the forces between quarks, and the forces that regulate radioactive decay are not yet as satisfactorily established. These are the frontiers of nuclear physics, of particle physics, and of certain parts of astronomy and cosmology. In all these fields we deal with nonterrestrial phenomena that are activated by energy exchanges much larger than those taking place on earth. It needed miraculous feats of technical skill to realize those extraterrestrial conditions on earth or to observe those phenomena in the universe with radio-eyes, X-ray eyes, and other vastly extended human sense organs. A whole new world of unexpected phenomena is being discovered in the very small and in the very large; in the manifestations of the dynamics of all those short-lived quark combinations as well as in the far reaches of the extragalactic universe.

The discoveries at the external frontier are important not only because they reveal entirely new ways of natural behavior, but also because they may lead to a deeper understanding of our own terrestrial world. For example, we have no idea yet why the electric charge of the electron and the opposite charge of the proton have a definitive value. This value is a decisive factor governing the behavior of the atomic world. If it were much larger or much smaller, our world would look different and behave differently. Furthermore, we are totally ignorant with regard to the reason the electron mass is about two thousand times smaller than the mass of the proton and the neutron. It makes the atomic nuclei very much heavier than the electron. The lighter the mass, the more diffuse are the quantum states. As a consequence, the atomic nuclei occupy well-defined positions within the molecules, whereas the quantum states of the electrons are spread out over the interspaces between them. The nuclei, therefore, form a kind of skeleton within the molecules, which gives rise to what one may call "molecular architecture." It represents the typical spatial arrangements of atoms within the molecules that are the basis of much of what is going on in our environment. The helical structure of the DNA molecule—the coil of life—is an example. The deeper reasons for that decisive mass ratio may at some time be found at the external frontier of particle physics. They are not known today.

An equally important question to be solved by further study of the basic particles is the relation between the fundamental forces of nature. At present we can identify four of them: electromagnetic forces between electrically charged particles, "strong" forces between quarks, the "weak" forces responsible for radioactive phenomena, and the force of gravity. The electromagnetic and the weak force have been found recently to be intimately connected. There are some indications that the strong force could also be brought into relation with those two other forces. To get a unified theory of all forces is still an attractive aim for the future.

Internal Limits of Science—The Creativity of Nature

Are there limits to the power of scientific insight? Are there any phenomena or experiences that may never be accessible to explanation or comprehension with the methods of science? Evidently, many phenomena and processes in nature outside and inside the human mind are still far from understood by contemporary science. The question arises, however, whether there are limits of scientific explanation that will never be transcended.

To make predictions is difficult, especially when they concern the future, as a Danish humorist said. Nevertheless it will be argued that such limits indeed exist. There are two rather different kinds of limits, internal and external ones; these terms refer to the relation of the limits to the conceptual system of science.

There are three aims of science: *comprehension, explanation, prediction*. Comprehension indicates the presence of a general idea of how a phenomenon comes about, what its general causes are, and how it is related to other parts of the natural world. It implies a demystification of the part of the natural world to which the phenomenon belongs. Explanation goes further; it tells us why the phenomenon or the process under consideration runs one way and not otherwise. Prediction, of course, is even more specific: it tells us what will happen to a well-defined system in the future when certain conditions are fulfilled. There is also such a thing as a prediction of the past, "retrodiction," when conclusions are drawn with regard to the yet unexplored previous history of a given set of objects.

The internal limits of science apply only to the possibilities of explanation and prediction. They do not restrict comprehension. The reasons for these limitations can be subsumed under the term "amplification effects," which implies that very small causes sometimes have very large effects. A simple example indicates what is meant. Consider the fate of a single molecule in a gas, say, in the atmosphere. Can we predict the fate of the molecule in the course of time? The answer is definitely in the negative. Very small changes in the initial conditions are quickly amplified at each collision with other molecules. Even if we knew its initial condition with great accuracy, its final position would be practically impossible to determine. Furthermore, quantum mechanics puts a limit to the accuracy of initial conditions.

This limitation does not seem worrisome. Who cares about the fate of a molecule? It is not relevant to the behavior of the gas. We care about pressure, temperature, the fluctuations of density, and so on, all problems for which the fate of one single molecule is irrelevant.

Similar examples are found in the development of star systems. The laws of gravity require the formation of clusters in the primal hot gas of the early universe. Small density fluctuations grow by attracting neighboring gas molecules. The larger clots are even more powerful, to attract more material. By this amplification process, the originally uniform gas separates into ever-increasing groups, which at a later time develop into galaxies and galaxy clusters. It is impossible to predict the exact nature of cluster formation, although one can predict that clusters must be formed as a result of gravitational amplification of small density fluctuations. Here, the situation is already more interesting: nature creates new shapes that cannot be predicted from the laws of physics, except in very general terms. We may be able to understand the occurrence of spiral arms and the like, but not the immense variety of details that we admire when we look at pictures of galaxies. They are examples of the creativity of nature.

Geology presents many instances of amplification effects. One example is the shape of mountain ranges. We comprehend the formation of such ranges by tectonic activities of the earth's crust, but we cannot explain why Mt. Blanc has the specific shape we see today, nor can we predict which side of Mt. St. Helens will cave in at the next eruption and what its shape will be afterwards. The resulting mountain shape will be an example of nature's creativity. It should be added that the geological sciences allow a good deal of retrodiction: many hypotheses on the development of our planet can be verified or falsified by searching for evidence concerning past events.

Things become more critical when we consider biological processes. In order to emphasize the difference, let us consider two experiments with a beam of X-rays. In the first, a crystal is exposed to it; in the second, a living bacterium. The effects on the crystal can be rather accurately predicted, since it is completely irrelevant by which atom the X-ray photon is absorbed. The effects on the bacterium, however, depend critically on the particular atomic group in the gene carrying part of the cell that is hit by the X-ray photon. Here, it is essential where it has hit, but it is unpredictable. Of course most such hits are detrimental or do not produce much change. But some may lead to the development of an offspring that is better able to cope with the environment. It is well known that such changes are retained and may displace the previous bacterium by the processes of replication and natural selection. Again, we have here a case of a relevant amplification process. In general, changes in the genetic constitution of a cell or a living species are introduced by many other causes besides X-rays, but always as an unpredictable molecular process with macroscopic consequences. These are typical examples of amplification effects.

The explanation of the specific paths of evolution is made all the more difficult because of the enormous number of possible combinations of nucleotides that make up the genetic constitution in the well-known DNA chain of molecules. It is true that the number of viable combinations is considerably smaller, but it is still very much larger than the number of those realized in nature. Therefore, it is impossible to explain why certain combinations are realized and not others, or to predict future evolutionary changes. Thus, again, the formation of the actual living species is an unpredictable act of the creativity of nature. We comprehend the general trend, but we cannot explain the specific events. Just as in geology, bioevolution also admits a certain amount of retrodiction. Indeed, much of the supporting evidence rests on successful conclusion of what would have to be found in fossils and how certain kinds of biochemical processes evolved by natural selection.

The evolutionary amplification effect acquired a new twist when the nervous system and the brain evolved. It represents a new way of communication between the external world and the living being. Although the phenotype was still determined by an amplification of the microstructure of the DNA, its behavior pattern depended as well on the reaction of the animal to sensual impressions. It also represents an amplification process, the microprocesses in the sense organs causing large-scale actions and reactions of the living beings. The interrelations between sensory input and behavioral output are most intricate because of the phenomenon of memory. It allows arbitrary time intervals between cause and effect, and permits a process called "learning," in which the relations between input and output become more and more sophisticated during the lifetime of an individual. It is an amplification system of a higher order, which makes it more difficult for scientific explanations or predictions of specific events. However, there should be no limit to the deepening scientific comprehension of the neurological and psychological factors involved.

With the development of the human species, a new feature entered: cumulative learning. It led to the development of new patterns of behavior quite different from those observed before. Previously, the behavior of an animal species remained essentially unchanged over very many generations, in spite of some learning. The death of an individual erased its learned experiences. Changes in behavior were caused mainly by changes in the natural environment or by genetic changes. Now, cumulative learning was possible; the death of an individual no longer erased the learned experiences because of the emergence of language and documents. It led to the formation of autonomous structures within the behavior patterns of the species; we call them cultures and civilizations. They evolved and decayed, but developed steadily toward higher degrees of sophistication. The cultural evolution differed from the biological one by its much faster time scale. It did not wait for changes in the natural environment or in the genes. The governing principles were no longer exclusively the survival of the species but also the survival of what we may call ideas. The amplification process has reached its largest extent. Individuals have the capacity to influence the course of the cultural evolution; they themselves are the products of the amplification of genetic, environmental, and cultural causes.

The difficulties encountered in efforts to explain and to predict become greater the more complex are the entities considered in the hierarchy of nature. The development of stellar systems or the properties of rocks, minerals, and mountain ranges are examples of amplified effects of small causes in the past history of the objects themselves. In the realm of life, we find amplified effects of cause that acted not only upon the object, but also upon the ancestors of the objects under consideration. Moreover, when the brain comes in, we must add the amplified effects of the environment on the sense organs. Finally, when we arrive at the emergence of humankind, the effects of individuals upon the course of events become relevant. These are the reasons a good part of the life sciences and most of the social sciences are more descriptive than predictive. It does not exclude the recognition of general trends or laws, but in so many biological and human phenomena, it is the specific that is relevant and not the general.

We must, however, avoid one misunderstanding. The occurrence of unpredictable events does not mean that the laws of nature are violated. On the contrary, the actual causes and the mechanisms of amplification are no "miracles" from the scientific point of view; they are comprehensible but unpredictable. This is why we called these limits the internal ones. Indeed, the laws of nature require that such amplification effects occur under certain conditions, like those that exist when life develops or when galaxies are formed. Once the amplification of some microscopic event has taken place, the chains of events that follow can be reasonably well predicted in many cases. The scientific approach does have some predictive power in respect to what will happen after the unpredictable event has occurred, a power that will increase with the further evolution of science. This is certainly true in the nonliving and in the biological realms; it may be questionable in the social realm, since the interference of individuals into the course of events becomes essential.

External Limits of Science—Human Creativity

The development of cultures and civilization among the human species has brought about a new escalation of possibilities and therefore a new barrier to any scientific predictability. Let us consider a specific form of cultural expression, books and paintings, in order to make a few quantitative considerations. The possibilities of combining words into a book, or color elements into a painting, are so enormous that their number would be overwhelmingly greater than the number of all possible gene combinations. Of course, the number of word or color combinations that make "sense," in any definition of the term, is very much smaller. Evidently, the existing books and paintings represent only a negligibly small part of them. That is why the scientific method encounters even more important limitations when it is applied to the creations and expressions of the human mind. We call these limitations external; they are extraneous to its own conceptual system. A special concept characterizes these limitations, the concept of complementarity.

There are important and relevant phenomena in human experiences that are "complementary" to scientific description. Niels Bohr used the concept of complementarity to describe situations in which there are several mutually exclusive approaches to reality. They represent different aspects, one excluding the other, yet adding to our understanding of the phenomena as a whole. Such complementary situations appear even within physics; for example, in respect to the description of an atom in terms of the quantum state or in terms of the location of its constituents. The quantum state evanesces if it is observed by a sharp instrument designed to locate the electron. The state is restituted when the atom is left alone and given enough time to return to its original form. Both aspects—quantum state and location—are complementary to each other; they are necessary concepts to provide a full insight into atomic reality.

Similar complementarities appear in all fields of human cognition, as Bohr often pointed out. There are different ways of perceiving a situation, ways that may seem unconnected or even contradictory, but they are necessary for understanding the situation in its totality. A simple example may suffice. A Beethoven sonata can be analyzed physically by studying the vibrations in the air; it can also be analyzed physiologically and psychologically by studying the processes at work in the brain of the listener. But there is another approach that gets closer to what we consider most relevant and essential in a Beethoven sonata: dealing with the immediate and direct impression of music.

Other complementary situations are indicated by the following pairs of human attitudes to different realms of experience: scientific–poetic, compassion–justice, neurophysiology–psychology, action–thought. The intention is not to emphasize the pair aspect of complementarity; on the contrary, the main thrust of this idea is the existence of many different approaches.

We assert that important parts of human experience cannot be reasonably evaluated within the scientific system. There cannot be an all-encompassing scientific definition of good and evil, of compassion, of rapture, of tragedy or humor, of hate, love, or faith, of dignity and humiliation, or of concepts like the quality of life or happiness. Certainly, it is possible and desirable to analyze the nervous and psychological processes and reactions that occur during the process of experiencing such ideas. Recent progress in neurophysiology and biochemistry promises much deeper scientific insights into that side of those human experiences. We may even acquire the means to influence, change, and evoke such reactions. But there remain important aspects of these experiences that are not touched by the scientific approach. Usually they are the ones most relevant to us.

Other approaches to the questions and problems of human experience are found in art, poetry, literature, and music; in forms of expression related to ethics, philosophy, and psychology; and in faith, religion, and mythology. They imply forms of human creativity different from the creativity that makes science possible. The contrast between science and other approaches is not necessarily that between rational thinking and emotional feeling. One can and does talk rationally about emotional impressions, about music and other arts, about ethical problems, dignity, and the quality of life. One also can talk emotionally about scientific matters: about the wonders of nature, the vastness of space, and the grand evolution from the primal bang to the present universe. Yet, within each approach is a specific type of discourse; it appears lucid and concise within its own intrinsic scale of values, but fragile and indefinite when judged by the peculiar requirements of a complementary approach. One view complements the other, and we must use all of them in order to get the full significance of our experiences.

Unfortunately, there is a certain resistance in the human mind to the recognition of complementary aspects. There is a strong trend toward clear-cut, universally valid answers that exclude different approaches. For example, the scientific approach is often considered the only serious and reasonable approach. No field of human experience seems to be in principle inaccessible to scientific study and comprehension, although the study of thought processes is still in its early infancy. Science may have a justified claim to completeness in this sense. But "complete" does not mean "all-embracing." Even if we reach a scientific comprehension of thinking and feeling, it will be necessary to use other methods of discourse to deal with our experiences. A system of thought such as science can be complete within its own framework of thought, but still leave out important aspects of experience. Indeed, in matters of human thinking, action, and feeling, those left-out aspects are often the most relevant ones. Some of the prejudices against science and technology are based on a half-conscious resistance to the implicit claim of completeness. The scientific approach is not the only legitimate and reasonable one.

Whenever one way of thinking is developed with great force and success, other ways are unduly neglected. It was aptly expressed by Marcus Fierz, the Swiss physicist-philosopher: "The scientific insights of our age shed such glaring light on certain aspects of human experience that they leave the rest in even greater darkness."

Here is an interesting example from a time when the scientific approach was repressed and the religious approach was dominant. In the year 1054, during the height of religious belief in Europe, a supernova appeared, brighter than any planet. It lasted for three or four months, yet not a single chronicle in Europe mentioned this phenomenon. In the Middle Ages, the appearance of a star brighter than all others was not considered a relevant fact worth registering.

The one-sided religious emphasis of the Middle Ages and the equally one-sided scientific-technological emphasis of our time have released creative forces of enormous power. Think of the medieval creations of art, architecture, and moral philosophy and of the development of science, natural philosophy, and technology in our era. At the same time, however, both one-sided approaches have led to serious abuses, such as the Crusades and the neglect of corporeal suffering in the Middle Ages, the development of weapons designed to produce massive annihilation and the emphasis on material values today.

As usual in the history of humankind, each emphasis has been distorted and used as means and reason for wholesale murder and destruction. Think of modern warfare and the nuclear arms race today—and of the reply of the papal legate Abbot Arnoud de Citeaux when he was asked what to do with the population of the town of Béziers after it was successfully conquered in the year 1205: "Kill them all. God will select those who should go to heaven and those who should go to hell!"

It must be pointed out that science itself has its roots and origins outside its own rational realm of thinking. In essence, there seems to exist a "Gödel theorem of science," which holds that science is possible only within a larger framework of nonscientific issues and concerns. The mathematician Gödel proved that a system of axioms can never be based on itself: statements from outside the system must be used in order to prove its consistency. In a similar manner, the activity of science is necessarily embedded in a much wider realm of human experience. Science would be impossible without the conviction of every scientist, and of society as a whole, that scientific truth is relevant and essential. The scientific observation of the supernova of 1054 was not regarded as important in medieval Europe.

Human experience encompasses much more than any given system of thought can express within its own framework of concepts. We must be receptive to the varied, different, and apparently contradictory ways of the mind when we are faced with the reality of nature, of our imaginations, and of human relations. There are many modes of thinking and feeling: each of them contains a part of what we may consider the truth. Science and technology comprise some of the most powerful tools for deeper insight and for solving the problems we face. Some of these problems, indeed, were created by the thoughtless applications of those very tools, such as the pollution of our environment and—first and foremost—the growing imminent danger of nuclear war. But science and technology are only one of the avenues toward reality: others are equally needed to comprehend the full significance of our existence. Indeed, those other avenues are necessary for the prevention of thoughtless and inhuman abuses of the results of science. We will need all approaches to deal with the predicaments of humanity that prevent so many of our fellow beings from having a life worth living.

III

Ideas in Physics

7

What Is Quantum Mechanics?

There is no doubt that the most outstanding development in modern science was the conception of quantum mechanics. It showed, better than anything else, the human capability to comprehend the fundamental principles that underlie the world in which we live—even when these principles run contrary to our experience in dealing with our everyday environment. The French philosopher-mathematician Henri Poincaré said, "It is hardly necessary to point out how much quantum theory deviates from everything that one has imagined until now; it is, without doubt, the greatest and deepest revolution to which natural philosophy has been subjected since Newton."

Much happened in physics between the time of Newton and the time of quantum mechanics. The discoveries and insights over the last three centuries share a characteristic feature: seemingly unconnected phenomena turned out to be manifestations of the same fundamental principle. It was a period of unification of disparate fields of experience. Here are some of the most important steps.

Newton showed that the motion of the planets is governed by the same law as the free fall of an object on earth. Thus, he unified terrestrial and celestial mechanics. In contrast to the belief of the ancients, he showed that the world of the earth and of the heavens is governed by the same laws.

Scientists in earlier days believed that heat was some peculiar substance called caloric, which flowed from a hot object to a colder one.

Physicists in the nineteenth century recognized that heat is the random motion or random vibration of the constituents of matter. Thus, thermodynamics and mechanics were unified. This feat is connected with the names of J. B. Mayer, B. Rumford, R. E. Clausius, L. Boltzmann, and J. W. Gibbs.

For a long time, the phenomena of electricity, magnetism, and light appeared to be unconnected. In the first half of the nineteenth century, one of the great unifications of physics took place. Faraday and Maxwell, together with many others, were able to show that all three phenomena are manifestations of the electromagnetic field. And so the field concept entered into physics. The simplest example is the electric field of an electric charge that exerts a force on another charge when the latter falls within its range. An electric current produces a magnetic field that exerts a force on magnetic materials. Such fields may even propagate through space independently of any charges or magnets, in the form of electromagnetic waves, of which visible light is one example. The field concept is less directly connected to our everyday experience than the concept of a particle, but it can easily be realized by our senses. For example, if one feels the attraction of a piece of iron by a magnet, one obtains the immediate impression that there is something surrounding the magnet that acts upon the iron. Finally, Einstein unified space, time, and gravity in his special and general theories of relativity.

Quantum mechanics also united two branches of science: physics and chemistry. But it did much more. In previous great developments in physics, fundamental concepts were not too different from those of our everyday experience, such as particle, position, speed, mass, force, energy, and even field. We often refer to those concepts as "classical." The world of atoms cannot be described and understood with those concepts. For atoms and molecules, the ideas and concepts formed in dealing with the objects in our immediate environment no longer suffice. Surprising forms of behavior were observed that not only needed a different language but required new concepts to understand the properties of atoms.

A small group of people conceived of and formulated these new ideas in the middle twenties of this century. The most important among them were W. Heisenberg, a German; E. Schrödinger, an Austrian; P. A. M. Dirac, an Englishman; W. Pauli, another Austrian; and M. Born, another German. They worked at different places, but the center of activities was in Copenhagen, where they met frequently under the leadership of the great Niels Bohr. Bohr was the ideal leader of such a group. Older than most of the others, who were then in their twenties or early thirties, he contributed enormously to the conception of the new ideas by his constant questioning, by his criticism, and by his enthusiasm. The crowd that assembled around him was a group of devoted forward-looking people who, free of the bonds of convention, attacked the deepest riddles of nature with a spirit of joy that can hardly be described. That joy of insight is a sense of involvement and awe, an elated state of mind akin to what you feel on top of a mountain after a hard climb, at the shore of the blue sea, or when you hear a great work of music. It comes not only after personal achievement, but also after finally understanding an important new insight gained by the work of others. For every real scientist, it is great compensation for the hard work and trouble he must endure (see Figure 1).

The quantum revolution changed our old concepts of reality in many respects. We are going to describe this drama in five parts—a prologue, plus four acts:

Figure 1 *Werner Heisenberg, Wolfgang Pauli, and Enrico Fermi at a conference in 1927, reflecting their enthusiasm for and joy of the new quantum mechanics.*

Prologue   Riddles of prequantum physics

Act I   Discovery of wave-particle duality

Act II   How wave-particle duality miraculously solves the riddles of prequantum physics

Act III   Significance of wave-particle duality and the new reality of the quantum state

Act IV   The quantum ladder: An extension of quantum mechanics to nuclear and subnuclear phenomena and to the history of the universe

PROLOGUE:
Riddles of Prequantum Physics

Before quantum theory was conceived, physicists were unable to explain some of the most ubiquitous phenomena in our environment. Here are a few examples: A piece of iron, when heated, becomes first red, then yellow, then white, but nobody could explain why. The different colors emitted by a piece of matter come from the irregular heat motion of the electrons in the atoms of iron. Fast motion emits higher frequencies of light than slow motion. The frequency determines the color of the light. The laws of thermodynamics tell us that any form of motion should receive the same amount of energy at a given temperature, an amount that increases when the temperature rises. Thus we expect only an increase of intensity of the emitted light, not a change from red to yellow to white. This change represented an unsolved riddle, somewhat like today's ignorance of the nature of memory. We use memory constantly, but nobody knows precisely what it is.

We can consider more examples of unsolved questions of that period: Why are copper and silver metals and oxygen a gas? Why do metals have properties so different from other solids, such as rocks? Why do these properties persist, even after heating, melting, evaporating, and subsequent cooling to the original temperature? Why do oxygen atoms bind to hydrogen atoms to form water? Why does sodium gas emit yellow light when heated? Why is it that burning 1 kilogram of coal produces approximately 6000 calories? Why is the size of atoms about a hundred millionth of a finger's breadth? No one could provide any answers to these questions at the turn of the century.

More problems were generated by the discovery of the electron by

J. J. Thomson in England and H. A. Lorentz in the Netherlands at the end of the last century and, in particular, by further discoveries by E. Rutherford and H. G. Mosely at the beginning of this century. They found that atoms consist of a heavy, positively charged atomic nucleus surrounded by much lighter electrons. Because the electric force between the positively charged nucleus and the negatively charged electrons is of the same form as the attraction between the sun and the planets, they concluded that atoms must be tiny planetary systems, with the nucleus as "sun" and the electrons as "planets." Moreover, it was found that all elements seem to have this planetary structure and differ only in numbers of electrons. For example, hydrogen has one electron; helium, two; iron, twenty-six; and uranium, ninety-two.

It was difficult to understand how elements that are so different— some are gases, some are metals, some are liquids—differ in their atomic structure by only a few electrons. For example, the element neon, which has ten electrons, is a chemically inactive gas; however, the element sodium, which has eleven electrons, is one of the most chemically active metals. An electron increase of 10 percent completely changes the character of the atom! No one could explain this apparent inconsistency between quantity and quality.

Four observations defied all understanding at the turn of the century.

1. The color of objects at various stages of heating (red, yellow, white).

2. The very different specific properties of elements whose number of electrons is almost the same.

3. The fact that atoms do not change their properties in spite of the many collisions and interactions that they suffer in a gas or in an ordinary piece of matter. They quickly resume their original qualities after the perturbation. Their stability and their ability to regenerate is completely at odds with what we would expect from a planetary system. If our solar system were to collide or pass another star at a close distance its orbits and patterns would be completely changed and it would not return to its original form.

4. The energy content of the atom is "quantized." An atom can assume a series of definite energies only and never a value in between. This most surprising fact was found at the beginning of this century and is also completely foreign to a planetary system. There is no reason

why the energy of planetary motion cannot change by arbitrarily small amounts, for example, when a meteorite hits a planet. An atom, however, can accept or lose only definite amounts of energy, those that would change its energy from one of the values in the series to another.

It became clear to prequantum physicists that the analogy between an atom and a planetary system breaks down completely when atomic properties and processes are examined in detail. On the other hand, these observations left no doubt that the atom consisted of a positively charged nucleus surrounded by electrons, which ought to form a planetary system, according to the laws of mechanics known at that time. Everything, including our own bodies, consists of atoms. Obviously, the most urgent problem for physics at that time was to resolve these contradictions and to achieve a better comprehension of the structure and behavior of atoms.

ACT I: DISCOVERY OF WAVE-PARTICLE DUALITY

Not until the first quarter of this century did physicists find the path to the solution. It all began with a series of startling discoveries that seemingly had no direct connection with atomic structure. These discoveries showed that light, believed to be a wave, exhibited particle properties and that electrons, believed to be particles, exhibited wave properties. Let us call it the wave-particle duality.

Often, when it is difficult to find an explanation for one group of strange findings, another group of unexplained observations helps us to resolve both difficulties. It's often easier to solve two riddles than one. Two different disturbing observations may lead more readily than one such observation to a solution. That was the case with the wave-particle duality, since it showed the way to understand the strange properties of the atomic world.

Let us first look at the duality itself. We have all learned in school that light is an electromagnetic wave. We perceive the different wave lengths, or frequencies of vibration of these waves, as different colors. Red has a longer wave length and lower frequencies than yellow or blue. How did we know that light is a wave? Let us look at water waves to learn about a characteristic property of waves: interference. When two wave trains merge, originating from two different points, they combine in a typical way. When the crest of one wave coincides with the crest of another, the two together create a stronger motion. When the crest of one wave coincides with the trough of another, the two wave motions cancel each other in a phenomenon called "interference." Figure 2 shows the interference of two water waves originating from two different points. We see that they reinforce each other in certain directions and wipe each other out in other directions. The same phenomenon was observed long ago by Thomas Young in light waves, as sketched in Figure 3 and shown in Figure 4. The two light waves are produced by illuminating a screen with two slits. Of course, there is a difference between water and light waves: In the former case, the water surface oscillates and in the latter it is the electric and magnetic field strength that oscillates in space.

Great was the surprise, therefore, when it turned out that the energy of a light beam cannot be subdivided indefinitely. An ordinary wave can be strong, weak, or still weaker, with no restrictions on its intensity or lack thereof. Not so with light waves! The observed light

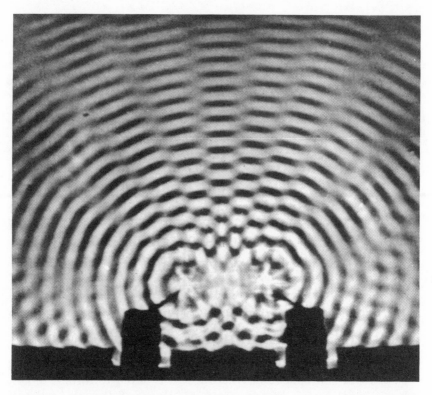

Figure 2 *Interference patterns produced by two water waves originating from two neighboring points. (Physical Science Study Committee, Physics, D.C. Heath, Boston, 1967).*

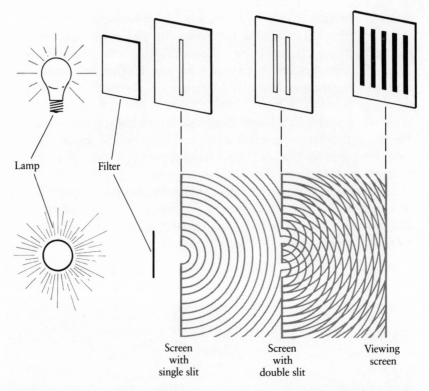

Lamp   Filter

Screen   Screen   Viewing
with   with   screen
single slit   double slit

Figure 3   *Arrangement for demonstrating interference of light. The first slit de-*
fines the incoming wave; the second has two openings, thus producing two waves;
the third shows the interference stripes seen on the screen at right. (After Atkins,
Physics, *Wiley, New York, 1965).*

energy seems to occur in lumps called light quanta, or photons. The
energy of a light beam is always a multiple of such lumps, never half
a lump or ten-and-a-quarter lumps. This is a strange finding. How
could it be that the energy of a wave cannot assume an arbitrary
value, but must be a multiple of a definite quantum? The energy of
a light wave is indeed quantized; this property was shown beyond
any doubt. Figure 5 is an example of how it could be observed. It is
a photograph of what we see when a light ray (in this case, an X-
ray—light of very high frequency) penetrates through a "cloud chamber," that is a container of saturated steam. The vapor is in a state
of pressure and temperature at which it is about to form droplets.
Just a bit of energy deposited here and there will form a droplet. If
the bit of energy is larger, a bigger droplet is formed; if smaller, a
tinier one will appear. Now, looking at the picture, we see (as we

Figure 4 *Patterns seen on the screen at the extreme right of the arrangement of Figure 3. Upper pattern with red light; lower pattern with violet light. The lower pattern is narrower because of the shorter wave length. (Physical Science Study Committee,* Physics, *D.C. Heath, Boston, 1967).*

might well expect) that the light ray gets weaker penetrating the liquid. However, it gets weaker in a special way: the droplets do not become smaller, but their number does. The unchanging size of the droplets indicates that light consists of quanta: the effect of each quantum is the same all along the light beam, but there are fewer droplets farther down the road (to the right of the picture) because part of the energy has already been used up. If the ray were a true wave, its intensity

Figure 5 *The cloud chamber shows the absorption of photons, one by one, and the weakening of the beam as photons are removed. The photons enter from the left and are absorbed by the argon atoms of the gas. They eject photoelectrons, whose tracks produce little droplets that show white in the photograph. You can see that the beam is weakened if you divide the photograph in half; there are seventeen tracks on the left half and only nine on the right. The "light" is actually an X-ray beam of a wavelength about 0.2 angstroms. (W. Gentner, N. Maier-Leibnitz, and W. Bothe,* Atlas Typischer Nebelkammerbilder, *Springer Verlag, Berlin, 1940).*

would have become weaker and would have produced smaller droplets. The weakening shows itself not by smaller drops but by fewer
ones. Each light quantum maintains the same strength, but there are
fewer of them when the beam becomes weaker. These and other similar observations reveal the "graininess" of light.

Light "grains" (photons, or light quanta) are very small indeed.
That is why they were not discovered earlier. Their energy was found
to be proportional to the frequency of light. This relationship is expressed in the simple formula, $E = hf$, where E is the energy of the
photon, f the frequency, and h is a famous number called Planck's
constant. If we measure energies in electron volts and frequencies in
ups and downs per second, the numerical value of h is 4×10^{-15}.
Let us keep this formula in mind since it will be a clue to understanding
many other riddles. Radio waves have very low frequencies and, therefore, very small quanta, according to this formula. The quanta are so
small that it is very difficult to observe them. Visible light has larger
quanta, but they are still extremely small. A million millions arriving
at the same place and time would be felt as a little prick on a finger.
The eye, of course, is very sensitive to them. X-rays are very high
frequency radiation, and so their quanta are much larger, but still
rather small.

The graininess of light, together with the series of definite energy
values of an atom, forces us to a new interpretation of the mechanism
of light emission by atoms. The atom may lose or gain energy only
by amounts that correspond to the differences between its definite
energy values. For example, when an atom happens to be in a state
of higher energy, it may get into one of lower energy by emitting a
photon. The photon would be such as to carry the energy difference.
Thus, an atom should emit light with very definite frequencies,
namely, those whose quanta are equal in energy to the *differences*
between the atomic energy values. This prediction turned out indeed
to be the case, and it explains the characteristic frequencies emitted
by each atomic species. Quanta of yellow light of a sodium lamp carry
an energy equal to the difference between the lowest and the next
higher state of the sodium atom. This regularity showed that there is
a logical connection between two mysterious facts: the quantized energy of atoms and the graininess of light.

What does this amount to? We come to the startling conclusion
that light has particle properties, in spite of the fact that so many
indications—interference, for one—have shown that light is a wave!

The mystery deepened considerably as a result of a second surprising discovery: particles—electrons, for example—have wave

properties! The French physicist L. de Broglie predicted this duality by ingenious intuitive insight, even before it was discovered by experiment. Under certain conditions, electrons emerging from two nearby points do not add their intensities but give rise to weaker beams in some directions and to stronger beams in others, similar to the interference of two water waves or light beams, as was shown in Figures 2 and 3. What we call a particle exhibits properties that we ordinarily ascribe only to waves. What is the electron, a particle or a wave? What is a light ray, a wave train or a beam of particles? Eddington found a telling terminology, calling photons and electrons "wavicles."

The fundamental relation between particle energy and wave frequency, $E = hf$, holds also for particles. A similar relation exists between the particle momentum and the wave number k (the number of wave lengths in one centimeter): $p = hk$. These relations are called "de Broglie relations." They both contain the fundamental number h, the Planck constant.

Obviously, we run into terrible difficulties and contradictions by assuming that something is a wave and a particle at the same time. A school of fish swimming in a lake is completely different from a wave on its surface. Each fish in the school is localized, as is each particle in a particle beam, whereas a wave is necessarily spread out over space. These contradictions will be raised in Act III of our drama. Such everyday concepts as particle and wave are not applicable in the atomic realm without restrictions. This will lead us to a new conception of reality. For the moment, let us assume that entities such as electrons and light are indeed "wavicles"—exhibiting both wave and particle properties—and see what follows from this assumption.

ACT II: HOW WAVE-PARTICLE DUALITY MIRACULOUSLY SOLVES THE RIDDLES OF PREQUANTUM PHYSICS

First, we can easily see why a solid material becomes first red, then yellow, then blue and white when it is heated to higher temperatures. What are heat and temperature? In a warm material, atoms and molecules perform irregular vibrations of all kinds. The energy of these random motions, thermal energy, is proportional to the temperature: the hotter the material, the faster the particles vibrate. Atoms and molecules contain electrically charged particles; when they vibrate, they emit light. But light is quantized; it comes in lumps of energy. If the thermal energy is not sufficient to produce a light quantum of a given color, that color *cannot* show up. Thus, a piece of iron at room temperature does not emit visible light because at that temperature the thermal energy is less than the energy of the quanta of visible light. (Iron, at room temperature, does emit infrared light, whose quanta are of lower energy; we cannot see it but we can measure it, and we feel it as a heat radiation.) At a higher temperature, thermal energy reaches the energy of a visible quantum. Red light has the lowest frequency and therefore the lowest quantum in the visible range; then comes yellow, then blue. Thus red is the first color to be seen when the iron is heated. As the temperature is increased, iron becomes yellow-red, then white, because the sum of red, yellow, and blue is white.

In 1900, Max Planck was the first to realize that quantum theory would lead to a correct description of the radiation of incandescent matter. His way of explaining it was different from the description given here and somewhat more involved. Nevertheless, his ideas gave impetus to the development of quantum theory.

What is much more impressive, however, is that the wave-particle duality also explains the stability and specificity of atoms and their special quantized states with definite energy values. The wave nature of electrons bestows properties on atoms that are quite different from what we expect of planetary systems.

To understand the difference, we must learn something about confined waves. When a wave is confined to a restricted region in space, it can assume only certain definite wave patterns. A violin string suspended between two end points can set up only those vibrations whose half wave length fits once or twice, or any integral number of times, into the space between the two points of attachment, as shown in Figure 6.

Not only are the shapes of the vibrations determined, but also the frequencies (the number of ups and downs per second), once the tension of the string is kept fixed. Each of the different vibrations that can be set up has its characteristic frequency; the string can vibrate only a set of selected frequencies. The lowest of these frequencies, the easiest to set up, is the one whose half wavelength just fits the distance between the fixed ends of the string.

The lesson learned from the string is generally true for all kinds of waves. Whenever waves are confined to a finite space, we observe special wave forms and a set of assigned frequencies that are characteristic of the system. Most musical instruments are built on this principle. Stringed instruments make use of the series of discrete frequencies characteristic of the string; a wind instrument is based on

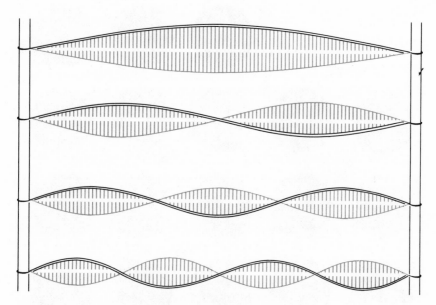

Figure 6 *Wave forms of a string fixed at both ends.*

natural frequencies of air waves enclosed in the pipe of the instrument, whether it is a trumpet or an organ pipe. Another interesting example of this phenomenon is a metal plate fixed at its center. If we use a violin bow to set it in vibration, we will find again a definite set of vibrations, with characteristic frequencies and shapes. We make these shapes visible by strewing sand on the plate. The sand accumulates at places where there is no vibration, thus delineating the shapes of the vibrations in "Chladni figures," as shown in Figure 7. It is entirely possible to calculate the shape of these patterns and predict at which frequency of vibration they will appear. All we need to know are the shape and elastic properties of the plate.

Can electron waves be confined too? Indeed, they are confined in an atom! The positive charge of the nucleus attracts the electron and prevents it from leaving the immediate neighborhood of the nucleus. Thus, the electron is confined to a space near the nucleus. Now we come to the most astounding part of the second act of our drama. In 1926, Erwin Schrödinger calculated the shapes and frequencies of the characteristic patterns that develop when electron waves are confined by the electric attraction of the nucleus. It is a straightforward problem of the dynamics of confined waves. What did he get? As expected, he found a series of distinct vibrations, each with its own definite shape and frequency. This is a big step toward solving the riddles of the

Figure 7 *Vibrations of a circular metal plate fixed in the center (Chladni figures).*

atom. It not only shows that there are indeed well-defined modes of vibration in the atom but also reveals a connection between the wave nature of the electron and the existence of discrete states in the atom. Here we are touching on the very nerve of nature. When an electron is confined to a limited region around the nucleus, wave properties of the electron permit only certain special, predetermined patterns of vibration.

The real success of this idea came about when Schrödinger calculated the wave patterns of the hydrogen atom—the simplest of all atoms, with its single electron confined by the nucleus. The result was overwhelming. He found a series of states of vibration that corresponded in every respect to the observed quantum states of the hydrogen atom. The extension of waves in space corresponded very well with the observed size of the hydrogen atom. But the most surprising and convincing result of his calculations concerned the energy of quantum states. How do we get at the energies of the different states of vibration? We use the fundamental relation between the frequency f and the energy E: energy is frequency multiplied by Planck's constant.

When Schrödinger calculated the frequencies of these vibrations and multiplied them by Planck's constant, he got exactly the observed energies of the quantum states of hydrogen! An incredible success. Everyone who contemplates this fantastic discovery sympathizes with Italian physicist Enrico Fermi, who used to say, when presenting this calculation in his lectures, "It has no business to fit so well!"

Confined electron waves in atoms cannot be observed directly. We can measure their extension, and frequencies (to be exact, we measure the differences between frequencies, which are observed as energy differences), but we cannot see them or photograph them because they would be destroyed by the light we would have to use in order to see them. This will be the topic of the next act in our presentation. One can make models, however, representing the results of Schrödinger's calculations. It is instructive and impressive to look at pictures of these models. Figure 8 shows the electron wave patterns, in order of increasing frequency, or energy, the successive quantum states of an electron confined by a nucleus. The lowest state, the ground state, is the simplest one; it has spherical symmetry. The next states have figure-eight forms; the higher the frequency, the more involved the patterns.

These are the fundamental patterns of matter. They are the shapes, the *only* shapes, that the electron vibration can assume under conditions prevailing in atoms—that is, under the influence of a central force (the attraction of the nucleus) that keeps the electron confined. We may call them "the primal shapes of nature." These patterns are the original building blocks from which nature combines and forms everything we find around us.

Let us see how the other properties of atoms are explained in terms of these patterns. We begin with the stability of atoms and the regeneration of their original shapes and properties after being disturbed. Take the hydrogen atom: under ordinary conditions, when temperatures and pressures are not too high, the atom is found in the quantum state of lowest energy: it vibrates in the simplest possible pattern, the uppermost one in Figure 8. To change from the lowest pattern to the next, the frequency, and therefore the energy, must be increased; for the hydrogen atom, the difference in energy is 10 electron volts (eV). Unless collisions or perturbations are able to deliver that amount of energy or more, a hydrogen atom stays unchanged in the lowest state or pattern. Since, at room temperature, thermal energy

1s

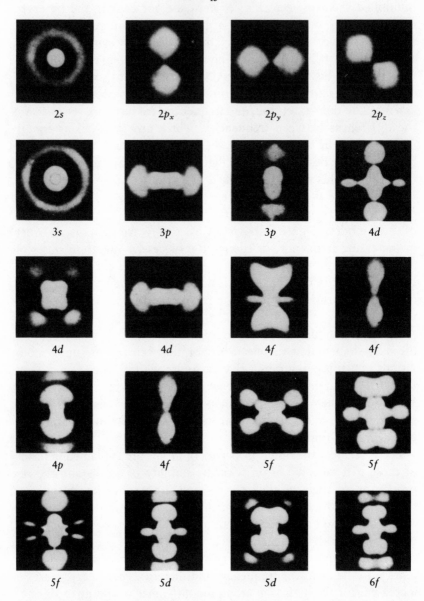

2s   2p_x   2p_y   2p_z

3s   3p   3p   4d

4d   4d   4f   4f

4p   4f   5f   5f

5f   5d   5d   6f

Figure 8 *Mathematical models of vibrations of electron waves confined by a central charge. (Adapted from Introduction to Atomic Spectre by H. E. White, McGraw Hill, 1934.)*

is only $\frac{1}{40}$ of an electron volt, collisions at room temperature cannot change the hydrogen atom's energy, or frequency. Under these conditions, the atom is stable. It remains in the lowest pattern.

Wave patterns also explain the regeneration ability of atoms. Say a hydrogen atom is deformed during a collision; it must assume the original pattern again when the perturbation is over. There are no other patterns available for the electron except at much higher energies. Let us look at a violin string: the player's finger presses down on the string; that pressure corresponds to a deformation. When the finger is removed, the string assumes its natural vibration.

How do these patterns explain the specificity of atoms and the variety of elements? Here, the "Pauli exclusion principle" enters. It says that no more than two electrons may vibrate in the same pattern and that those two must have opposite spin. Therefore, while the hydrogen atom, with its single electron vibrates in the simplest possible pattern in its lowest state of energy, other atoms exhibit more complex patterns, even in their state of lowest energy. Each second additional electron must assume the next higher pattern of the scale. This accounts for the variety of nature, because otherwise electrons in all atoms would vibrate in the lowest pattern and all elements would have roughly the same properties: the world would not contain as many different materials and forms.

Pauli discovered his principle empirically by analyzing the properties of atoms. But later on he was able to show that it follows from the fundamental laws of quantum mechanics. Unfortunately, his conclusions are too complicated to be explained in the frame of this essay.

The Pauli principle is the reason why neon, with ten electrons, is so different from sodium, with eleven. Since no more than two electrons are allowed to assume the same pattern, the ten electrons in the neon atom vibrate in five different patterns, the first five shown in Figure 8. As it happens, these five patterns fit together in such a way that the atom has a rounded shape, without any indentations or elevations. That is why neon is chemically inactive. The sodium atom, however, is irregular because the additional eleventh electron is forced to vibrate in a different pattern, according to the Pauli principle. This "isolated" electron is loosely bound and therefore ready to interact with electrons around other atoms. Sodium, therefore, is chemically active. When an atom's electron patterns fit into a nicely rounded shape, or "closed atomic shell," the atom is an inactive gas. The atom with the next higher number of electrons can be expected to be a chemically active substance, with very different properties coming from the new occupied pattern. Atoms having one or a few electrons over and above the closed shell are those that form metals, such as sodium. The additional electrons jump easily from atom to atom and therefore give rise to the high electric and thermal conductivity of metals. That is why they feel cold when we touch them. Body heat is quickly carried away by the additional electrons.

Atomic structure provides interesting examples of how quantity determines quality. From the number of electrons in an atom, we can deduce the kind of properties a particular atom will have in its ground state by combining the various patterns of vibration. A telling instance happened when plutonium was produced in nuclear reactions for the first time. (Plutonium does not exist in nature because it is radioactive and decays into other elements in about 40,000 years.) The amounts of plutonium that were created were too small to permit any observation about its properties; however, it was known that the plutonium atom contained ninety-four electrons. Thus, we were able to determine its properties from the patterns of the electrons vibrating around the nucleus. It was found that it must be a metal; it must have specific weight of about 20 grams (g) per cubic centimeter; it must be brown; it must have a certain electric and thermal conductivity and elasticity. All this information could be obtained from the single number ninety-four. It was a great moment when the first cubic millimeter of plutonium was finally produced and these projections were confirmed. This incident illustrates the tremendous predictive power of atomic quantum mechanics.

The connection between quantity (number of electrons) and quality (properties of the atom) points to an essential difference between quantum mechanics and classical physics. In the classical science, there is no well-defined state of lowest energy. If the electrons around the plutonium nucleus followed classical laws, the state of the plutonium atom would depend on the initial positions and velocities of the ninety-four electrons. No two plutonium atoms would be really identical. The same would be true, even for the hydrogen atom, with one electron since there are an infinite number of different ways for the one electron to circle the nucleus with a certain energy. There isn't even a lowest energy. The wave nature of electrons has changed all this. There is only *one* wave of lowest frequency (frequency determines energy), the one at the top of Figure 8. In plutonium (as in any other atom) there is only one way to put the electrons in pairs into the wave forms such as those shown in Figure 8—at the lowest possible energy.

We therefore conclude that atoms with a fixed number of electrons are all alike; they behave identically. Gold, with seventy-nine electrons, has the same properties in the United States as in the Soviet

Union because there is only one unique way of putting seventy-nine electrons into patterns of the kind shown in Figure 8 and obtain the lowest possible energy, the ground state. There are, of course, other ways to distribute the seventy-nine electrons, but then we would obtain higher energies: higher quantum states of gold. They represent a series of energy values—the spectrum of gold—the lowest of which is 2.3 eV above the ground state. These states occur only at very high temperatures, but there will always be the same series of states.

Quantum mechanics introduced a concept that does not exist in classical physics: the concept of exact identity between atomic systems. In the classical picture we can always imagine arbitrary, small differences between atoms. In quantum mechanics, these are either exactly alike or measurably different—an important trait of nature.

The patterns shown in Figure 8—and their inherent symmetries—determine the behavior of atoms. They also help us to understand how atoms combine to form molecules and how atoms form regular arrays in crystals. The simple beauty of a crystal reflects the fundamental shapes of the atomic patterns on a larger scale. Ultimately, all the regularities of form and structure that we see in nature, ranging from molecular structure to the hexagonal shape of a snowflake or the intricate symmetries of living forms in flowers and animals, are based on the symmetries of these atomic patterns. The world abounds in characteristic forms and shapes, but only quantum mechanics can tell us—at least in principle—where they all come from.

Electron patterns also explain why 6000 calories of heat are produced from burning a kilogram of coal. Energy is gained when carbon dioxide is formed from a carbon atom (in coal) and an oxygen molecule (in air) because the electron patterns of carbon and oxygen fit together better in carbon dioxide and therefore have lower energy than in the oxygen molecule and the carbon crystal. The amount can be calculated, and when multiplied by the number of atoms in a kilogram of coal, the result is 6000 calories. The reason why oxygen combines so easily with hydrogen to give water is that the eight electrons of oxygen are just two electrons short of the closed shell that we found in neon. Thus, they form a round shape when the two holes are filled with the electrons of two hydrogen atoms, so we get H_2O!

Even the phenomena of life are based upon the characteristic electron patterns and their stability. The structure of DNA comes from the specific way in which electron patterns of carbon, hydrogen, oxygen, nitrogen, and other atoms fit together and form the well-known helix. They are resistant to thermal motion at room temperature; more energy is required to change those patterns and to disentangle them.

Consequently, the DNA helix has its own stability, which explains why the same flowers emerge every spring and children resemble their parents.

Schrödinger's calculations and the subsequent tremendous development of our understanding of the properties of atoms, molecules, gases, liquids, and solids have shown that the structure of matter in our environment is based on the electric force between atomic nuclei and electrons and how the wave-particle duality of the electrons respond to it.

There is an interesting historical relation. Kepler thought that planetary orbits in the solar system had very definite size ratios. He connected them with the size ratios of simple polyhedrons. In fact, it is not so, for the sizes of the planetary orbits are, to a large extent, accidental. But now Kepler's idea reappears in the atomic world, where it is clearly understood as a typical property of electrically confined waves. There is a kind of harmony among the different frequencies of the electron patterns, a "chord" that can be considered a rebirth of the Pythagorean harmony of the spheres. These harmonies may not be particularly pleasing as musical chords to our ears, but they certainly appeal to our intellectual ears when they offer so much insight into the structure of the material world.

ACT III: SIGNIFICANCE OF WAVE-PARTICLE DUALITY AND THE NEW REALITY OF THE QUANTUM STATE

Act II demonstrated that the wave-particle duality plays a decisive role in the dynamics of atoms. The wave nature of electrons permitted us to understand the puzzling properties of atoms, such as the stability, specificity, and discrete energy states. But the fundamental question remains: How can the electron be a particle and a wave at the same time? It is not a true particle, because it exhibits wave properties, and it is not a true wave, since its amplitude is fixed in the following sense: if the electron assumes one of the wave patterns of Figure 8, it vibrates with a certain intensity. It cannot vibrate with half that intensity, since that would correspond to half an electron and there is no such thing. It is neither a wave nor a particle.

Its wave nature is exhibited not only in the patterns of Figure 8. Beams of free electrons that are not bound to atoms also show wave and particle properties. As mentioned before, electrons emerging from two nearby points exhibit interference under certain conditions, similar to the water waves in Figure 2. On the other hand, the intensity of the wave representing an electron beam cannot assume any value, as an ordinary wave would, but only those values corresponding to a definite number of particles. Furthermore, when two electron beams cross each other and the electrons of one beam are scattered by the other, scattered electrons have just the momenta and energies we would expect from two *particles* colliding; however, the directions in which they emerge are distributed according to the scattering laws of waves!

Why can't we find out, by exact observations, whether an electron is a wave or a particle? Couldn't we try to follow the electron motion in the atom, step by step, to see whether it is a localized particle moving along an orbit or a vibrating wave spread over a region? This question goes to the heart of quantum physics. One of the features of classical physics is the "divisibility" of physical processes, the idea that a process can be thought of as a succession of particular partial processes. According to that idea, each process can be followed, step by step, in time and space. The orbit of an electron around the nucleus would be thought of as a succession of small displacements. In contrast, a wave would be thought of as a continuous oscillatory movement spread over a region of space.

Here we meet one of the basic concepts of quantum mechanics. There are fundamental reasons why such tracing cannot be carried out. The idea of divisibility of motion is in serious trouble, and the trouble comes from the graininess of light. In order to see the details of the electron motion in the atom, we must use light waves with a very small wavelength, the size of the atom. Such light, however, has a high frequency and therefore a large energy quantum. In fact, light whose wavelength is as small as an atom has a quantum of energy that would be far more than enough to tear the electron away from the atom. When light hits an electron, it will knock it out of the atom and destroy the very object of our examination. This is so, not only when light is used to observe an object, but quite generally all measurements that could be of use to decide between the wave and the particle nature of the electron have the same result. If we attempt to perform these measurements, the object changes its state completely.

The quantum nature of light or of any other means of observation introduces a coarseness that makes it impossible to decide between wave and particle. It does not allow us to subdivide the atomic orbit into a succession of partial motions, whether they are particle displacements or wave oscillations. If we force a subdivision of the process and try to look more accurately at the wave in order to find out where the electron "really" is, we will have destroyed the subtle individuality of the atom that gave rise to all its characteristic properties. The argument that an entity cannot be both a wave and a particle, because a wave is spread over space whereas a particle is concentrated at a definite position, no longer holds within atomic dimensions. The habitual concepts of "location" and "spread" are no longer applicable; any effort to observe them would destroy the object.

Here quantum mechanics enters as a new and revolutionary concept. The great new insight of quantum physics is the recognition that individual states of the atom—we call them quantum states—are each indivisible wholes that exist only as long as they are not attacked by penetrating means of observation. The quantum state is the state the atom assumes when it is left alone to adjust itself to the prevailing conditions. If we try to measure the location of an electron with those penetrating means, we not only will destroy the quantum state, but will indeed find the electron at some place, but that place is not predictable.

Electrons do not have a predictable position in the atom, because "position" is a classical concept, not directly applicable in the atomic realm. The results of our physical measurements, however, are always classical magnitudes; that is, we measure magnitudes of position, velocity, and energy. Therefore, we should not be surprised if, in some cases, all we can predict are probabilities; furthermore, the quantum state has been thoroughly changed after measurement. What we should be surprised about is that physicists were able to construct a mathematical formalism (quantum mechanics) for dealing with quantum reality that allows us to calculate those probabilities.

The restrictions to the application of classical concepts, such as position, velocity, and momentum, are codified by the famous Heisenberg uncertainty relations. When we ask what is the position or the velocity of an electron in a quantum state, we cannot always expect a definite answer. The Heisenberg uncertainty relations tell us, for example, to what degree, within a quantum state of an atom, the location and the velocity of an electron is left undetermined. They are the warning posts that advise us how far we are allowed to apply habitual classical concepts before we get into trouble with reality. "Up to here and no further may you apply your old-fashioned concepts."

An important consequence follows. Certain statements about the atom must remain probabilistic because our concepts—for example, "electron position"—are not appropriate in the atomic quantum state. If we force the concept on the atom, we get only a probability for an answer: the electron will be found here with this probability and there with another probability. The phrase, "If you ask a silly question, you get a silly answer," should be applied in this form: "If you ask an inappropriate question, you get a probabilistic answer." Outside the confines of the Heisenberg relations, however, for objects much larger than atoms, we can still apply classical concepts without trouble. The orbit of an earth satellite can be calculated and predicted with practically unlimited accuracy.

The quantum state has a more subtle individuality than ordinary macroscopic states of matter. Reality exhibits different, seemingly contradictory properties, when examined in different ways. In the words of David Bohm: "The electron may be regarded as an entity that has potentialities for developing either particle properties or wave properties, depending on the type of instruments with which it interacts."

Some philosophers like to say that, according to quantum mechanics, the world around us is not real and depends on our minds, because our observations disturb and change the objects. I disagree. True enough, typical quantum properties unfold only if atoms are not subject to methods of observation that penetrate their interior. But they are not exposed to such perturbations under ordinary conditions, and that is why characteristic quantum properties are manifest everywhere: in the color of objects; in the structure of crystals; in the mechanical, electrical, and chemical properties of different substances; and, in the last instance, in the phenomena of life. In most of our studies of material properties, we try to maintain, not to disturb, the quantum states, since they give rise to the reality of interest to us. Sure enough, if an atomic phenomenon is observed too closely by our clumsy instruments, we destroy the very object of interest, its quantum state, with all its seemingly contradictory properties. But just these properties are responsible for the behavior and appearance of matter in our environment. Hence, it is the quantum state that is "real" and exists independently from us. If close observations destroy it, and if we cannot describe it with our everyday concepts, too bad for those observations and concepts! What is real are the objects and their quantum states, since they represent nature. The inapplicability of some of our concepts does not make the objects less real.

Although an unambiguous description of atomic reality is impossible with our ordinary concepts of material processes, we have an unambiguous mathematical scheme that gives the right predictions and probabilities for any observation. A physical description, however, must make use of such seemingly contradictory concepts as the wave picture and the particle picture. Neither can give a complete description, but both are necessary to understand the phenomenon in its entirety. Each of these mutually exclusive perspectives gives only a partial, one-sided view; both are needed for a full understanding. Niels Bohr introduced the term "complementarity" to describe this novel situation. This is why we face a richer reality in the quantum world than the classical picture has ever been able to describe.

ACT IV: THE QUANTUM LADDER
An extension of Quantum Mechanics to Nuclear and Subnuclear Phenomena and to the History of the Universe

After its conception, quantum mechanics developed in two distinct directions. The first, broadest development was toward a better understanding of the properties of agglomerations of atoms, such as molecules, liquids, and solids. Quantum mechanics turned out to be the key to many previously unexplained properties of materials—such as their behavior at high and low temperatures—and of chemical reactions and molecule formations. Knowing the quantum states of atoms made it possible to understand what happens when atoms are joined to molecules, liquids, or solids. Electrical and optical properties of metals, for example, turned out to be consequences of peculiar properties of electronic quantum states in the regular array of atoms in metal. The disappearance of electric resistance in some metals at low temperature (superconductivity) could now be explained. New forms of electric conductors, semiconductors, for example, were found and understood. These new insights led to the invention of the transistor and the microchip, which revolutionized electronic technology.

The other development of quantum mechanics is less broad but deeper: it goes into the depth of the structure of matter, into the structure of the atomic nucleus, and later into the structure of the constituents of the nucleus. The same quantum mechanics that once explained atomic behavior is now found to operate on a deeper level within atomic nuclei and even within their constituents.

Let us look at the atomic nucleus. It is a very small, massive, positively charged entity, roughly speaking, about 10,000 times smaller in diameter than the atom. It is responsible for the structure of atoms, since its positive electric charge attracts electrons and keeps them confined in the atom. That confinement produces the characteristic quantum states, such as those depicted in Figure 8.

Rutherford, who in 1911 discovered the internal structure of atoms, observed in 1917 that atomic nuclei also have an internal structure. He found that they contained protons. The proton itself is nothing other than the nucleus of the simplest atom, the hydrogen atom. The additional constituent contained in other nuclei was recognized by Chadwick, who in 1932 discovered the neutron—a particle very similar in mass and character to the proton, except that it carries no electric charge, whereas the proton carries one unit of positive charge. Atomic nuclei were found to be composed of protons and neutrons, with the positive charge of a nucleus provided by its protons.

With this discovery, a new branch of physics began: nuclear physics. First of all, the mere existence of a conglomerate of protons and neutrons suggests the action of a new kind of force. Electric forces could not keep protons and uncharged neutrons together; indeed, protons would be driven out because charged particles of equal sign repel each other. There must be a strongly attractive force acting between neutrons and protons to keep them together in such a small entity as the nucleus. We call it the nuclear force—such a force was indeed observed and measured.

Then, in the 1930s, a repeat performance of quantum mechanics took place. Protons and neutrons are also subject to the wave-particle duality, as are all particles. The nuclear force confines them into a small area of space. Confinement produces characteristic wave patterns, not unlike those shown in Figure 8. Thus, nuclei, like atoms, are expected to exhibit typical quantum states, with properties such as stability and regeneration, except that the relevant energies and energy differences are much larger.

Here we come to an important principle of quantum mechanics: the energy–size relation. It refers to the energies of quantum states of a confined system of particles. The smaller the size of the system, the greater are those energies and energy differences between quantum states. They also depend on the mass greater of the constituents: the higher the mass, the smaller the energies. We will concentrate on the size dependence here; it is the more important one.

The nucleus is very much smaller than the atom. Therefore, the energies of the quantum states and the energy intervals between them are much greater. We call nuclear physics the next higher rung of the quantum ladder, the lowest rung being atomic and molecular physics. Indeed, it takes millions of electron volts (a unit of one million is a mega-electron-volt or MeV) to lift a nucleus from its lowest quantum state to the next one, whereas in an atom, it takes only a few electron volts (roughly between one and ten). Nuclear reactions imply energy exchanges of millions of electron volts, whereas chemical reactions between atoms deal with exchanges of only a few. This is why nuclear explosives are so much more powerful than ordinary ones.

When a nucleus performs a transition from a higher to a lower quantum state, the energy difference is emitted in the form of a photon, just as it is in an atom, but the "nuclear light" called gamma rays is much more energetic than "atomic light." In the nuclear regime, another kind of emission appears: sometimes, instead of a photon, a pair of particles is emitted, an electron and a neutrino, in a process known as radioactivity. It could not have occurred in the atomic regime, because it requires energies not available in atomic processes. An electron and a neutrino must be created. According to Einstein's famous equivalence of energy and mass—$E = mc^2$—the creation of an electron requires the availability of at least $\frac{1}{2}$ MeV, which is the energy corresponding to the electron mass. A neutrino is massless; it does not require a minimum energy to be created. Such energies as the mass energy of the electron are not available in transitions between atomic quantum states, but they are available in transitions between nuclear quantum states.

Because of the large difference in energy, nuclear processes occur under very different conditions from atomic or molecular ones, processes that require energy exchanges of only a few electron volts. This is approximately the energy of photons coming from the sun. Therefore, the surface of the earth abounds with phenomena based on interactions of atoms and molecules. The atomic nuclei necessarily stay in their lowest quantum state under such conditions and therefore act as unchanging entities. In our terrestrial world, nuclei never get naturally excited; they are never lifted into their higher quantum states; and they appear completely stable. Nuclear physics is dormant on earth. We observe nuclear phenomena only when we construct machines—cyclotrons, synchrotrons, and other particle accelerators or nuclear reactors—that can produce the necessary energies.

The nuclear processes found on earth, apart from man-made ones, are the decays of some naturally radioactive substances, such as radium, thorium, or uranium, responsible for much of the heat produced deep in the interior of the earth. But they are not of terrestrial origin. They were produced when the matter that now constitutes the earth was ejected with tremendous energies by a supernova explosion seven billion years ago. They represent the last embers of the great nuclear fire that created the elements.

The places of nuclear processes in nature are those regions where millions of electron volts are available. That happens in the interior of stars and in the explosions of supernovas. Indeed, nuclear reactions in the center of the sun are the sources of solar heat. They are the nuclear fire in which hydrogen nuclei are burnt to helium nuclei (not unlike the burning of coal to carbon dioxide in a coal fire). It will last four or five billion years before burning out.

There is an even higher rung of the quantum ladder. Certain strange occurrences in cosmic rays, unaccountable on the basis of nuclear physics, had already been observed in the 1930s. The decisive discovery was made in 1950, when E. Fermi and his collaborators found that the proton has an excited quantum state. Soon thereafter, many more quantum states of the proton and neutron were discovered, pointing toward an internal structure of nuclear particles. Like the atom and the nucleus, they seemed to be a composite system made of some constituent particles that are combined by some kind of force and form typical wave patterns that lead to discrete quantum states.

These discoveries opened up a new world of phenomena: the third rung of the quantum ladder, the subnuclear realm. As expected from the energy–size relation, the relevant energies are much larger. They are measured by the giga-electron volt (GeV), that is, a billion electron volts. The first excited state of the proton is 0.3 GeV above the ground state. This is the reason why subnuclear phenomena are dormant, even in the nuclear realm. New types of accelerators of many GeV are needed to observe them.

It turned out to be a most surprising world, not yet fully exploited and understood. The constituents of the proton and neutron were identified. They received the ugly name "quarks." A very strong new force was identified that holds quarks together within the proton. So far, the picture turned out to be similar to the one at the lower ranges of the quantum ladder. The different quantum states of the proton and neutron could again be interpreted as confined waves of quarks.

There are a number of unexpected new features that are to some extent still surprising and difficult to explain. For example, it seems to be impossible to extricate a quark from a proton or neutron. They cannot be liberated from confining bonds, but they can be observed to move within the proton and neutron, in contrast to the situation on the lower rungs: the atom can be decomposed into nucleons and electrons; the nucleus can be decomposed into protons and neutrons.

Furthermore, a number of new short-lived entities show up: mesons and heavy electrons. Both entities need gigavolt energies to be created. They exist only for a short time. They transform themselves quickly into other known particles, such as ordinary electrons, neutrinos, and photons.

Antimatter comes to play an important role on the third rung: What is it? For every particle there is a corresponding antiparticle with exactly the same mass but opposite charge. There are antiatoms made up of positive antielectrons and negative antinuclei composed of antiprotons and antineutrons. But antimatter cannot exist together with ordinary matter, because an antiparticle and a particle annihilate each other on contact and transform themselves into energy. This is a transformation of one kind of energy into another kind of energy, since mass, according to Einstein, is a form of energy. Inversely, if energy in sufficient concentration is available, it can transform itself into a pair consisting of particle and antiparticle. The energy concentrations necessary for such processes are very high and available to a sufficient degree only at the third rung of the quantum ladder, so as to make antimatter an important ingredient of the subnuclear phenomena.

The existence of antimatter is another triumph of quantum mechanics. In the early 1930s, the British physicist P. A. M. Dirac showed that the equations of quantum mechanics and relativity theory required that there be an antiparticle to every particle. It also followed that particle-antiparticle pairs can be created from other forms of energy and annihilated into energy. Dirac could not believe that result because, at that time, antimatter had not yet been found. He was deeply astonished by these strange consequences of his calculations. These equations seemed to him "more intelligent than their author." It was an unusual feat of the human mind to predict the existence of antimatter by pure intellectual insight before it was actually observed in nature.

Let us return to the subnuclear world, which is revealed with the help of very high energy beams produced by powerful accelerators. When a particle carrying many gigavolts of energy impinges upon a target, an explosion of newly created particles takes place: protons, antiprotons, electrons, antielectrons, mesons, and other particles emerge all over. Figure 9 gives a telling picture of the variety of such events.

In the past three decades, the quantum ladder has acquired a new significance. There seems to be a connection between the infinitely small, the elementary constituents of matter, and the infinitely large, the origin and history of the universe as a whole. The connecting link is the discovery of the expansion of the universe. There are a number of indications that celestial objects move away from each other. The farther the object is, the faster it seems to move away. If this is so, we would expect that in the distant past, the concentration of mass ought to have been much greater. Indeed, about fifteen billion years

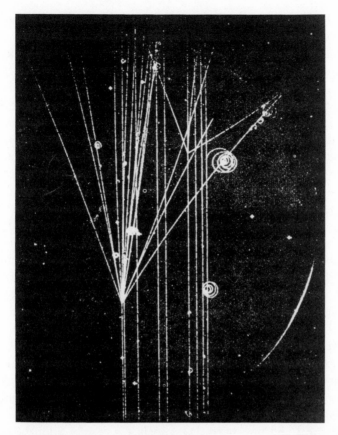

Figure 9 *A bubble-chamber picture of a 25-GeV proton beam impinging on a hydrogen atom and producing new particles. (Courtesy of CERN, Geneva, Switzerland.)*

ago, all space should have been filled with almost infinitely concentrated matter. Such concentration would have to be accompanied by extremely high pressure and temperature. Thus, we are led to the tentative conclusion that the universe started with a "primal bang," where all space was filled with highly concentrated matter of extremely high temperature and energy, which decompressed and diluted itself, first quickly and then more slowly, until it reached its present state.

One of the most uncanny discoveries of the last decade was the observation of a pervading cool radiation coming from all directions in space, with all the properties of an optical reverberation of the radiation emitted during the initial hot period in the life of the universe. It was another indication of the great happening at the beginning of the universe.

Developments from the primal bang to our present state are intimately connected to the quantum ladder. In the first instants after the bang, energy concentration was indeed so high that the phenomena of the third rung of the quantum ladder was the order of the day, or more appropriately, the order of the microsecond. At that time, space was filled with quarks, antiquarks, gluons, electrons, antielectrons, and neutrinos and with an intense light radiation of extremely energetic photons. Then, as the universe expanded, energy concentration diminished rapidly. Particles and antiparticles annihilated, producing more radiation and short-lived mesons. After a few microseconds, a slight surplus of quarks over antiquarks (not quite understood today) remained, and the quarks assembled into protons and neutrons. Then the temperature dropped further because of the expansion. After about 10 seconds, some protons and neutrons assembled into helium nuclei. We now step down to the second rung of the quantum ladder: the nuclear realm. It probably took several hundred thousand years to cool down sufficiently to allow electrons to be bound by the nuclei to form atoms, arriving at the first rung. It then took billions of years to reach the present situation. Galaxies and stars were formed, and on the surface of some planets, the atomic and molecular world developed the great variety of forms and materials we now see on earth.

This view of the development of the universe is to some extent hypothetical and unproven. It is much less certain than the validity of quantum mechanics and our knowledge of the properties of molecules, atoms, and nuclei.

The quantum ladder symbolized the steady increase in depth of our knowledge about the structure of matter. It started with ordinary chunks of matter composed of atoms and molecules, whose structure was revealed on the first rung. It then proceeded to the structure of atomic nuclei and—finally today—to the quarks as constituents of the proton or neutron. There may exist yet unknown higher rungs of the ladder. The development of the universe happened in the opposite direction, down the quantum ladder, as it were. The very beginnings are shrouded in the unknown, since we know nothing about the higher rungs of the ladder that may come into play in the first, extremely short time intervals. But we have clearer ideas about the evolutionary history of the world from a microsecond after the primal bang to the present universe. It was a series of gradual steps, from the simple to the complicated, from the unordered to the organized, from the hot, formless gas of elementary particles to the cooler, structured atoms and molecules; still further to the more structured liquids and solids, and finally to sophisticated self-reproducing living organisms. Steps in this history that are still hidden in ignorance and guesswork include what happened immediately after the "primal bang," the mechanisms forming galaxies and clusters of galaxies, and the details of the origin and development of life on our planet.

The drama of the development of quantum mechanics has not ended, but we have arrived at the present limits of our knowledge. This limit lies far beyond what could have been expected at the turn of the century, when quantum mechanics was conceived. Ingenious use of accelerators and instrumentation revealed even deeper structures of matter, still subject to the rules of quantum mechanics in more developed forms. It is certainly an encouraging thought that we were able, in our laboratories, not only to understand the deeper structure of matter, but also to recreate the processes and phenomena that, in all probability, happened in nature only in the first instants of its existence.

8

What Is
An Elementary Particle?

The concept that matter consists of some simple and unchanging elementary constituents is deeply ingrained in our way of thinking. We observe that matter appears in enormous varieties of different realizations, qualities, shapes, and forms, transforming and changing from one into others. In these changes, however, we observe many recurrent properties, many features that remain unchanged, or if changed, return under similar conditions. We find constancies and regularities in the flow of events; we recognize materials with well-defined properties, such as water, metals, rocks, or living species; we conclude that there must be something unchanging in nature that causes these recurrent phenomena.

NEWTON'S IDEA

This recognition is the origin of the idea of elementary particles. Newton expressed it very succinctly in his *Opticks*:

> All things being considered, it seems probable to me that God in the Beginning formed Matter in solid, massy, hard, impenetrable, moveable Particles, of such Sizes and Figures, and with such other Properties, and in such Proportion to Space, as most conduced to the End for which he formed them; and that these primitive Particles being Solids, are incomparably harder than any porous Bodies compounded of

them; even so very hard, as never to wear or to break into pieces; no ordinary Power being able to divide what God himself made one in the first Creation.

And then he goes on to say, "Changes of Corporeal Things are to be placed only in the various Separations and new Associations of Motions of these permanent Particles."

Newton clearly and distinctly expresses the idea that matter is composed of elementary particles. This conception was corroborated by the chemists of the nineteenth century, who found that the tremendous variety of natural materials could be considered as being composed of only ninety-two different substances, which we now call elements. These are composed of small particles called atoms. There are also ninety-two different kinds of atoms, one for each element. During the nineteenth century, each atom was thought to be indivisible, and this lack of divisibility was exactly what Newton had in mind when he said that primitive particles were "incomparably hard." In fact, the word "atom" itself comes from Greek and means nondivisible.

STRUCTURE OF THE ATOM

The fundamental idea of an incomparably hard, elementary particle that could not be divided was not destined to last. In 1911, Rutherford made a decisive experiment that heralded a turn away from this concept. He showed that atoms do, in fact, contain smaller constituents. He literally took apart what, according to Newton, no ordinary power could divide. Furthermore, he showed us what we all know now very well, that an atom is a planetary system, with a nucleus in the middle, surrounded by scurrying electrons.

With Rutherford's discovery, physics and chemistry faced an extreme crisis. The first aspect of the crisis was to understand how an atom could be incomparably hard and unchanging if it consists of a planetary system. The stability of matter demands that atoms be hard and unchanging, yet a planetary system is easily changed if something disturbs it and changes completely if it collides with another planetary system. For example, if our solar system were to collide with another, both systems after the collision would be quite different. Yet atomic systems do not behave in this way. When two atomic systems collide, as happens frequently in a gas, atoms become distorted in the collision, but afterward, they return to their original condition, with all the properties—such as shape and size—they originally possessed intact. So this aspect of the crisis asked how it was possible for atoms to be planetary systems and yet, at the same time, be capable of regeneration.

The second aspect of the dilemma was the discovery that the energy of an atomic system can assume only a series of discrete values (energy levels), corresponding to the "quantum states" of the system. Atoms can absorb or emit energy only in discrete amounts. This happens usually with an absorption or emission of a light quantum. Such behavior contrasts strongly with that of a planetary system, which can absorb or lose energy in any amount it pleases. There is no succession of energy levels in a planetary system as there is in an atomic system.

It took physicists some two decades to resolve this crisis through the development of quantum mechanics. This was one of the most revolutionary periods in our quest to understand nature (see my essay, "What Is Quantum Mechanics?" in this collection).

It is important to note that there is a finite energy step between the lowest state and the first, excited state of an atom. It is of the order of several electron volts. Such finite energy is very important because it is in terms of this energy that we understand the incomparable hardness of Newton's fundamental particle. In Newtonian terms, a "hard" atom can be neither destroyed nor changed. But this is insured by that finite energy step. As long as the surrounding conditions are not energetic enough, that is, as long as they do not contain energies larger than this threshold energy, the atom must stay in the lowest state. Under these conditions, the atom is stable and has unchanging properties, namely, the properties of its lowest state.

Our understanding of the incomparable hardness of atoms, in terms of the finite energy difference between the lowest state and the first excited state, reveals an aspect of hardness unknown to Newton—an aspect that may be called conditional elementarity. Atoms act like elementary particles; that is, they are incomparably hard, but only in an environment that is not too energetic. When the environment contains energies much greater than the threshold energy between the ground state and the first excited state, then the atom has a good chance of becoming excited, and its properties change. That is, it no longer acts as if it were incomparably hard.

Quantum mechanics allows us to calculate the size and energies of an atom. In an atom there is a kind of equilibrium between two tendencies: (1) the electric attraction of the positively charged nucleus and the negatively charged electrons, which keeps the electrons near the nucleus, and (2) the tendency of quantum state is to expand in size. Quantum states resist compression. The smaller their volume, the larger the energy necessary to maintain it in that volume. The equilibrium between those two tendencies determines the size of the atom and its energy levels. Based on these ideas, it turns out that the radius of an atom is of the order of h^2/me^2, the Bohr radius, and the energy of the lowest atomic level is of the order of $-me^4/h^2$. In these formulas, m is the mass of the electron, e is the charge of the electron and h is Planck's constant. The main point of all this is that quantum mechanics allows us to calculate the properties of nature at the atomic level.

The dominant force in the structure of atoms is the electromagnetic force, that is, the force that charged particles exert on one another. Rutherford showed that the atom consists of a heavy, positively charged nucleus surrounded by electrons. Electrons are attracted to it, and quantum mechanics predicts what kinds of quantum states will be produced. The heavy nucleus in the center plays a small but decisive role, keeping the electrons around so that they assume the quantum states characteristic for the atom. In some ways, quality is reduced to quantity, because if I tell you, "Here is an atom with fifteen electrons and a charge of plus fifteen in its nucleus to keep these electrons around it," then all the atomic properties of this atom—its size, its color, the way it combines with other atoms, whether it is a solid or a gas—are, in principle, determined.

The manner in which atoms bond chemically to form molecules can be explained, at least in theory, by the electromagnetic force, together with quantum mechanics. I say in theory because many of the processes are very complicated, and we do not understand them in detail. But the principle is understood. The chemical bond results from the interaction of quantum states of different atoms.

Every molecule has a definite structure—a structure possible only because nuclei are heavy, weighing several thousand times more than electrons. In quantum mechanics, the heavier a thing is, the more localized it can be. So in a molecule, nuclei are localized because they are so heavy, whereas much lighter electrons are not. The quantum states of the electrons are smeared out over the molecule and act as a sort of glue keeping the molecule together.

STRUCTURE OF THE NUCLEUS

In order to understand the next step in the development of physics, it is good to remember what might be called the energy–size relation. It is a consequence of quantum mechanics that the smaller a system is, the higher its energy requirements will be to get it out of its ground state, where it cannot change its properties, and into one of its excited states, where its properties are different. As I have already pointed out in connection with atomic systems, such excitation energy is the basis for conditional elementarity. If a system is small, then a large amount of energy is required to excite it, and if such energy is not available, the system will act like an elementary particle; that is, it will act like a particle that Newton described as unchanging or incomparably hard.

The next development in the search for nature's elementary particles was Chadwick's discovery of the neutron in 1932. He revealed that neutrons are constituents of atomic nuclei. Their importance may be appreciated by considering what elementary particles appeared to be. Before Chadwick's discovery, if physicists were asked what the elementary particles of physics, the unsatisfactory answer would have been electrons and nuclei. But the trouble is that all ninety-two elements have different nuclei, and each nucleus carries a different charge. Hydrogen has one charge unit; oxygen, eight; uranium, ninety-two; and so on. We also know that for a given charge there are so-called isotopes, so that in reality we have something like 250 different nuclei. Could they all be elementary particles? Of course, people never really believed that they could be. However, because the nuclei are so small, it takes high energy to excite them. So people believed that not enough energy had been developed to find out what was going on inside. When Chadwick in England discovered the neutron, it was obvious that nuclei were not elementary particles but were instead systems very hard to excite. It is now known that nuclei consist of neutrons and protons, two particles of almost equal mass, the proton carrying a positive charge unit and the neutron electrically uncharged. But nuclei are so small and the forces that keep them together so strong that it takes millions of electron volts to get them excited—roughly 100,000 times more energy than is needed to excite atoms.

The neutron revealed that nuclei are not elementary, in the sense of being incomparably hard, but consist of protons and neutrons. They have many excited quantum states, just like atoms. But, their energy difference is very much greater, counted in mega-electron-volts (MeV), whereas atoms are counted in electron volts. This is why they appear elementary when they are exposed to energies of less than a mega-electron-volt.

With the discovery of the composition of nuclei, a new world opened, a new realm of phenomena. This world, which I call the nuclear world of the nuclear realm, deals with the phenomena that are connected with the internal structure of the nucleus—a structure dormant in our environment because the threshold energy is not available under terrestrial conditions. An ordinary fire, or even a chemical explosion, exchanges only a few electron volts between the atoms. Nuclear reactions require more than a million times as much energy. On earth, energies of this kind can only be obtained by accelerators, by cosmic rays, in nuclear reactions, and, unfortunately, in nuclear-bomb explosions.

Many new phenomena have been observed here. Nuclei react with each other. In nuclear fusion, they merge and form a larger nucleus; in nuclear fission, some heavy nuclei split into two, yielding a great deal of energy. Both processes yield energy. Indeed, the fusion of hydrogen to helium nuclei is the energy source that keeps the sun hot. We are entering a new realm of nature, the exploration of which is one of the most significant developments of the physics of this century.

One phenomenon that is the subject of this exploration is the nuclear force. If the nucleus is composed of protons and neutrons (called nucleons) and the neutrons are not charged, the electromagnetic force between charged particles cannot hold them together. There must, therefore, be a new force, a reasonably strong force, to bind these particles together. That force is called the nuclear force. It was found to be attractive over a distance of two or three 10^{-13} cm, that is, a distance of 1/100,000 of an atomic size, and repulsive when the nucleons get closer than 0.5×10^{-13} cm.

In another important process in the nuclear world, neutrons turn into protons and protons into neutrons. Neutrons and protons are just two states of a single particle known as the nucleon. The neutron state of this particle can change into the proton state, and vice versa, with the emission of a new type of radiation. Evidently, such radiation must carry charge, since the neutron acquires a positive charge when it becomes a proton. Therefore, something negatively charged must be emitted in order to conserve charge. What is emitted is an electron (negative) and a neutrino, or "lepton pair." The word "lepton" is a common name for electrons and neutrinos. A neutrino is an uncharged particle of probably zero mass. If its mass is not zero, it is certainly very much smaller than the mass of the electron. Conversely, a proton can turn into a neutron with emission of a positron (positive electron) and a neutrino. When this process occurs, a nucleus emits a lepton pair. It is called radioactivity and the nucleus then is radioactive.

There are two ways in which a nucleus performs a transition from one quantum state to another. One is the emission of light quanta, the same as in atomic transitions. The cause for that kind of transition is the electric charge of the protons in the nucleus when the electric configuration changes from one state to the other, producing electro-

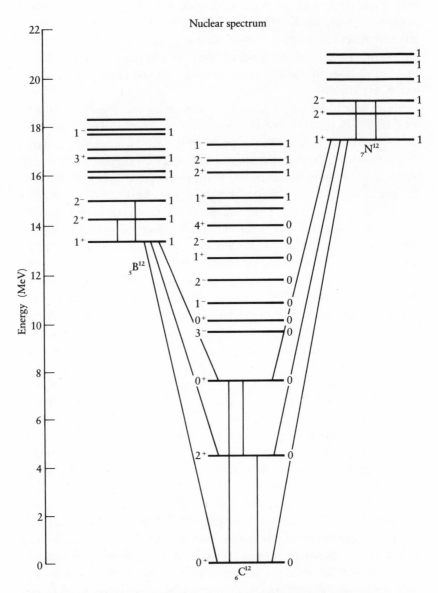

Figure 10 *The level spectrum of the twelve-nucleon system. The numbers on the left of each level give the angular momentum J and parity, and the numbers on the right give the isotopic spin. The connecting lines are the most important transitions—the vertical ones are electromagnetic, and the skew ones are lepton-pair emissions. In this figure, $_5B^{12}$ stands for boron with five protons, $_6C^{12}$ stands for carbon with six protons, and $_7N^{12}$ stands for nitrogen with seven protons. All three are examples of twelve-nucleon systems.*

magnetic radiation that appears as an emitted light quantum. That is also the mechanism producing the emission of light in an atom.

In the other kind of transition, a lepton pair is emitted from the nucleus. Necessarily, in such transitions the nucleus changes its charge. These transitions are much slower than those emitting light quanta. This is why interaction leading to lepton-pair emission is called "weak interaction."

Figure 10 shows the spectra (excited states) of three nuclei, all consisting of twelve nucleons. Actually, they are all the same nucleus, since replacing a neutron by a proton (or vice versa) can be considered equivalent to changing the quantum state of the twelve-nucleon system.

At this point it is interesting to note a difference between the nuclear and the atomic realm. Within the atom we find a heavy nucleus and light electrons—a situation we could almost characterize as an authoritarian regime. The heavy, highly charged nucleus decides what happens. By the same analogy, the nucleus can be characterized as a democratic regime. Protons and neutrons are practically the same weight and exert the same nuclear force.

SUBNUCLEAR STRUCTURE

We have now traced the development of the idea of an elementary particle roughly up until the 1930s, when physicists lived in what can be described as a fool's paradise. They believed they had found all the elementary particles: protons, neutrons, electrons, and neutrinos. They also believed there were four forces in nature: the electromagnetic force, keeping electrons and nuclei together in the atom; the nuclear force, keeping protons and neutrons together in the nucleus; the weak force, producing transitions between protons and neutrons; and gravity, acting between large bodies. It was a fool's paradise because it turned out that it was not so. To understand why, we introduce the concept of the "quantum ladder." Molecules consist of atoms. Atoms consist of nuclei and electrons. Electrons do not yet seem to be composite, but nuclei consist of nucleons, that is, protons and neutrons. Now what about the nucleon? What does it consist of?

To answer this question we already have a model to guide us through atomic systems: atoms attract each other to form molecules, just as nucleons attract each other to form nuclei. By comparing the force between atoms with the force between nucleons, we may be able to get a clue to help us understand this latter force. When we look at the force holding atoms together in molecules, we find that it is not unlike the nuclear force. Atoms, as well as nucleons, are attracted at a certain distance and then repelled at closer distances. There are, however, certain differences. The chemical force is much weaker. The energy units for the chemical force are only electron volts and not millions of electron volts, as in the case of the nuclear force. Distances are much longer—angstroms, not fermis, meaning 10^{-8} cm, instead of 10^{-13} cm. Still, the character of the two forces is strikingly similar, so we may be able to understand the nuclear force in the same way we understand the chemical force. The chemical force comes about because atomic quantum states interact and produce a bond between them. Before we could understand the nature of the chemical bond, we had to recognize that the internal structure of atoms was composed of electrons and nuclei. Now, since the nuclear force has the same basic shape as the chemical bond, there is hope that we can understand it in a similar fashion, that is, in terms of the internal structure of a nucleon, analogous to the internal structure of the atom. Of course, the analogy is not exact. The nuclear force is not identical to the chemical force in all respects, only in general outline. But the analogy is good enough to give us hope that a search for the internal structure of a nucleon would be profitable.

The first experimental evidence of the internal structure of the nucleon came in 1952 when Enrico Fermi and his collaborators in Chicago were able to excite a proton to its first excited state. This result led to a new world, a third realm of phenomena that we call the subnuclear world (see Figure 11).

Now let us explore the strange, unexpected phenomena lying dormant under ordinary conditions. Because protons are smaller than nuclei, the energy–size relation of quantum mechanics discussed before dictates that the energy we need to excite these particles will be greater than the amount needed to excite the nucleus. Fermi and his colleagues needed a cyclotron of 400 million eV, several hundred times more than the usual threshold of nuclei, in order to obtain the first excited state of the proton. Once enough energy is available to excite these nucleons, we find not only excited protons and neutrons, but also some new entities called mesons, heavy electrons, different kinds of neutrinos, and antimatter. Particles are produced in lavish numbers, but most of them, having very short lifetimes, decay into previously known particles.

The next four figures illustrate some of these discoveries. First, let us look at the excited states of the nucleon. Figure 12 gives the nucleon spectrum, as it was known about ten years after Fermi's first discovery. The ground state is the proton and the neutron indicated by *P,N*.

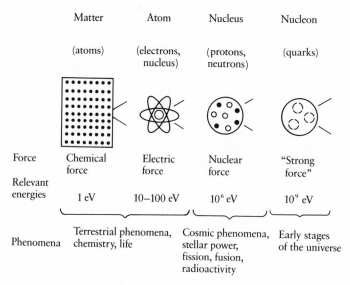

	Matter	Atom	Nucleus	Nucleon
	(atoms)	(electrons, nucleus)	(protons, neutrons)	(quarks)
Force	Chemical force	Electric force	Nuclear force	"Strong force"
Relevant energies	1 eV	10–100 eV	10^6 eV	10^9 eV
Phenomena	Terrestrial phenomena, chemistry, life		Cosmic phenomena, stellar power, fission, fusion, radioactivity	Early stages of the universe

Figure 11 *The quantum ladder.*

Fermi discovered the first excited state, which is the lowest one in the second column and called it Δ. The other states were discovered later. In fact, these data are more than twenty years old. There are many, many more levels now known than are shown here. New quantum numbers, such as "isotopic spin" I and "strangeness" S, had to be introduced to bring order into this array of levels. Notice that the energy scale is in gigaelectron volts, which means a billion electron volts—much higher energy than needed at atomic or nuclear levels. There are some new kinds of transitions taking place in the subnuclear level.

Figure 13 illustrates some of these transitions, compared with those seen at atomic and nuclear levels. In atoms, transitions are accompanied by emission of light quanta; in nuclei, gamma rays (energetic light quanta) and lepton pairs are emitted. In transitions between levels of the nucleon, in addition to gamma rays and lepton pairs, new entities, such as π- and K-mesons, are emitted.

It soon was found that π- and K-mesons were not the only mesons. There are many more. Figure 14 plots the most important members of the meson spectrum, of which the π- and K-mesons are only a sample. Mesons are rather ephemeral entities that decay in about a billionth of a second, or less, into less exotic particles. Figure 15 shows how some of the different mesons decay. Notice that π- and K-mesons

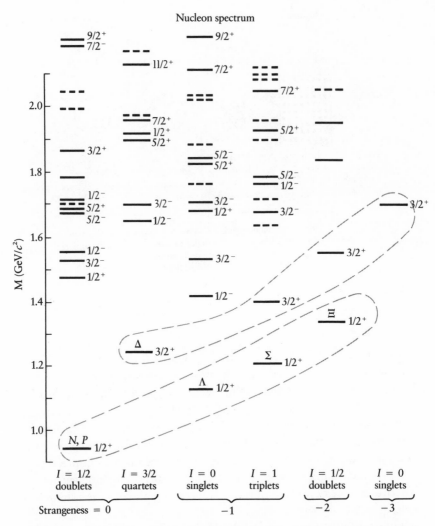

Figure 12 *The levels spectrum of the nucleon. The numbers on the right of the levels indicate the angular momentum quantum number and the parity. The broken lines encircle states that differ only in the type of quarks they are composed of, but not in the wave patterns of those quarks.*

decay into gamma rays (that is, light) and into lepton pairs. It turns out that the electron appears in several forms, a normal electron and heavy electrons. Heavy electrons are known as muons and tauons. They are unstable and ultimately decay, as shown in Figure 15. The third electron, the tauon, is much heavier than the other two and also

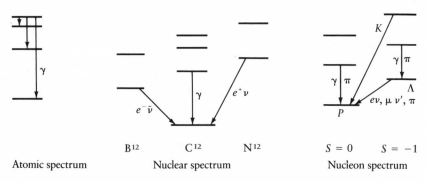

Figure 13 *The different kinds of transition between the levels of excitation in the different spectra. The symbol γ refers to photons.*

decays quickly into lighter particles. Why these three types of electrons exist is still unknown. When he heard about the discovery of the muon, I. I. Rabi quipped, "Who ordered this?"

And what about antimatter? In the 1920s, physicists were surprised to discover that atoms consisted of positively charged nuclei and negatively charged electrons. They wondered why there were not atoms in which the nucleus was negatively charged, surrounded by positively charged electrons. "Why is nature so asymmetrical?" they asked. Some physicists believed that nature was just that—unsymmetrical. Then came one of the most dramatic developments in the intellectual penetration of nature. In England, P.A.M. Dirac was attempting to adjust quantum mechanics to special relativity. This was not easy. In the course of his work, Dirac came upon an equation that frightened him, as he later admitted, because it was so infinitely rich in information. It showed why the electron has a spin that can assume only two opposite values, why it has a magnetic moment. But, if you read the equation correctly, it also revealed that, besides the negative electron, a positive electron (the positron) must also exist; equally, besides the positive proton, a negative proton must also exist. In other words, Dirac's equation had symmetry built right in it: for every particle there must be an antiparticle. Dirac could hardly believe it and thought that he must have interpreted something wrong, because no one had yet seen a positive electron or a negative proton. But only a few years later, in 1932, Anderson and Neddermeyer discovered the positive electron, and twenty-five years later Segre and coworkers discovered the antiproton. These and many subsequent experiments confirmed the existence of Dirac's particle-antiparticle symmetry.

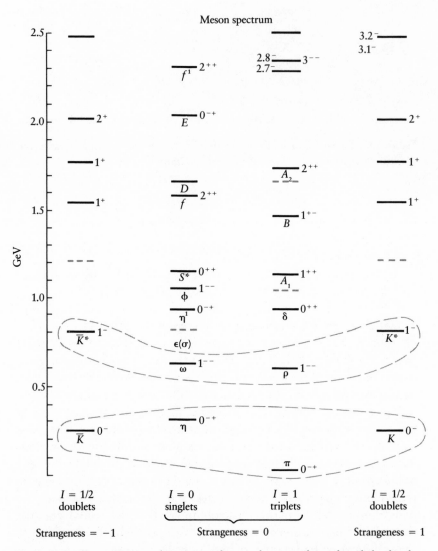

Figure 14 *The spectrum of mesons. The numbers on the right of the levels indicate the angular momentum quantum number, the parity sign, and, in some cases, the charge-conjugation sign. The broken lines encircle mesons that differ only in the type of quarks they are composed of, but not in the quantum states of those quarks.*

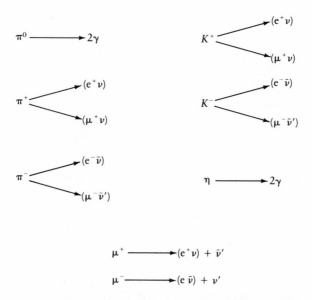

Figure 15 *Some meson and heavy-electron transformations into other forms of energy.*

Particle-antiparticle symmetry is linked with another strange phenomenon: the production and annihilation of subatomic particles. Annihilation of particle-antiparticle pairs can form other types of energy. For example, protons and antiprotons can annihilate each other to produce light or mesons. Particle-antiparticle pairs can be created from pure energy, or light. For example, light can be transformed into electron-positron pairs or proton-antiproton pairs. Such interactions explain why we do not see antimatter under ordinary conditions. If antimatter were to emerge into our world, it would annihilate ordinary matter to produce light or mesons. So under ordinary circumstances, we see only the ordinary matter that is left after antimatter has been annihilated. Either kind of matter can be stable in a region of space if none of its antimatter is present at the same time. If both kinds are present, they will interact and annihilate each other.

In the subnuclear realm, production of antimatter poses great difficulties for physicists. Obstacles arise because at this level we are dealing with extremely high energy. A great amount of energy is required for particle-antiparticle production because enough energy must be available to produce the rest mass of each particle. To produce an electron-positron pair, at least twice the rest mass energy of the electron is needed. Under ordinary conditions in the atomic world, we do not have sufficient energy. That is why antimatter is produced only under exceptional conditions in the atomic or nuclear world. But when we come to the subnuclear world, the energy indeed is great enough. This places us in a very strange situation. I shall describe the difficulty using an analogy. Take a couple of good Swiss watches. If you want to know what is inside them, you can hurl them together so strongly they break open, revealing their wheels, springs, and other parts. Basically this is the method physicists have used to find out what is inside atoms and nuclei. But it does not work with nucleons. If two nucleons are hurled together strongly enough to reveal what is inside them, not only is the internal structure of the nucleons exposed, but also a lot of particles and antiparticles are created. The difficulty lies in deciding which particles come from the internal structure of the nucleon and which are merely being created because of the high energies available. (Indeed, this difficulty is true even for Swiss watches, because when you hurl them together with enough strength to break them open, luminous sparks fly from them. No one thinks of the light emitted as having been in the original watches!)

Data from our experiments with subnuclear particles are given in Figures 12 and 14. Figure 12 shows some of the many excited states that the proton and the neutron can assume; Figure 14 covers mesons. The question that these data pose is: What is the underlying structure from which this plethora of excited states arises? It reminds us of the situation when we had to face ninety-two different nuclei. We found that there really are only two kinds of nuclear particles, protons and neutrons, and that the ninety-two nuclei are combinations of these.

QUARKS

Murray Gell-Mann and George Zweig recognized in 1960 that the numerous excited states of the nucleon (and also of the mesons) can be explained in a similar way. They suggested that there are a few fundamental nuclear particles, which Gell-Mann dubbed "quarks," whose combinations give rise to the observed nucleon states and mesons. Their idea was that the nucleon consisted of three quarks and the mesons of a quark and an antiquark. To arrive at the observed great variety of quantum states of such quark systems required the introduction of at least five (probably six) different types of quarks—referred to by the letters u-, d-, s-, c-, b-, and t-, with such whimsical names as up, down, strange, charmed, bottom, and top, to describe their properties. They carry certain new quantum numbers: u- and d-

quarks carry what is called isotopic spin $+\frac{1}{2}$ and $-\frac{1}{2}$, respectively; s-quarks carry strangeness; c-quarks carry a property distinct from the others, dubbed charm; the b- and t-quarks carry properties called bottom and top. These properties are expressed in quantum numbers that remain unchanged in processes involving collision of the entities made of quarks.

In order to arrive at the right electric charges of quark combinations, we have to make a most unusual assumption. Quark charges are fractions of the fundamental unit of electric charge, which is the charge e of the proton. The upper part of Table 1 shows the assignments.

The proton and the neutron consist of a triplet of only u- and d-quarks. The proton is the triplet uud, and the neutron is ddu. We see that the charges add up, as they should, to e in the former case, to zero in the latter. The higher states in Figure 12 are either combinations of u- and d-quarks in excited states, not unlike electrons in excited states of the atom or combinations where quarks other than u and d are involved. For example, the triplet uds would give the state denoted by Λ in Figure 12, with the total charge zero, but it carries strangeness because of the presence of s.

Mesons are pairs of quarks and antiquarks: for example, three mesons, called pions π^+, π°, and π^- are the pairs $u\bar{d}$, $u\bar{u}$ (or $d\bar{d}$), and $d\bar{u}$, making up a triplet with electric charge $+1$, 0, and -1, in units of e. A bar over a symbol signifies an antiquark carrying the opposite charge. Mesons have a short lifetime because quarks and antiquarks annihilate each other. Thus, mesons decay into other particles, such as photons, electrons and neutrinos. Excited states of protons and neutrons also have short lives, but they perform transitions that finally end in the proton, which is stable. Subnuclear physics abounds in short-lived entities.

Today, the existence of quarks is well assured. One can even "see" quarks inside a nucleon this way: when a beam of very energetic electrons is directed at a proton, the beam is slightly scattered because of the overall charge e of the proton. But occasionally we observe rather strong scattering that can be explained only by a near encounter of an electron with a particle within the proton. The nature of these scatterings indicates what kinds of particles have done it. Indeed, the analysis of such scattering leads to the conclusion that they are small entities of fractional charge, as indicated in Table 1. We may call this "seeing the quark" because when we see with our own eyes, we also analyze the scattering of light by the object seen.

Strangely enough, and perhaps unfortunately, we cannot prove that a proton consists of three quarks simply by hitting it hard enough to release a quark—the method used to prove that the nucleus consists of protons and neutrons and that atoms consist of a nucleus and electrons. The extraction of a constituent is the best proof of the inner structure of an entity: remember the example of the Swiss watch. But this extraction turned out to be impossible with quarks. The reason will become clear when we analyze the force that keeps quarks together.

Quarks are subject to several forces: electromagnetic forces, because of their electric charge; "weak" forces, which transform one quark type into the other with the emission of a lepton pair. For example, if a neutron becomes a proton with the emission of a lepton pair, what really occurs is that a u-quark in the proton becomes a d-quark, accompanied by the emission of a lepton pair. Since the proton is a *uud* combination, we would then get a *udd* combination which is the neutron. Furthermore and most important, quarks are subject to the "strong" force, which keeps them together in nucleons and mesons. Of course, they are also subject to gravity, as is any massive or energy-carrying object.

In order to understand the nature of the strong force between quarks, we must analyze the force concept at a deeper level. A force is usually described by a force field. For example, the attraction of the planets by the sun, is ascribed to a gravitational field surrounding the sun, and any object within the range of that field is acted upon by that field, pushing it toward the source. An electric charge is surrounded by an electric field acting on another charge within its range, attracting it when the second charge is opposite and repelling it when it is equal. We also ascribe fields to the strong and the weak force; the strong field is called the "glue field" (it glues the quarks together); the weak force is transmitted by the "weak field," with a very short range.

According to the quantum mechanics of fields, known as quantum-field theory, there exist field quanta, little entities of the field that play an important role in the actions of the field. Sometimes, these appear as particles, but with properties different from those of particles such as electrons or quarks. Field particles are called "bosons," whereas electrons and quarks are "fermions." Often, a field appears in the form of a wave—as in electromagnetic or gravitational waves—with field quanta called photons (or light quanta) in the former case and gravitons in the latter. Strong and weak fields form waves under extraordinary conditions only. Their quanta, known as "gluons" in the strong case and "W- and Z-bosons" in the weak case, are instrumental in producing field effects. All field quanta have zero rest mass and therefore move with light velocity. The great exceptions are the W- and Z-bosons, which have great mass, even comparable to a silver nucleus. Since such heavy entities cannot propagate any distance, except when extremely high energies are available, weak forces have a very short range.

We now return to the "strong force" between gluons, with its most surprising properties. Where does the force come from? We know that the source of gravity is mass (or energy); the source of the electromagnetic force is the electric charge; the source of the weak force is something we call a weak charge, shared by quarks, electrons, and neutrinos. (Detailed study of the weak source has had an interesting result: it has led to a unification of electromagnetic and weak fields as components of an overall field. We will not go into the details of this theory.) The source of the strong force is a new property of quarks that has received the name "color" but has nothing to do with ordinary color. Electric charge is characterized by a single number, either positive or negative. Electric charge is also bound to the particle, whereas an electric field does not carry any charge. Color charge is three-fold and symbolically described as red, blue, and yellow. The essential point is that quarks can transmit color to the glue field. For example, quarks produce a field by changing from red to blue, with the emitted gluon taking color along. When the field acts on another quark, it changes the color of the other quark. The theory that describes these interactions is called "quantum chromodynamics," providing an analogy to quantum electrodynamics, the theory of electromagnetic effects.

There is an important similarity between color and electric charge. The combination of two particles with opposite electric charge is neutral; it carries no net charge. For example, a hydrogen atom consists of a positive proton and a negative electron and therefore has no net charge. When combined, the three color charges also cancel each other. The combination of three quarks, each with a different color, is neutral, colorless, and will not produce a color field. Here we have an analogy to ordinary color: the three fundamental colors combine to create white. Furthermore, quark-antiquark combinations (mesons) are colorless because antiquarks possess the anticolor of a colored quark, the sum of the two other colors. In the analogy to common color, anticolor is the complementary one that produces white when added to the color. Thus, three quarks of different color and the quark-antiquark pairs are the only combinations that produce a colorless whole.

These are more surprising consequences of "chromodynamics."

First, field quanta carry color charge; therefore, some gluons attract each other and occasionally form entities called glue balls. Second, the strong force transmitted by the gluon field does not decrease with distance, as electric, gravitational, and weak forces do, but becomes stronger. We cannot explain that reversal in simple terms—it has to do with the spread of color charge from the source into the field— but the consequences are obvious. If attraction increases with distance, it is impossible to remove a quark from a proton or a meson since it would require infinite energy to do so.

The increase of attraction with distance explains the emission of a meson by an excited proton. The surplus energy of excitation has this effect: the bond that holds one of the quarks becomes stretched and acquires more energy, until it can produce a quark-antiquark pair, the antiquark forms a meson with stretched quark, and the quark replaces the latter in the proton. What we get is a nucleon and a meson (see Figure 16).

It becomes clear now why we find quarks only in combinations of three of different color or in quark-antiquark pairs. Only those com-

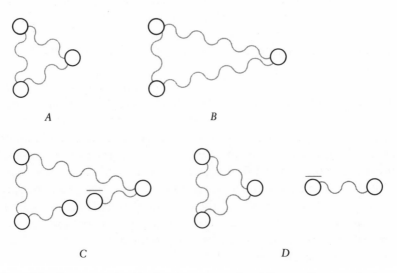

A

B

C

D

Figure 16   *Meson production from a proton after delivery of energy. A. A nucleon. B. Energy is fed into the nucleon and the bonds of one quark are stretched. C. The stretched bond creates a quark-antiquark pair. D. The newly formed quark returns to the two quarks of the original proton and forms a nucleon again; the rest becomes a meson.*

binations are colorless as a whole. When they are well separated from each other, the forces between the quarks of one entity and those of the other cancel out. However, if two nucleons come close to each other, the strong forces between quarks no longer cancel completely, because distances between quarks of one nucleon and quarks of others vary for different pairs. This is the origin of the nuclear force, quite analogous to the chemical force between atoms. Each atom is electrically neutral, so there is no net force at large distances. At closer distances, however, a net attraction may occur when the constituents of one atom interact with those of another.

UNSOLVED PROBLEMS

We have presented a greatly simplified sketch of our present view regarding the inner structure of matter, from atoms to quarks. The main features of this view probably are correct, but many details are still the object of intensive research. Although we are able to explain atomic, nuclear, and subnuclear phenomena much better than before, a number of fundamental questions remain unanswered.

One of them is the question of the numerical value of the elementary electric charge e. There is a remarkable numerical ratio between the square of the charge e and the two fundamental constants of nature: Planck's constant h and the light velocity c. It turns out that $hc/e^2 = 137.04$. We have no idea why this relation holds. If that number were different, the properties of matter would deviate considerably from what they are. Our environment would be changed. Another number is the ratio M/m of the mass M of the proton and the mass m of the electron. The proton is 1836 times heavier than the electron. This is a most important number for the world in which we live. It makes the nucleus of the atom so much heavier than the electrons surrounding it. This circumstance gives the molecule a definite structure, since the heavier nuclei are well-located with a molecule, whereas the electrons are distributed over large parts of the molecular volume. The high value of M/m, therefore, is responsible for molecular architecture, for the specific structure of molecules. The functioning of life depends on the characteristic structure of proteins and DNA molecules. We do not know why the electron is so light compared with the nucleus.

What is more, the problem of particle masses is still unsolved. Practically none of the mass values of elementary particles can be explained or derived from a theory or arrived at without measuring them. Only the zero-mass of the photon, gluon, and graviton follows necessarily from electrodynamics, chromodynamics, and the theory of gravity.

Are the four fundamental forces independent or are they somehow components of one fundamental force? A fundamental relation was found to hold between the electromagnetic and weak forces, but the other forces have not yet been found to be so clearly related, although some promising attempts are now being made to bring them together.

Finally, are the "elementary" particles listed in Table 1 really elementary? Will quarks or electrons perhaps exhibit some inner structure when we apply higher energies than those available today? Are quarks or electrons made up of smaller parts? We do not know today. The only way to find solutions to these unanswered questions is further research. We have not yet reached the end of our quest into the innermost structure of matter.

Table 1. Elementary Particles

Fermions (particles in a narrow sense)

	Quarks					
Letter	u	d	s	c	b	t
Name	Up	Down	Strange	Charm	Bottom	Top
Charge	$+\frac{3}{2}e$	$-\frac{1}{3}e$	$-\frac{1}{3}e$	$+\frac{2}{3}e$	$-\frac{1}{3}e$	$+\frac{2}{3}e$
$\approx$ Mass (MeV)	~ 0	~ 0	~ 150	~ 1500	~ 5000	?

Leptons

Electrons

Name	Ordinary	Muon	Tauon
Charge	$-1e$	$-1e$	$-1e$
Mass (MeV)	0.51	106	1784

Neutrinos

Name	Ordinary	Muon	Tauon
Charge	0	neutrino	neutrino
Mass (MeV)	~ 0	0	0
		~ 0	~ 0

Bosons (field quanta)

Name	Field	Mass (GeV)
Photon	Electromagnetic	0
Graviton	Gravity	0
Gluon	Strong	0
W-boson ⎫	Weak	⎧ 81
Z-boson ⎭		⎩ 95

Let us return to the question of the title of this essay: What Is an Elementary Particle? We don't know whether we have reached the bottom of elementarity. What we can say now depends on the energy scale applied to matter, involving what we call conditional elementarity. If we are dealing with energies of less than about 0.1 eV, then molecules such as we find in the air around us are elementary particles. At these energies, molecules remain unchanged and appear infinitely hard; collisions will not change them. At higher energies, atoms are elementary particles. And at still higher energies, nuclei and electrons are elementary particles. If you go into energies in the millions of electron volts range, then elementary particles are protons, neutrons, electrons, and neutrinos. Finally, if you go into the subnuclear realm, you have quarks, electrons, heavy electrons, and neutrinos. As far as field quanta are concerned, you find photons at all energy ranges, but gluons and the W- and Z-bosons appear only at the subnuclear levels. Gravitons should exist at all energies, but they are hard to observe and, so far, have escaped discovery. Table 1 presents a list of elementary entities as they are believed to exist today.

Let us end by quoting Newton again. In his book, *Opticks*, from which we quoted at the beginning, Newton made farsighted speculations which are astoundingly similar to our present findings as indicated in brackets:

> Now the smallest Particles of Matter may cohere by the strongest Attractions [quarks], and compose bigger Particles of weaker virtue [nucleons], and many of these may cohere and compose bigger Particles whose virtue is still weaker [nuclei], and so on for the diverse Successions until the Progression end in the biggest Particles on which the Operations in Chymistry, and the colours of natural Bodies depend [atoms, molecules], and which by cohering compose Bodies of sensible Magnitude.

And later he says, "There are therefore Agents in Nature able to make the Particles of Bodies stick together by very strong Attractions [the forces of nature]. And it is the business of experimental Philosophy to find them out."

9

Contemporary Frontiers in Physics

Physics has become such an enormous field of science that a short summary of work at its frontiers must, of necessity, be incomplete and biased. (And because the names of the contributing physicists obviously cannot be quoted in extenso, I have not mentioned any names except where they are necessary to identify a theory or an experiment.) Today, every physicist is a specialist in some narrow part of the field, and it is impossible to have critical insights into the whole of our science. I ask indulgence from those whose fields are not treated adequately here. Still, we must not forget that the unity of science remains the main tenet of every scientist and the basis of his view of nature. We believe in the existence of fundamental laws that govern everything in nature. Some of the great unifying principles of physics are listed in Table 2.

Although quantum mechanics is listed among the unifying principles, it also brought about a division of physics into different realms of phenomena. This is because there exists a threshold of excitation for any dynamical system. The threshold becomes higher as the dimensions of the system decrease. I refer to this ordering principle as the quantum ladder (see Table 3). The first rung is the atomic and molecular realm, in which energy exchanges are so low (up to a few thousand electron volts) that atomic nuclei remain unexcited and therefore all nuclear (or subnuclear) processes remain dormant. The second rung is the nuclear realm, which becomes active when energy

Table 2. Unifying Principles of Physics

Principle	Author or theory
Unity of natural laws in heavens and earth	Newton
Unity of heat and mechanics	Mayer, Helmholtz, Joule
Unity of electricity, magnetism, and optics	Faraday, Maxwell
Unity of space, time, matter, and gravity	Einstein
Unity of physics, chemistry, and materials science	Quantum mechanics
Unity of atomic, nuclear, and subnuclear phenomena (?)	Unified field theory (?)

exchanges between atomic units reach the order of 1 million electron volts (1 MeV). The third is the subnuclear realm, which is activated around energies of 1 billion (10^8) electron volts (1 GeV). In general, at a lower rung we can forget about processes at a higher rung, except when we employ them intentionally as tools, as Rutherford did when he used alpha particles to determine the structure of atoms and as we do today, for example, when we study molecules by use of nuclear magnetic resonance.

Thus the quantum ladder divides physics into more or less independent parts, such as atomic physics (including the physics of atomic aggregates), nuclear physics, and subnuclear or particle physics. The first part is the most extensive and richest one, both because it deals

Table 3. The Quantum Ladder

Subject	Energy range (eV)	Main location
Atomic and molecular realm		
Chemistry, optics, materials, biology, complexity, organization, order-disorder	Up to 1000	Earth and planets of other stars
Nuclear realm		
Radioactivity, nuclear reactions, fission, fusion	10^5–10^7	Interior of stars
Subnuclear realm		
Antimatter, mesons, heavy electrons, short-lived entities, quarks	10^8 to ?	Big bang, neutron stars, unknown

with our immediate environment and because the electrical neutrality of atoms and the vast possibilities of forming electron states around several nuclei permit an enormous variety of structures and combinations. We have molecules, macromolecules, atomic clusters, gases, liquids, solids, membranes, and, finally, living structures with all their complexity and organization.

RECENT DISCOVERIES

The last decades have been unusually fruitful in almost all parts of physics. Many important discoveries have been made and a few fundamental insights have been gained. There is a special reason why so many new discoveries were made in these decades, namely the exuberant growth of new instrumentation and the maturing of many previous innovations, which became ready for full exploitation. A partial list of examples includes lasers, plasmas, new types of microscopes, synchrotron radiation, low-temperature techniques, rockets, accelerators, colliding beam devices, detectors, and, most important, computers.

The laser made it possible to produce large concentrations of highly excited atoms and molecules, to observe collective phenomena of excitation such as superradiance, to produce nonlinear effects of light in matter, and to create tremendous concentrations of electromagnetic energy.

The techniques of plasma production, handling, and analysis have been widely developed. New types of instabilities have been found and effects of trapped particles have been studied.

Among new microscopes, I include the scanning electron microscope. I also include the use of focused particle beams to study small regions of matter by observing the emitted secondaries, as well as new image intensifiers.

Synchrotron radiation has provided us with X-ray intensities about 10^4 times stronger than those of the best conventional machines. The study of extended X-ray absorption fine structure (EXAFS) makes it possible to investigate a molecular environment with a resolving power down to almost 0.1 angstrom (Å).

New techniques of low-temperature physics have opened up wider perspectives in the realm of superconductivity and superfluidity. Of particular interest is the study of superfluid helium-3, and the recent discovery of superconductors at about 100K. Both phenomena exhibit amazing properties that lead to new vistas of collective behavior in condensed matter.

Rockets have changed the character of astronomy by making it possible to conduct direct observations outside the atmosphere with all kinds of probes and, in the nearest future, with space telescopes.

Accelerators are now able to produce proton beams with energies of up to a tera-electron-volt (10^{12} eV), and the technique of colliding electron and proton beams has been developed. New types of particle detectors (wire chambers, streamer chambers) allow us to study particle collisions with much greater precision and sensitivity.

Last, but perhaps foremost, the development of computer hardware and software has made it possible not only to deal with the deluge of data streaming from new devices, but also to study previously unsolvable problems of nonlinear relations appearing in almost all fields of physics. Modern physics without modern computers is unthinkable.

NEW INSIGHTS

New insights into the workings of nature won in the last decades are more difficult to pinpoint. My judgment may differ from that of my readers, and our common judgment may turn out to be mistaken. Nevertheless, I would certainly include the new approach by L. Kadanoff, M. Fisher, and K. Wilson, which finally has shown a suitable way to deal successfully with the problems of critical phenomena. It leads to a deeper understanding of what happens at the critical point and gives an accout of the different powers n by which the various parameters change with $(T - T_c)^n$, where T is temperature and T_c is the critical temperature. This approach showed that the problem is largely independent of the special properties of the systems.

In order to appreciate the role of chaos in physics, I would like to mention a few recent attempts to understand how chaotic situations may develop.

I would include the successful attempt by S. Weinberg, P. Higgs, G. T. Hooft, J. Ward, and A. Salam to unify weak and electromagnetic interactions; their predictions are being verified one after another. I would include the recognition of the quark structure of protons, neutrons, and mesons, which has become increasingly convincing as more experimental evidence has been gathered. I would also include quantum chromodynamics, an attempt to describe the strong interaction between quarks by analogy with quantum electrodynamics.

Other more tentative ideas are being discussed that aim at a new fundamental view of things. Examples are the ideas of supersymmetry and superstring theory; the quantum treatment of the black-hole phenomenon, which indicates a possible new type of particle creation; and the use of nonlinearities in the field equations (corresponding to solitons and instantons) to obtain structures that might be models for elementary particles. At best, these daring attempts are promising beginnings.

Let us look into the future. Of course, it is impossible to predict advances in basic science. A major advance might best be defined as one that was not foreseen. Indeed, I suspect that the most significant steps forward will occur where we expect them least. All I can do here is describe a number of growth points in physics—that is, areas in which some new discoveries or insights are probable in the near future. Again, the list will be incomplete, and biased by my restricted knowledge and experience. The order in which the growth points are listed has nothing to do with their relative importance.

DISORDER

It has long been known that the deviations from ideal order in solid crystals have a decisive effect on the properties of materials. Still, we do not have a systematic way of describing grain boundaries, dislocations, and other lattice defects or of predicting the circumstances under which they occur. Furthermore, it has been found that amorphous solids have properties that were previously ascribed only to crystals. We are beginning to understand the reasons. The effects of random distributions of spins and of foreign atoms and the like are being studied in greater detail, and a theoretical treatment of such problems has become possible. The previously mentioned studies of chaotic behavior belong in this category. To quote Philip Anderson: "The next decade is very likely to be the most 'disorderly' decade in theoretical physics."

SURFACES

The structure and composition of surfaces is becoming increasingly interesting to theorists and experimenters. New instrumentation methods permit much more accurate investigations of surface phenomena, and there are new theories to deal with them. J. M. Kosterlitz, D. V. Thouless, and A. Berezinski showed that new states of aggregation should be expected in two-dimensional arrays, and some of their predictions have been verified. The process of melting of a two-dimensional system has now been investigated theoretically and experimentally, and the results may help us to understand three-dimensional melting better. Clearly, the study of surfaces is important for understanding catalysis and action of membranes.

NONLINEAR PHYSICS

Whenever nonlinear relations occur in physics, mathematical understanding becomes difficult. Therefore the description of natural phenomena always begins with the parts where linear dependencies are predominant, or where nonlinearities are small. Nonlinearities can then be considered as perturbations and treated by successive approximation. This is the reason why quantum theory has had so many successes. Because of the principle of superposition of wave functions, the behavior of many simple systems can be described by linear relations with small nonlinear perturbations. Furthermore, because of the smallness of the coupling constant e^2/hc (where e, h, and c are, respectively, the electron charge, Planck's constant, and the speed of light) for the interaction with the electromagnetic field, the most important interactions—the electromagnetic ones—can be treated by successive approximations. But in contemporary physics, we more frequently encounter problems where that method no longer works. When nonlinearities become important, instabilities occur and new forms of behavior set in. One finds examples in almost every field, but the best known is turbulent flow. Plasma physics abounds with such instabilities. It is an illustration of how nature is much more varied than we guess, even when we know the fundamental equations that underlie the processes.

Nonlinearities are important in particle physics because of the strong interactions between quarks, which are not amenable to approximation methods, except at very small distances between the interacting particles. Among new forms of behavior introduced by nonlinearities are the so-called solitons—large local disturbances of a field that behave not unlike particles. They may even turn out to be what we observe as elementary particles. In all fields of physics, new methods developed to deal with nonlinear relations by means of computers may become important tools to understand still unexplained phenomena.

COLLECTIVE PHENOMENA

I expect that our understanding of collective phenomena will greatly increase in the near future. Many-body problems are receiving much more attention than before and are encountered in almost every field of physics. In the solid state and in the liquid state, increasingly complex collective phenomena have been discovered and are only partially understood.

One of the most surprising discoveries was made in 1986, when materials were found that became superconducting at unexpectedly high temperatures, such as 70 kelvin (K) and higher. Such occurrences cannot be explained by the interactions of the conduction electrons with lattice vibrations (the current explanation of superconductivity of certain metals or alloys at very low temperatures of a few kelvins). Theorists are now challenged to explain high-temperature superconductivity, phenomena with important technical applications.

The physics of the liquid state, plasma physics, nuclear physics, and astronomy are full of unsolved problems of collective behavior. A new method invented in one field may help to solve problems in others. Unfortunately, there is not enough cross-fertilization today, and the same idea is often reinvented in different fields.

HEAVY-ION PHYSICS

The study of energetic collisions between heavy nuclei opens up new vistas in nuclear physics. It enables us to observe nuclear matter at high compression. Under these conditions, it is no longer possible to describe it as an assembly of protons and neutrons. The pressure causes the appearance of excited nucleons and pions, and a phenomenon called pion condensation may occur. Indeed, the simple proton-neutron description of nuclei has turned out to be insufficient even to account for more precise measurements of the charge distributions in ordinary nuclei. In the future, physicists studying nuclear structure will have to take into account the existence of excited states of nucleons and mesons; nuclear structure therefore will be much more closely connected with particle physics than it is today.

Furthermore, a collision between nuclei of high atomic number Z creates temporarily a nucleus with an abnormally high charge: $Z > 150$. Such charge concentrations are expected to produce strange effects, not only by way of vacuum polarization but by the appearance of negative electron clouds around the nucleus, which reduce the effective charge. Future experiments may test these unusual consequences of quantum electrodynamics.

ASTROPHYSICS

Until fifteen or twenty years ago, the sky was considered essentially unchanging except for planets, comets, and very rare events, such as novas and supernovas. Today, when studied with radio antennas, infrared receivers, and X-ray telescopes, the sky presents an ever-changing picture of fluctuating intensities within almost any time interval, from milliseconds to months. If this were translated into visible light, the sky would present a dramatic picture of stars, clusters, and nebulae flaring up and fading away. Some of these phenomena are understood, but many are still mysterious or are open to various interpretations.

As mentioned before, further use of rockets and the introduction of space telescopes will greatly extend the range of "seeing" in astronomy. We may expect the wave of new cosmic discoveries to continue unabated for some time.

The discovery of pulsars and their interpretation as neutron stars of very high density are already familiar. This was a momentous development—starting with the observation of small, regular flickerings and growing into the recognition of the existence of large chunks of dense nuclear matter. Knowledge gained about the most abnormal state of matter from so few observations is impressive. It led to new ideas, not only about nuclear matter in general, but also about what happens to a star that has exhausted its nuclear fuel: it explodes and implodes at the same time, producing a supernova and a neutron star. The compression of ordinary magnetic fields during the gravitational collapse to a neutron star produces fields of the order of 10^{12} gauss, which would completely distort atoms to elongated electron tubes. Much new information about the physics of supernova explosions and about nuclear matter under high gravitational compression will be gained in the near future by further studies of these phenomena.

The existence of black holes follows from an extrapolation of Einstein's theory of gravity by many orders of magnitude beyond the range for which its validity has not yet been established beyond doubt. Rarely has a theoretical idea been extended so far, but Einstein's ideas are so convincing that most experts in this field consider black holes to be a real possibility. The present indications of their existence should be confirmed or refuted in the foreseeable future.

X-ray astronomy is now an established observational method, and the X-ray sky has been thoroughly investigated. Many new X-ray sources have been found, some of them double stars, where matter streams from one partner to the other; the latter may be a neutron star or perhaps even a black hole, as in the X-ray source Cygnus X-1. Future extensions of these observations may reveal many new and unexpected cosmic phenomena. Observations of infrared light are just beginning to add to our knowledge of what is going on in stars and nebulae. Infrared studies will soon develop into an essential branch of astrophysics.

It is generally believed that energy production in stars such as the sun is well understood as a process of fusion of hydrogen to helium, but failure to detect the neutrino flux from the sun, which had been predicted on the basis of this model, is a problem. It now seems well established that too few neutrinos from beryllium reach the earth. Possibly, this effect could be explained by assuming a transition of some neutrinos in another kind of neutrino when they penetrate the sun. To be sure, the undetected neutrinos are supposed to result from a side effect of the fusion process, and it should soon be possible to measure neutrinos produced when deuterons are formed from two protons, which is part of the direct process of energy production. These neutrinos are not energetic enough to be changed into other types. If such neutrinos also are not detected, our knowledge of stellar structure would be deeply shaken.

Perhaps the most impressive, if not uncanny, recent discovery was the observation of blackbody radiation of about 3 K filling all space. It is tempting to interpret this radiation as an optical remnant of an early stage of our universe, after the big bang about 15×10^9 years ago—to construe it as direct evidence for the creation of the universe from an extraordinarily high concentration of energy. Future research, observations, and theories not only may bring us closer to understanding the very beginning of the universe but may also resolve the question of the average density of mass, a value that determines whether the universe will endlessly expand or will undergo periodic expansions and contractions, with an unending series of big bangs. The question of the mass density has been complicated further by indications that the universe contains much more mass than is contained in luminous objects. The nature of this "dark matter" is unknown. It may be as much as ten times the amount of luminous matter.

There always remains the possibility that all we now hypothesize about the early universe and its development is based on a wrong interpretation of the observed facts and that the evolution of the universe is completely different from what we now believe.

Nevertheless, the observed 3 K radiation determines an absolute coordinate system, at least within the observable universe, the one in which it appears to be isotropic. Small deviations in isotropy have been found that indicate motion of our solar system—not only the expected rotation around the center of the galaxy, but also motion of the galaxy toward the Virgo cluster. The dream of Michelson and Morley has come true—to find the absolute motion of our solar system, in respect not to an ether, but to a gas of photons.

PARTICLE PHYSICS

Two decades ago the view that quarks are the constituents of baryons and mesons (hadrons) was considered a vague hypothesis, perhaps only a simple ordering scheme of hadron families that had little to do with reality—the hadrons behave "as if" they are made of quarks. Now there is hardly any reason to question their existence. There is not much doubt today that the nucleons and their excited states are composed of three quarks and that the mesons are made up of quark-antiquark pairs. A turning point was reached with the results of J. Friedman, H. Kendall, and R. Taylor, who observed deep inelastic scattering of fast electrons with nucleons at the Stanford Linear Accelerator Center (SLAC). The observations showed all the characteristics of electrons being scattered by charged subnuclear particles much smaller than protons. It was the Rutherford experiment of subnuclear physics, since it revealed the existence of small concentrated charges within the nucleon. The quarks were indeed seen, just as Rutherford saw the atomic nucleus.

Similar deep inelastic scattering studies were later made with beams of neutrinos, which were scattered by quarks through weak interactions. These experiments confirmed and extended the findings of the electron-scattering experiments and thus provided additional support for the quark hypothesis. Quarks were found to be particles with spin $\frac{1}{2}$; they carry fractional charges such as $+\frac{2}{3}$ and $-\frac{1}{3}$. Several different types ("flavors") of quarks were identified, with different masses. Protons and neutrons consist only of the first two types, the so-called u and d quarks, but it was necessary to introduce more types—three more so far—in order to explain the numerous heavier short-lived mesons and baryons found in nature. Different quark types transform into each other only through weak interactions. Moreover, it was necessary to ascribe an internal degree of freedom to each quark—a trivalued spin called color—that permits the quark to exist in three distinct quantum states.

So far it has not been possible to "ionize" the hadrons, that is, to liberate a quark from a hadron and observe it as a free particle. However, in high-energy collisions, jets of mesons have been observed with a large momentum exactly in the direction in which quarks should have been ejected. This process of "mesonization" of quarks is, to some extent, understood as the creation of a trail of quark-antiquark pairs by the ejected quark. The behavior of quarks has led to the conclusion that the forces holding them together are soft, that is, weak against a large momentum transfer (actions at small distances) and strong against a smaller momentum transfer (actions at larger distances). Indeed, the confinement of quarks (impossibility of isolating them) indicates that the potential of the quark binding force goes to infinity for large distances.

Quantum chromodynamics (QCD) goes a long way toward explaining some of these features. It describes the strong interactions between the quarks by a non-Abelian gauge-field theory, a generalization of quantum electrodynamics in which the quarks are the sources of a "gluon" field and their "charge" is given by their trivalued color degree of freedom. In this theory, the field carries charge, a feature that is characteristic of a non-Abelian field theory. So far, the calculable results of this theory seem to agree with observations such as the weakness of interactions for large momentum transfer, but the most important feature of quark-quark interactions, the confinement of quarks, has not yet been derived from this theory in a completely satisfactory way. There are strong indications, however, that this is the fault not of the theory but of our inability to find satisfactory solutions to the equations. The next decade may produce many new insights into this mysterious subnuclear realm of nature.

Such new understanding is essential because QCD cannot tell us how many quark types exist and what their masses are. It does not deal at all with this question. Indeed, the fact that there are more than two types of quarks is already a deep riddle. The two quark types with the lowest mass are the constituents of neutrons, protons, and pions: they make up nuclear matter as we know it under terrestrial and most stellar conditions. It is completely unknown why nature needs the heavier quarks that are the constituents of the "strange" and "charmed" hadrons, which are all short-lived products of energetic collisions that quickly decay into more-ordinary particles such as nucleons, electrons, and neutrinos. The number of known quark types probably will increase at least by one. A sixth quark, the "top" quark, is expected to exist; it would fit well into the scheme of particles.

Two new quarks discovered within a period of four years should be enough, but physicists have also discovered a new heavy electron, the τ particle of a mass near 1.8 GeV, which together with the e and the μ now form a triad of charged leptons. The future will show whether it also has its own neutrino, as do the other two electrons. The existence of at least three electrons differing only in their mass is a tantalizing problem. Here, too, we have no idea about the role in nature of these heavy electrons, which decay by weak interactions into ordinary electrons after emitting suitable neutrinos. Just as QCD does not tell us why there are several quark types, quantum electrodynamics does not offer any explanation for this proliferation of electrons.

Recently, a number of exciting experimental and theoretical developments took place in the field of weak interactions. They are connected with the construction of a unified theory of weak and electromagnetic interactions, which I mentioned earlier. An attempt was made to unite these two phenomena by introducing a common field transmitting these interactions. The field has several components, one representing the photons as carriers of electromagnetism, others representing the carriers of the weak interactions. This unification not only solved some of the internal contradictions in the previous theory of weak interactions, it also required the existence of neutral currents, that is, weak interaction processes without transfer of charge. During eighty years of study of weak interaction processes it was assumed that they are all connected with a charge transfer: a radioactive nucleus changes its charge when it decays, and the charge is transferred to the emitted electron. Processes without charge transfer escaped discovery, but a few years after their prediction by the unified theory, such processes were observed in neutrino-induced reactions, first at CERN and then elsewhere. The theory predicted these and other weak-interaction phenomena with astonishing quantitative accuracy.

It was a great triumph for that theory when the carriers of weak interaction, the W- and Z-bosons, were indeed found at CERN in 1986. They are, as the theory predicted, massive entities, almost as heavy as the silver nucleus. If the theory is right, weak and electromagnetic phenomena will merge at high energies in a predictable way, and a new type of particle (the Higgs particle) will appear. Time will tell whether the theorists are on the right track, but one thing is almost certainly true: at these high energies (center-of-mass energies of 100

GeV or higher), both the weak and electromagnetic phenomena will exhibit properties very different from those to which we are accustomed.

Unquestionably, particle physics, like all other fields of physics, is in a state of flux. New discoveries bring about new problems. The answers will be found by more observations and by clever theories. The great progress of physics in recent decades was based on the development of better, larger, and finer tools and instruments and of new theoretical ideas. So will be the progress of physics in the future. To paraphrase Teilhard de Chardin in *The Phenomenon of Man,* "The history of natural science can be summarized as the elaboration of ever more perfect eyes within a cosmos in which there is always something more to be seen."

10

*The Origin
of the Universe*

The question of the origin of the universe is one of the most exciting topics for a scientist to deal with. It reaches far beyond its purely scientific significance, since it is related to human existence, to mythology, and to religion. Furthermore, it deals with questions that are connected with the fundamental structure of matter, with elementary particles. Today, the science of the very large—cosmology—is linked to the science of the very small—elementary particle physics. Therefore, we start with a short review of what we know about elementary particles, in order to understand how today's ideas about the origin of the universe have been arrived at.

The structure of matter can be analyzed according to increasingly more fundamental levels of organization. Table 4 shows this in an elementary way. A piece of metal, for example, is made of atoms, which are kept together by a chemical force that does not contain very high energies. Using electron volts (eV) as a measure of energy, we would need only a few electron volts to separate an atom from the piece of metal. If we look at one of the atoms, we see that it consists of a nucleus surrounded by electrons. These constituents are kept together by the electric force, which is somewhat stronger than the chemical force. From ten to a few hundred electron volts are needed to tear a few electrons from an atom. The size of the atoms is about 10^{-8} centimeter (cm). Now let us look at the nucleus, which is considerably smaller, of the order of 10^{-12} cm. The nucleus consists

Table 4. Fundamental Structural Levels of Matter

	Constituent particles	Binding force	Relevant energies
Matter	Atoms	Chemical force	1 eV
Atom	Electrons, nucleus	Electric force	10–100 eV
Nucleus	Protons, neutrons	Nuclear force	10^6 eV
Nucleon	Quarks	"Strong force"	10^9 eV

of protons and neutrons kept together by the nuclear force, a force that is much larger than the chemical and electric forces; about 10 million eV (10 MeV) are required to tear a proton or a neutron from a nucleus.

We know today that protons and neutrons, the so-called nucleons, are themselves not elementary but probably consist of three elementary particles that carry the unhappy name "quark." One wishes that a better sounding name had been chosen, such as "parton," for example, but "quark" has taken hold. The forces that keep the quarks within the nucleon are again much stronger. The size of the nucleon is about 10^{-13} cm, and the effects of the forces involve energies of the order of 1 billion eV (1 GeV). The nuclear force that binds protons and neutrons in the nucleus is understood today as a consequence of the "strong force," which keeps quarks together. The relation of the nuclear force to the strong force is not unlike the relation of the chemical force between atoms to the stronger electric forces within atoms.

The analysis outlined in Table 4 brings us to two related concepts that play an important role in many theories of the history of the universe: the quantum ladder and the "conditional elementarity" of particles. We may distinguish three different realms in nature, three levels on the quantum ladder. The first is the atomic realm, which includes the world of atoms, their interactions, and the structures that are formed by them, such as molecules, liquids and solids, gases, and plasmas. This realm includes all the phenomena of atomic physics, chemistry, and, in a certain sense, biology. The energy exchanges taking place in this realm are of the order of a few electron volts. If these exchanges are below 1 eV, such as in the collisions between molecules of the air in a room, then even atoms and molecules can be regarded as elementary particles—that is, they have "conditional elementarity" (see Table 5)—because they keep their identity and do not change in any collisions or in other processes at these low energy exchanges. If

Table 5. Conditional Elementarity of Particles

Particles	Energy limit
Molecules, photons	<0.1 eV
Atoms, photons	<1 eV
Nuclei, electrons, photons	$<10^4$ eV
Protons, neutrons, electrons, neutrinos, photons	$<10^9$ eV
Quarks, electrons, muons, tauons, W, Z, gluons, photons	$>10^9$ eV

one goes to higher energy exchanges, say 10^4 eV, atoms and molecules will decompose into nuclei and electrons; at this level, the latter particles must be considered as elementary. The structures and processes of this first rung of the quantum ladder are found on earth, on planets, and on the surfaces of stars.

The next rung is the nuclear realm. Here the energy exchanges are much higher, of the order of mega (million) electron volts (MeV). As long as we are dealing with phenomena in the atomic realm, such amounts of energy are unavailable, and the nuclei are inert: they do not change. However, if one applies energies of millions of electron volts, nuclear reactions, fission and fusion, and the processes of radioactivity occur; our elementary particles then are protons and neutrons, together with electrons. In addition, radioactive processes produce neutrinos, particles that have no detectable mass or charge. In the universe, energies at this level are available in the centers of stars and in star explosions. Indeed, the energy radiated by the stars is produced by nuclear reactions. The natural radioactivity we find on earth is the long-lived remnant of the time when earthly matter was expelled into space by a supernova explosion.

The third rung of the quantum ladder is the subnuclear realm. Here we are dealing with energy exchanges of many gigavolts (GeV), or billions of electron volts. We encounter excited nucleons, new types of particles such as mesons, heavy electrons, quarks, gluons, and also antimatter in large quantities. Gluons are the quanta of the strong force that keeps quarks together. As long as we are dealing with the atomic or nuclear realm, these new types of particles do not occur and the nucleons remain inert. But at subnuclear energy levels, nucleons and mesons appear to be composed of quarks, so that quarks and gluons figure as elementary particles. It is an interesting question whether the elementary particles established so far are indeed truly elementary. It may well be that they are also conditional and that the list has to be extended further and further. We will come back to this exciting question at the end of this essay.

Most of the entities that are found in the subnuclear realm have a very short life. They are created and disappear again after transforming themselves into other forms of energy. Matter and antimatter, particles and antiparticles occur when large amounts of energy are exchanged, annihilating each other when they collide, their mass-energy appearing in other forms. These phenomena occur in nature only during great cosmic cataclysms, such as supernova explosions, in neutron stars, and mainly during the primal bang, where they play an important role. Of course, they also can be produced in laboratories by means of high-energy accelerators.

A list of elementary particles is found in the essay "What Is an Elementary Particle?" in this collection. Today we know of five quarks, usually referred to by the letters $u, d, s, c, b;$ they are of different character, which we will not describe in any detail. (A sixth quark is likely to exist.) They carry electric charges that are fractions of the unit charge, one-third or two-thirds, and their masses differ; we have not the slightest idea where these masses come from. It is interesting that we find quarks occurring only in groups of three, such as in the nucleons, or occurring as a pair of a quark together with an antiquark, such as in the mesons. The electric charges of these groups are zero or ± 1. It has so far turned out to be impossible to detach a quark from these groups; the force between quarks seems to be of a character that does not allow a quark to be removed from these combinations, although we are not yet quite sure of this fact.

The list of elementary particles also includes leptons, whose main representatives are electrons. The ordinary electron, we believe, has an infinite life. There also exist heavy electrons, the so-called muons and tauons (μ and τ), which differ from ordinary electrons only by having much higher masses; they have a short life and transform themselves quickly into normal electrons by emission of neutrinos and, in the case of tauons, of mesons. Also included among the leptons are the neutrinos, which are believed to play an important role in the universe. It seems today that there are three types of neutrinos, one for each electron.

The other elementary particles are the carriers of interactions between particles we have mentioned so far. These interactions take the form of forces between particles and are transmitted by "force fields." On the basis of quantum field theory, each of these force fields is carried by certain particles, so-called field quanta. In the case of electromagnetic forces, field quanta are the well-known photons; in the case of weak interactions that produce radioactive phenomena, they are particles of high mass, the so-called W- and Z-bosons, which have been found recently at the European high-energy laboratory CERN in Geneva; the field quanta of the strong interaction between quarks are called gluons. The field quanta of gravity are the so-called gravitons, which will not be of great interest to us. Recent theories have demonstrated that the electromagnetic force and the weak force are intimately connected.

THE UNIVERSE TODAY

What I am going to describe, in a greatly simplified form, is the so-called standard model of the development of the universe, which, in spite of its unsolved riddles and shortcomings, gives a good overall picture of that history, with the exception of the very first moments. It should be emphasized that all discussions of the development of the cosmos are hypothetical, because it is very hard to make empirical observations regarding the totality of the universe, and therefore we do not know whether we have caught the real facts. No existing view of the development of the cosmos is completely satisfactory, and this includes the standard model, which leads to certain fundamental questions and problems. I will discuss some of these questions, as well as some of the ways the standard model has been revised and altered in the last few years to answer them.

In order to understand the history of the past universe, it is necessary to account for certain important facts regarding the present universe. These facts can be conveniently divided into four groups.

The first fact to be accounted for is that today's universe consists essentially of hydrogen and helium. Ninety-three percent of all atoms in the universe are hydrogen atoms, about 6 percent are helium, and the rest—about 1 percent—are atoms of the other elements, such as oxygen, carbon, iron, and so on.

The second fact is one of the most surprising phenomena to have been discovered in the last 100 years: the expansion of the universe. Today we can say almost with certainty that the universe indeed expands; the further that objects, such as galaxies, are from us, the faster they move away from us.

The third fact concerns the distribution of matter in the universe. This is a very difficult problem, because we see only radiating matter, and we do not know how much matter exists that cannot be observed directly. However, we can draw some conclusions about nonradiating matter by its gravitational or light-absorbing effects. We are less interested in the detailed distribution, such as galaxies or clusters of galaxies. What concerns us is the density of matter, averaged over large regions containing many galaxies. We believe that the average number of protons or neutrons per cubic centimeter is, very approximately, 10^{-6}, taking the average over very large distances. Of course, the density is much higher in the interior of galaxies and much lower between them. But averaged out, the density of 10^{-6} nucleons per cubic centimeter, or one per cubic meter, seems to be the same over all the observed parts of the universe.

The fourth fact is of great importance: the whole of space is filled with a thermal radiation that approximately corresponds to a temperature of 3 K, which is 3° above absolute zero. In all probability this radiation was emitted at a very early period of the universe and in this sense can be considered as the optical reverberation of the primal bang that still fills the universe. It is certainly one of the most impressive discoveries of modern science that we can still "see" the primal bang, as it were.

We will now look at some of these points in greater detail. Let us begin with the expansion. It will be assumed, in this context, that the universe is infinite. This is not necessarily so, for if the average density of matter is high enough—higher than the one given earlier—the universe would be finite, according to Einstein. It would be a finite universe without any limits, in analogy to the surface of a sphere in two dimensions. For our considerations, it will suffice to assume that the universe is indeed infinite, as is probably the case.

The expansion of the universe was discovered when it was found that cosmic objects move away from us with speeds that are greater the farther away the object is located. The speed at which objects move away from us increases by about 20 kilometers (km) per second for every 10^6 light years distance from us; this value is not precisely known, but it is of this order of magnitude. In the standard model, the expansion must be imagined, not as the penetration of a limited amount of matter into empty space surrounding it, but as an increasing dilution of matter everywhere in the universe. The matter density becomes thinner with time, all over infinite space. Each point can be considered as the center of this dilution. Indeed, regardless of his location in the universe, an observer would see exactly the same thing with respect to the objects around him, as is illustrated in Figure 17; that is, objects would recede from him at the rate of 20 km per second/ 10^6 light years. The expansion of the universe does not distinguish any point and is that same all over space. This assertion will be some-

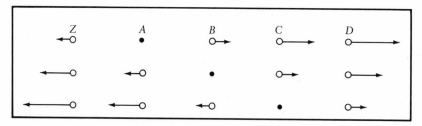

Figure 17 *In an infinite universe that is expanding, every point, represented here one-dimensionally by points Z, A, B, C, and D, can be considered as the center and would, in fact, appear to be so. If our solar system were at point A (top row), we would see B and Z moving away in opposite directions; the more distant C would be moving away at a greater velocity (represented by the longer arrow), and D at an even greater velocity. If we were at points B or C (middle and bottom rows), we would observe precisely the same effect with respect to the points adjacent to us. (Adapted from* The First Three Minutes, *by Steven Weinberg, Basic Books, 1977.)*

what altered by some recent ideas about the early moments of the universe. We will come to these ideas later on.

This expansion or dilution leads to a most remarkable conclusion when we try to extrapolate it toward the past: we can easily calculate that about 17 billion years ago the density of matter must have been infinite. Actually, the figure of 17 billion years is a bit too large since it does not take into account the fact that the expansion must have been faster in the past and has been slowed down by the mutual gravitational attraction of matter. By calculating the size of this effect from the present mass density, we arrive at the result that the event of infinite density, that so-called singularity, must have occurred less than 17 billion years ago, since the expansion was more rapid at the beginning. The date was, rather, about 13 billion years before the present. It is interesting that we can indeed calculate approximately the date of the primal bang. From now on we will call the moment of the primal bang the "zero" of our time scale and will use a modern chronology: the time after the primal bang.

It is important to keep in mind that the primal bang is not a local phenomenon, at least in the standard model. The descriptions of it in the popular literature are often grossly misleading; it is wrong to imagine that the primal bang occurred at a given point in space, matter being expelled in all directions. Actually, the primal bang was the beginning of a decompression of an infinite universe. This means that the whole universe, the infinite space, was filled with an extremely high density of matter shortly after time zero. With the passage of time, density decreased further, until it reached the present value. On average, this density was the same all over space; the universe expands equally at all points, and the density decreases equally in the whole universe. We may ask how this is possible. Where does all the matter go? Space is infinite is the answer, and ten times infinite is again infinite. Thus let us remember that in the standard model the primal bang was not localized. It happened simultaneously all over space.

These considerations are valid for an infinite universe. If the universe is finite, but without limits, it would indeed have shrunk to a point at the time of the primal bang. But then the whole universe would be that point and there would be no other points "outside" it. In this sense it would still be possible to say that the primal bang happened all over space and not as an explosion from one point into a previously empty space.

Now we come to a new concept: the "radius of communication." Today, we see many stars that are very far away. But we can get the light only from distances that are smaller than a certain length R_C, the radius of communication—distances smaller than R_C could have been traversed by light in the time since the primal bang. Thus, the radius of communication must be no more than about 13 billion light years today and was smaller in the past. For example, 6.5 billion years ago it was just half as big, since only half the present time had elapsed since the big bang. For the sake of clarity, the situation described here has been oversimplified. The numbers for the radius of communication are actually somewhat larger than these, because the expansion of the universe carries the light along with it.

A significant implication of the radius of communication is that what we see today at a limit of 13 billion light years may never before have been in contact with us. It could not have been in our picture because the light did not have enough time to arrive. For example, the 3 K radiation coming to us from all directions originated so far away that today is the first time we are in communication with the objects that radiated it. This has an important consequence, as we will see later.

The intensity of the 3 K radiation that fills space is pretty much what we would expect of thermal radiation at that temperature, about 1000 photons per cm^3. This is a billion times more than the average number per cubic centimeter of protons today, but in terms of energy it is not very much because photons of 3 K radiation carry a very small amount of energy. Indeed the energy of this radiation is about 1/4000 of the mass-energy, mc^2, of ordinary visible matter in space.

The temperature of 3 K must be considered as the present temperature of the universe; the temperature of hot stars is completely negligible when one averages over space. The radiation determines the temperature.

It is significant that the 3 K radiation seems to be totally uniform, having the same intensity from all directions; it seems to fill space evenly in a homogeneous way. This makes it possible to observe the motion of the earth, of the solar system, and even of our galaxy by means of the Doppler effect of this radiation. Indeed, we find the frequencies of the radiation a little higher in a certain direction and a little lower in the opposite one. This must be caused by our own motion in that direction. Measurements tell us that our velocity is about 300 km per second and is directed toward the constellation Virgo. This motion is nothing other than the sum of the motion of our solar system within the galaxy and the motion of the galaxy toward the center of the Virgo cluster of galaxies.

It is remarkable that we now are justified in talking about an absolute motion, at least within the observable universe, and that we can measure it. The great dream of Michelson and Morley is realized. They wanted to measure the absolute motion of the earth by measuring the velocity of light in different directions. According to Einstein, however, this velocity is always the same. But the 3 K radiation represents a fixed system of coordinates. It makes sense to say that an observer is at rest with respect to the visible universe when the 3 K radiation appears to have the same frequencies in all directions. Nature has provided an absolute frame of reference.

THE HISTORY OF THE UNIVERSE

What can we infer from the present facts about the past of the universe? Obviously, the universe is not static; owing to the expansion, the density of matter decreases all the time. Figure 18 demonstrates the change of density and the related change of temperature with time. In order to represent these changes in a quantitative way, we consider the past history of all matter that is within our present-day radius of communication; this matter is included in a sphere of radius R. Today, about 6×10^{17} seconds after the bang R is equal—by definition—to the present radius of communication, R_C, about 13 billion light years; at half the time, 3×10^{17} seconds after the bang, R was 0.63

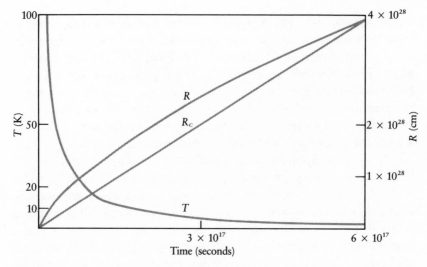

Figure 18 *Since the primal bang, the temperature and density of the universe have been decreasing from their infinitely high values. In this graph, the temperature of the universe* T, *the radius* R *of all matter that today is within our radius of communication, and the radius of communication* R_C *are plotted against the time since the bang. We see that the curves of* T *and* R *are inversely proportional to each other. The downward curve of* R *reflects the slowing effect of gravity on the expansion of the universe. The fact that* R *is greater than* R_C *in past times means that some matter has come within our radius of communication today for the first time since the primal bang. The curves are for a qualitative orientation. They are inaccurate for early times.*

times its present value, whereas R_C was only half as large. This is because R_C grows with light velocity, whereas R, the radius of the presently visible universe, grows because of the expansion, which is less than light velocity. R_C always lies below R between the primal bang and the present. This has the special significance already mentioned, that the outer parts of matter within the present radius of communication had not yet communicated with us in the past.

Figure 18 also shows that the temperature of the universe is always inversely proportional to the radius. When matter expands, light also takes part in the same expansion, wavelengths become larger, and frequencies become correspondingly smaller. The temperature of a thermal radiation is proportional to the frequency of light. This means that an expansion to twice the radius is equivalent to halving the temperature. Thus when the radius R was half as big as it is today, the temperature was twice as great, 6 K.

Now we turn to the events that took place at very short times after the bang, much shorter than can be shown in Figure 18. In order to examine what happened at these times, we use in Figure 19 a logarithmic time scale that indicates time in powers of 10—from 10^{-6}, which is a millionth of a second, to "today" being 6×10^{17} seconds after the bang.

We see in Figure 19 that there was a change in the development of the universe at about 10^{13} (300,000 years after the bang). At that time, the temperature was of the order of 1000 K, equivalent to about 0.1 eV. At such temperatures, the radiation energy of the photons in space is just about equal to the mass energy of visible matter. The number of photons was the same as today, but the photons were much hotter, that is, more energetic. Therefore, at times earlier than 300,000 years, the radiation energy dominates. Thus, another regime was prevalent before that moment, the "radiation regime." After that moment, until today and in the foreseeable future, the energy contained in

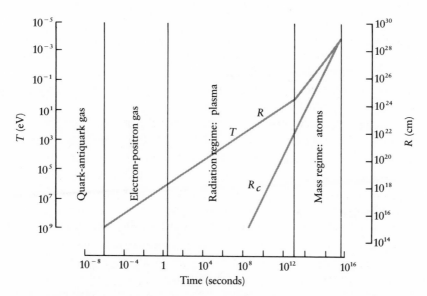

Figure 19   *The very early history of the universe is represented in this graph in logarithmic units. The vertical axis on the right indicates the values of R and R$_C$ in centimeters; the axis on the left indicates the values of T, the temperature measured in equivalent electron volts (1 K ≈ 10^{-4}eV). The scale of R increases upward, that of T downward, and since the temperature is the reciprocal of the radius, both magnitudes can be represented by the same curve in a logarithmic plot. The break in the curve at 10^{13} seconds indicates the transition from a universe dominated by radiation to one dominated by matter.*

matter in the form of mass has been greater than the radiation energy, which is why we call this period the "mass regime." Before 10^{13} sec, most energy was in the form of radiation.

Furthermore, at the temperatures that existed before 10^{13} seconds, hydrogen and helium atoms could not exist, because the heat energy was high enough to separate the electrons from the nuclei. A plasma of nuclei and electrons was present, and such a plasma is impenetrable to light, in contrast to the atoms, which are transparent when they occur in concentrations lower than solid matter. An interesting consequence of the lack of transparency of the universe before that point is that what we observe today as the 3 K radiation is not the radiation of the primal bang itself but rather the radiation that was present 300,000 years after the bang. The radiation was able to propagate freely and unhindered through space only after that moment. The expansion of space since then has reduced its temperature from about 1000 K to 3 K.

Note that this radiation was emitted about 13 billion years ago from distant regions. This shows that the primal bang and the subsequent development occurred all over space and not at one point, because otherwise we would not be receiving today the messages of that development from far away, coming to us from all directions. This statement must be qualified. We can conclude only that the primal bang occurred all over the space that we can look at today. It may not be all space.

Another important point in the history of the universe occurred 10 seconds after the bang, when the temperature was equivalent to about 1 MeV. Before that moment, when the temperature was still higher, space was filled not only with light radiation but also with electron pairs, positive and negative. The creation of a pair needs just 1 MeV, and when the temperature is higher than that, space is filled with a dense gas of electrons and positrons. We had then an extended radiation regime, not only light but something that may also be called radiation: electrons and positrons in thermal equilibrium.

The next important point in time is a millionth of a second after the bang. At that point, the temperature was several billion GeV, and it had been higher before then. Even at later times, when the temperature was equivalent to only 1 MeV and higher (this is before 100 seconds), helium nuclei were all dissolved into protons and neutrons. But at temperatures equivalent to 1 GeV and higher, the energy density was so high that pairs of nucleons and antinucleons must have been produced in large numbers—so dense that the nucleons and antinucleons merged to form a dense, hot gas of quarks and antiquarks.

This gas also contained many gluons, the quanta of the force field that acts between the quarks.

Before a microsecond, the universe was filled with a combination of gases: a quark-antiquark gas, a gluon gas, an electron-positron gas, and the optical heat radiation (photon gas). When the temperature fell under 1 GeV, a few microseconds later, gluons and quark-antiquark pairs disappeared, annihilating and transforming themselves into light radiation. All that was left then were a very few supernumerary quarks that combined into protons and neutrons. Remember that today we find far fewer nucleons than photons: the ratio is about 1 to a billion. The number of photons at previous times was always about the same as today, but they were more energetic. The number of gluons and quark-antiquark pairs before a microsecond was also about the same as the number of photons since they can be considered also as a kind of radiation in thermal equilibrium. In other words, only a very small quark surplus combined and formed protons and neutrons.

Here a point must be mentioned that has so far been neglected. At very high temperatures, neutrinos are also produced. We therefore must add another gas or radiation, the neutrino-antineutrino gas. Because neutrinos have a very weak interaction with matter, the universe became "transparent" to neutrinos at a somewhat earlier period than to light. This is why, most probably, space today is filled with the neutrino gas freed a few seconds after the bang. The expansion should have reduced the temperature of that neutrino radiation to about 2 K. So far, it has not yet been observed.

It is very difficult to know what happened at periods earlier than about 10^{-6} seconds. At that time the temperature was more than 1 GeV and was higher the nearer we come to the time of origin. We know very little about the properties and the behavior of matter under such conditions.

Let us now summarize the development of the universe from the beginning to the present acording to the standard model. The universe was always filled with light: at the beginning it was light of tremendous intensity and temperature, whereas today it is cold light. At 10^{-6} seconds, the temperature was 10,000 billion K and space was filled with a dense gas of quarks, antiquarks, gluons, electrons, positrons, and neutrinos, in addition to hot light. After 10^{-6} seconds, the gas had cooled down so that quark-antiquark pairs annihilated themselves and gluons disappeared. A few surplus quarks combined and formed protons and neutrons. After further expansion and cooling to less than a billion degress, 10 seconds after the beginning, the electrons and positrons annihilated themselves, leaving only a few electrons, just as many as there were protons. After about 100 seconds, neutrons combined with part of the protons to form helium nuclei. The universe remained in this situation for a relatively long time, about 300,000 years, but a short time compared to its total life. Then its temperature decreased to about 1000 K and hydrogen and helium atoms were formed. The universe continued expanding and cooling until it reached present density and temperature. Matter assembled in clusters of different sizes; stars, galaxies, and clusters of galaxies formed. The composition of matter remained unchanged, except for elements other than hydrogen and helium that formed in relatively small amounts in the centers of the stars and during star explosions.

UNSOLVED PROBLEMS

It should be emphasized again that the foregoing sketch of the origin of the universe, according to the standard model, is very hypothetical. Furthermore, there remain a number of fundamental problems showing that the standard model cannot be valid at times much earlier than a microsecond. These problems can be divided into six groups: the horizon problem, the simultaneity of the primal bang all over space, what happened before 10^{-6} seconds, the origin of the proton surplus, the critical density of matter, and what existed before the primal bang.

We begin with the first point. We have already emphasized that the 3 K radiation is uniform and homogeneous. Furthermore, in our standard model, today is the first time that we are in contact with those regions from which this radiation originated, the first time that we have "known" something about what is going on there; never before could a signal have reached us or any interaction have taken place. Moreover, those regions that have sent radiation to us from opposite directions could never have been in contact with each other before, because they have been farther away from each other than light could have traveled since the universe began. Indeed, a little calculation shows that only regions in the sky that are less than 2° of arc apart could have been in contact with each other when the 3 K radiation was emitted, 300,000 years after the beginning.

The question then arises, how is it possible that the radiation coming from all these regions is uniform? It looks as if "somebody" has arranged it so that the density of matter is the same all over, even in places that would not have had any possible communication or interaction with one another. It is also possible that the laws of nature are such that only one density could have been realized at a very early moment; then, because of the same subsequent expansion all over the universe, the density would be the same on the average at all points in space. This would be a satisfactory explanation from a scientific point of view, but since we do not know what happened before 10^{-6} seconds, no such conclusion can be drawn. At that time, energy exchanges took place that are far higher than the ones we have studied. We therefore do not know at all what the laws of nature are for such energy exchanges, and we can neither confirm nor deny that there was only one possible value for the density at an early moment.

Related to the very difficult problem of the uniformity and homogeneity of the universe is the equally difficult second question: Why did the universe start simultaneously all over infinite space? Time and space play a different role in the standard model: the universe was assumed to be uniform over large distances in space but not in time. It supposedly started all over at the same moment and changed in time when it expanded and cooled.

An interesting attempt to find an answer to some of these problems is the idea initiated by Alan Guth at MIT in 1981 of an "inflationary" universe. Guth's idea can be considered as a way to describe the primal bang. It is based upon the concept of a "false vacuum." In contrast to the true vacuum which contains no matter and no energy, a false vacuum contains energy but no matter. According to Einstein's general theory of relativity such a false vacuum is not stable, but undergoes a sudden explosive expansion that can be very much faster than the present expansion of the universe, if the energy content of the false vacuum is high enough.

Before the primal bang, space was in the state of a true vacuum: "the world was without form and void, and darkness was upon the face of the deep." However, according to quantum theory, we must expect energy fluctuations in the true vacuum. At any given moment some small region of the void will fluctuate into a false vacuum with a high energy concentration. This region then expands almost instantly and creates a much larger region filled with energy. We need not worry about energy conservation, because the negative energy arising from the gravitational attraction between the expanding positive energy balances the total amount. When the ultrarapid expansion is over, the energy in space transforms itself into hot particle gases such as quark-antiquark gases, electron-antielectron gases and photons. That would be the point when the standard model takes over and "normal" expansion begins, which is much slower than the explosive expansion. Such a development would solve the horizon problem. The energy density and the subsequent particle density would be uniform over the whole region because all points of the region were in contact before the explosion and expanded uniformly during the explosion.

The inflationary-expansion hypothesis would also solve the problem of the simultaneity of the primal bang all over the universe. The sudden inflationary expansion would start at some point in space and would stop when it reached a certain size. Then it would develop further according to the standard model and would have reached today a size that is much larger than the universe that we can see, but it would not be infinite. Another inflationary universe may have exploded at a different time and space. Perhaps, in billions of years, such other universes may intrude into ours; then the space-filling radiation would no longer appear uniform.

The inflationary-universe hypothesis also tells us what might have happened before 10^{-6} seconds, even before the primal bang. It introduces the view that our universe began with an explosion from one definite point—a view which we declared as wrong, according to the standard model. However, after an incredibly short time, when the explosion stops and the standard model takes over, our universe would be a uniform hot, highly compressed assembly of matter that goes on expanding slowly, not explosively, until it reaches the state in which we see it today. It is not infinitely large, as was assumed in the standard model, but probably very much larger than what we can see and observe today. In *our* universe, the primal bang took place all over *our* space, which, in this new view, is not total space. There would be other universes that started with a big explosion earlier or later than ours in other parts of space. In some ways, the new view is "Copernican," whereas the standard model is "Ptolomaic." According to that view our universe is not the only one; it is not unique. Its beginning is not the beginning of everything. It is on an equal footing with many other universes. However, we must keep in mind that this is an unproven hypothesis that may turn out to be pure fantasy. Nevertheless, the idea is impressively grand.

Now we come to the fourth unsolved problem: the surplus of protons. We are pretty sure from our observations that the universe today contains matter but very little if any antimatter. In the standard model of the universe, the dense gas of qarks and antiquarks that existed in the first microsecond later transformed itself into radiation by the mutual annihilation of particles and antiparticles. But a few quarks must have been left over in order to form the protons and neutrons of today. Therefore, there must have been a few more quarks than antiquarks in the gas—a tiny surplus because the number of nucleons is only about a billionth of the number of quark pairs in the hot gas.

Where did this surplus come from? One would expect that the world should have been completely symmetric at the very beginning. Why should matter have been favored over antimatter by such a small amount? It could be that "somebody" put a little more matter than antimatter into the pot at the outset. But one prefers to assume that there was full symmetry at the beginning.

In order to obtain a small surplus of matter from a symmetric beginning, there must exist processes that favor matter over antimatter a little—only a little since we are speaking here of a surplus of 10^{-9}. Indeed, such a process has been found. It is the so-called violation of the *CP* invariance, which is the mirror invariance *P* and the particle-antiparticle invariance *C* in the laws of nature. There are definite indications that some processes are not completely symmetric in respect to matter and antimatter and could perhaps be the cause of the surplus of protons. We do not yet have the right methods and ideas to confirm this from our present theories and observations.

We now come to the fifth problem: the critical density of matter. We mentioned earlier that the average density of matter in the universe is not well known. However, it seems that it is near a critical value. If the actual density today were higher than that value, the expansion of the universe would end after a certain future time, because the attraction among matter would then be strong enough to turn the expansion into a contraction. If this were to happen, the universe would then become denser, and the highly concentrated situation of the beginning would be reached again after a long period. The whole process, expansion and subsequent contraction, could perhaps repeat itself forever and ever. Conversely, if the actual density today were below the critical value, then the gravitational attraction would not be strong enough to turn the expansion around, and there would be no end to the expansion. If the density were exactly the critical one, the expansion would go on and on but would slow down asymptotically to zero without every turning around.

It seems that the actual density is very close to this critical value. Actually, the average density of matter seen in stars and galaxies is less than a tenth of the critical value. But there is some evidence that the universe contains a large amount of "dark matter," some of which makes itself felt by its gravitational effects. It may be as much as 90 percent of all matter. Its nature is not known. Probably it is different from the ordinary particles of which luminous matter consists. If neutrinos possess a small but finite mass then the neutrino gas that supposedly fills the universe would make a considerable contribution to the mass density. Whatever that contribution may be, the question still comes up why nature has chosen a mass density that is so near the critical one. Even if the deviation from critical density is relatively large today, say 10 percent or more, it must have been incredibly small at early moments of the universe, because at that time the density itself was very much larger.

The theory of an explosive, "inflationary" universe may possibly give an answer to this problem also. In order to get a glimpse of that explanation, we must take into account that the critical density corresponds to a "flat" universe, whereas a larger density implies a curved, closed universe, and a smaller density a curved, open one. This can be pictured in two dimensions: a plane is flat, a spherical surface is curved and closed, a hyperbolic saddle surface is curved and open. The explosive expansion increases the relevant dimensions in space by such a big factor that any curvature becomes negligible in that part of space that is our present universe.

The theory of the inflationary universe is still beset with a number of difficulties. If it turns out to be incorrect, the answer to the problem of critical density may again lie in the form of as yet unknown laws of nature determining the behavior of matter at the very extreme temperatures of the beginning of the universe.

We now come to the more philosophical question: What existed before the primal bang? The problem may be somewhat different if the mass density is higher than the critical one. Under these conditions, the events before the primal bang would correspond to a contracting universe, and we would have a universe that periodically contracts and expands forever. The hypothesis of the periodic universe is not without its own problems. It is not clear whether the concentration produces the same primal situation every time. It could well be that the entropy of the universe increases each time, in which case we again arrive at the problem of a real beginning: the first primal bang.

If the mass density lies below or at the critical value, the beginning of our universe would indeed be a primal bang about 13 billion years ago. If the inflationary hypothesis is correct, this universe would have started with a quantum fluctuation of a special kind of field that produces very high energy concentrations in space. In that case, the universe before the primal bang was empty space, ready for quantum fluctuations here and there, the strong ones leading to the development of universes more or less like ours.

This essay began with a remark about how strongly our topic is connected with other human interests, with philosophical, mythological, and religious concerns. It hits us in the heart, as it were. The origin of the universe can be talked about not only in scientific terms, but also in poetic and spiritual language, an approach that is complementary to the scientific one. Indeed, the Judeo-Christian tradition describes the beginning of the world with the creation of light on the first day and the sun on the fourth day. It seemed contradictory to have light created before the sun. However, the present scientific view does indeed assume that the early universe was filled with various kinds of radiation long before the sun was created. A remarkable musical description of the primal bang is found at the beginning of Joseph Haydn's oratorio *The Creation*. A choir of angels sings darkly and softly, "And God said, 'Let there by Light'." The entire choir and the orchestra burst into a fortissimo C-major chord at the last word of "And there was Light." There cannot be a more beautiful and impressive artistic rendition of the beginning of everything.

IV

Two Physicists

11

Wolfgang Pauli

We older disciples of the great Wolfgang Pauli remember with pleasure and nostalgia the prewar years when we had the privilege to work with him. It was one of the most interesting, stimulating, and productive periods in physics. At the same time, however, Europe saw events that were among the most terrible and depraved actions of man against man. The coincidence in the history of humankind of the greatest achievements and the worst evils has always impressed and depressed me deeply. As Dickens said: "It was the best of times, it was the worst of times."

Let me begin my tale a little earlier. In 1932, I received a Rockefeller grant for one year, to study at places of my choice. I wanted to divide my time between Copenhagen and Cambridge, England, to learn from the two great men Niels Bohr and Paul A. M. Dirac. In Copenhagen, I not only profited greatly from Bohr's overwhelming personality—everyone who spent some time with him was deeply influenced by his way of thinking and living—but I also met my wife there, so the division of my Rockefeller time was somewhat biased toward Copenhagen.

My stay in Cambridge was also very important to me, but not so much because of Dirac. It was not easy to learn from him; he worked for himself and did not have much contact with other physicists or would-be physicists. It was in Cambridge that I met Rudolf Peierls, who also had a Rockefeller grant. He was a few years older than I, and I learned much from him. Two or three years are not much, but they make a big difference when one is young and, sometimes, at the end of one's life. He introduced me to relativistic field theory—how to make calculations with the Dirac equation, a skill that was called "alpha gymnastics."

Peierls's stipend was $200 a month, whereas, to my slight annoyance, mine was only $150. I hasten to add that either amount represented at that time undreamed-of riches for an average European. The reason for the difference was that he was married, whereas I was only on the way to be. The Rockefeller Foundation asked us to send in reports on our achievements during the time of support. As proof of some of his activities, Peierls sent the foundation an announcement of the birth of his first child; of course, I was unable to match this. The officials in New York didn't appreciate Peierls's sense of humor, we heard.

HOW TO DEAL WITH PAULI

At that time—it must have been May or June of 1933—a letter came from Pauli asking me to be his assistant in Zurich, replacing Hendrik Casimir, whom Paul Ehrenfest, shortly before his suicide, had called back to Leiden. What could be better for a young physicist than to work with Pauli? It was the fulfillment of a dream. Why did he take me and not other, more experienced people such as Hans Bethe? I found out later.

Now, I had something else to learn from Peierls, who had been Pauli's assistant before. Of course, I asked him about his experiences. He said, "It is a great thing, but you must be prepared." Hence, Peierls taught me not only quantum electrodynamics, but also "how to deal with Pauli." Here is one example of the good advice he gave me: "Be very careful when you give a talk at the Zurich colloquium. Pauli likes to interrupt a speaker when he thinks he is wrong or inconsistent. The best method to counteract this is: The day of your talk go to Pauli in the morning and tell him what you are planning to say. If he does not like it, he will tell you in the strongest terms how silly it is, that it is all wrong or that it is trivial and known to every child, etc., etc. Then in the afternoon at the colloquium," continued Peierls, "you say exactly what you intended to say in the first place. You don't need to change anything, except if you really have been convinced by him. Pauli will sit in the first row, and when you come to the critical points, he will almost inaudibly mumble to himself: 'I've told him already, I've told him anyway!' So it won't be so bad at all."

I found out why Pauli took me instead of Bethe when I came to Zurich to begin my duties in the fall of 1933. I knocked several times at the door of Pauli's office until I heard a faint, "Come in." I saw Pauli at his desk at the far end of the room and he said, "Wait, wait, I have to finish this calculation." (*Erst muss ich fertig ixen.*) So I waited several minutes. Then he said, "Who are you?" "I am Weisskopf, you asked me to be your assistant." "Yes," he said, "first I wanted to take Bethe, but he works on solid-state theory, which I don't like, although I started it." This, then, was the reason.

I made a contract with him. I said, "Of course, I am more than delighted to work for you but, please, that new stuff you are working on, the Klein-Kaluza approach to general relativity, that I am unable to understand. I don't want to deal with it, but I am ready to work on everything else." He accepted the condition because he was already somewhat bored by it. (Today it seems to be the *dernier cri* of the most sophisticated particle theorists.) Pauli then gave me some problem to study—I have forgotten what it was—and after a week he came and asked me what I did. I showed him and he said, "I should have taken Bethe after all." I was well prepared by Peierls for events like this and I took it for what it was: a challenge to get a deeper understanding of physics.

The numerous Pauli anecdotes circulating among physicists give a distorted impression of Pauli's personality. He is seen as a mean character who wanted to hurt his weaker colleagues. Nothing is further from the truth. Pauli's occasional and highly publicized roughness was an expression of his dislike of half-truths and sloppy thinking, but it was never meant to be directed against any person. Pauli was an excessively honest man; he had an almost childlike honesty. What he said were always his true thoughts, directly expressed. Nothing is more reassuring than to live and work with somebody who says everything that is on his mind—but you must get accustomed to it. Pauli did not want to hurt anybody, although he sometimes did, without intention. He disliked half-truths or ideas that were not thought through, and he did not tolerate talking around a half-baked idea. He was, as many people said, the conscience of physics. He wanted people to understand things thoroughly and express them correctly. He never tired of answering questions and explaining problems to anybody who came asking. He was not a good lecturer before an audience because he did not have the ability to judge how much the crowd could take in, and his listeners did not often dare to interrupt him with questions. Once a student did so and said, "You told us that conclusion is trivial, but I am unable to understand it." Then

Pauli did what he did frequently when he had to think things over during a lecture: he left the room. After a few minutes he came back and said: "It is trivial!"

When you came to him and said, "Please explain this to me, I don't understand it," he would explain it with great patience and pleasure. We often said, "For Pauli every question is stupid, so don't hesitate to ask him whatever you want." He loved simple and illustrative explanations, but they had to be correct, and not misleading. Once, his colleague in experimental physics, Paul Scherrer—an excellent lecturer and a lover of simple conclusions—came to him and said: "Look, Pauli, I would like to show you how I explained that effect in my course. You see, here the spin is up, and there it is down and then they interact . . . isn't that simple?" Whereupon Pauli answered: "Simple it is, but it is also wrong!"

Pauli loved people and showed great loyalty to his students and collaborators. All of Pauli's disciples developed a deep personal attachment to him, not only because of the many insights he gave us, but because of his fundamentally endearing human qualities. It is true that sometimes he was a little hard to take, but all of us felt that he helped us to see our weaknesses. Ehrenfest expressed it well after J. Robert Oppenheimer came to him as a young postdoc in the late 1920s. Ehrenfest was unhappy because Oppenheimer always gave quick answers to questions, and Ehrenfest felt that the answer was not always correct but he was unable to reply fast enough. So he wrote to Pauli: "I have here a remarkable and intelligent American but I cannot handle him. He is too clever for me. Couldn't you take him over and spank him morally and intellectually into shape?" (*Zurecht prügeln.*) We all were spanked into shape by dear Pauli and we loved it.

There was one person to whom Pauli acted quite differently. When Arnold Sommerfeld, his former teacher, came to Zurich for a visit, it was all, "Yes, *Herr Geheimrat*, yes, this is most interesting, but perhaps I would prefer a slightly different formulation, may I formulate it this way. . . ." It was much fun for us victims of his aggression to see him well behaved, polite, and subservient; a completely different Pauli.

CALCULATIONS AND PUBLICATIONS

There were not many regular duties for Pauli's assistants to perform. Pauli himself made up the homework problems for his course, and we assistants only had to grade them. Our main duty was to be ready for discussion of his work and of new developments. He took this very seriously, and it was not easy to get permission to leave Zurich during the term. Once I asked him with great trepidation, "May I go to Copenhagen for a week?" "Why?" he asked impatiently. I answered, "I intend to marry and come back with my wife." To my great relief he replied, "I approve of that, I am going to get married also!" (*Ich heirate nämlich auch.*)

Pauli's assistants had another pleasant duty. Pauli's wife asked him to change his eating habits because of his proverbial bulk. But Pauli loved sweets and cakes, and many afternoons he wanted to continue our discussions in a nearby *Konditorei* where one could get delicious pastries. One of my duties was to promise never to mention these secret outings to his wife.

Of course there were also more serious duties. A lively correspondence was taking place between Werner Heisenberg and Pauli about the problems of quantum electrodynamics. Some of these problems, such as the unavoidable infinities, were quite serious and were solved only much later. Many of them, however, could be straightened out at the time. Whenever a letter came from Heisenberg, Pauli discussed it with me and frequently asked me to draft an answer: "You write it, I will correct it, and then we will send it to him." A letter once came from Heisenberg and Pauli was terribly dissatisfied with its content: "Such silly statements; it is all stupid and wrong. You must tell this to him in your letter!" What could I do? Well, I started out explaining our disagreements as well as I could, and then I quoted Leporello in *Don Giovanni*: "My master wants to tell you, myself I would not dare to." Then I was able to repeat literally all of Pauli's curses.

It was the time of an unhappy episode in my career as a physicist. Pauli asked me to calculate the self-energy of the electron on the basis of the positron theory to see if this energy is less divergent in that theory. I found that it diverges equally badly and I published this result. A few weeks after the publication I received a letter from Wendell Furry, who worked with Oppenheimer at the time, informing me that I had made a simple mistake of a sign in my calculation. If it is done correctly, the divergence is only logarithmic. The positron theory improved things considerably, in contradiction to my paper. I was down and depressed to have made and published a silly mistake in such a fundamental problem! I went to Pauli and said that I wanted to give up physics, that I would never survive this blemish. Pauli tried to console me: He said, "Don't take it too seriously, many people published wrong papers; I never did!"

What followed shows how decent the relations between physicists were at that time. I asked Furry by letter to publish his result under his name or at least to coauthor a paper correcting the mistake. But Furry was a gentleman. He answered, no, I should publish a correction in my name only and mention him as the person who drew my attention to the error. Since then, the logarithmic divergence of the self-energy of the electron goes with my name and not with Furry's. Yes, times have changed and so have the attitudes of physicists toward publication by others. I remember having shown Pauli a newly published paper on a subject of his interest. He said, "Yes, I thought of that too, but I am glad he worked it out, so that I don't need to do it myself."

Let me now say a few words about the origin of the paper that Pauli and I wrote in *Helvetica Physica Acta* (1934) about quantum electrodynamics with Bose particles. In 1934, I was playing around with the so-called Klein-Gordon equation, which is the relativistic wave equation of particles with zero spin. I was struck by the fact that the wave intensity $|\psi|^2$ is not conserved in the presence of electromagnetic fields, whereas the expression for the charge density is different from $|\psi|^2$ and fulfills the charge conservation laws. I felt there might be something like a lack of conservation of particle number in that equation, and that this might lead to pair creation or annihilation. In spite of what I learned from Peierls in Cambridge, I was not able to deal with this problem. It required what was called "second quantization," or the quantization of the wave field, something with which I was not very familiar at that time.

I went to Pauli for help. It was just after his separation from his first wife, and he was in a very bad mood. I tried to explain to him my difficulties and my tentative conclusions, but he was very impatient and repeated over and over how silly my remarks were. Finally, I quoted to him a verse from Wagner's opera, *Die Meistersinger*, that said approximately, "Oh master, why so much excitement and so little repose; I believe your judgment would be more mature if you would better listen." He looked up to me and asked, "What is that?" I said it is from *Meistersinger,* whereupon he replied, "Wagner, I don't like at all!" So ended the discussion.

The next day he was in a better mood and I repeated my story. He said: "That's interesting. Why didn't you tell it to me yesterday?" This began a wonderful time for me, when I learned from Pauli in detail how to deal with second quantization. We found that the quantum electrodynamics of spinless particles indeed leads to antiparticles, pair creation, and annihilation—and all of it came out without the necessity of filling up negative-energy states with particles, as Dirac did to get these phenomena from his equation. Pauli never liked that trick and frequently referred to our paper as the anti-Dirac paper. Of course, later on it was shown that the trick of filling up negative-energy states was not necessary even with the Dirac equation.

Pauli asked me to calculate the pair creation and annihilation cross sections of spinless particles according to our theory. The calculation was not too different from the one for ordinary electrons and positrons that Bethe and his collaborators had carried out shortly before. I met Bethe at that time at a conference in Copenhagen and asked him to show me how to do the calculations. I wondered how long it would take to get to the final result and he told me, "It would take me a few days, it will take you a few weeks." It did. Moreover, I made a mistake of a factor of four. Again a proof that Pauli should have taken Bethe.

THE EXCLUSION PRINCIPLE

Our paper was little more than an interesting formal exercise, because at that time no particles with zero spin were known to exist. However, some years after I left Pauli, he used some of the ideas for his famous proof of the connection between spin and statistics: particles with half-integer spin must fulfill the Pauli exclusion principle; those with integer spin must have Bose statistics. This achievement shows Pauli in his greatness. He discovered the exclusion principle in 1925 from a careful analysis of atomic spectra and was not satisfied until, fifteen years later, he was able to show how it followed by necessity from quantum field theory.

One day, in the course of my work as assistant, I came across an interesting note that Pauli had made a couple of years before his discovery of the exclusion principle. It was one of my lighter duties to keep Pauli's collection of reprints in reasonable order. In doing so, I browsed through older papers and found a copy of Bohr's famous paper about the *Aufbauprinzip,* in which he explained the periodic system of elements as an effect of electronic shell structure. Everybody who teaches this wonderful triumph of quantum theory uses the Pauli principle to explain the way in which the electron shells are filled when going from one atom to the next one with an additional electron. However, when Bohr published his paper on the periodic system, the exclusion principle was not yet known! It was a testimony to Bohr's unfailing intuition that he nevertheless got the right results. Browsing through Pauli's copy of that paper, I looked at the page on which

Bohr says, "Going from neon to sodium, we must expect that the eleventh electron goes into the third shell . . ." and my attention was caught by a remark that Pauli had written in the margin in big letters: "How do you know this? You only get it from the very spectra you want to explain!" Three heavy exclamation marks followed. It took Pauli two more years to tell us why.

MORAL INTEGRITY

Pauli was in Princeton during World War II. To stay in Switzerland would have been too dangerous because he was not yet a Swiss citizen; he carried an Austrian passport and was considered a German national, after the Nazis took over Austria. The Swiss consented to give him citizenship, only after his Nobel prize in 1946. He wrote a letter to Oppenheimer asking him whether he was obliged to join the war effort as a guest of the United States. After some discussion in Los Alamos, we decided that he would not have felt at ease in a large team. His pure character would make it difficult for him to work in a project aimed at a deadly weapon. Moreover, nuclear physics never interested him very much, even though he discovered nuclear spin and predicted the existence of neutrinos. We thought it important that at least one of the great physicists continue with pure research, facilitating the resumption of our activities after the end of the war.

When the war was over, Pauli was indeed of great help to all of us. He was asked to give a series of lectures about the latest ideas in particle theory. He brought us back to fundamental physics. Shortly afterward, he returned to Zurich. He wanted to keep in touch as closely as possible with American physics, and he asked me and others to write to him about the newest developments in theory and experiment. I remember a letter of mine reporting Chien-Shiung Wu's preparations to test the conservation of parity in weak interactions. Pauli wrote back that in his opinion, this was a waste of time; he would bet any amount of money that parity is conserved in any process. When the letter arrived, I had just heard the news that parity was strongly violated. My better self won, and I did not send a telegram saying, "Bet for $1000 accepted," but reported to him the surprising result of Wu's experiment. Overseas telephone calls were not yet used for physics. Pauli was completely flabbergasted. He wrote back expressing his astonishment that "God is a weak lefthander," since the experiment showed that in weak interactions, particles with left-handed spin are favored. He added: "I am glad that I did not conclude our bet. I can afford to lose some of my reputation but not some of my capital."

Pauli mellowed much in his later years, largely because his second wife, Franca, was able to make his life bearable and even pleasant. This was not an easy task. Pauli had a very difficult character, was easily depressed, and often felt thoroughly unhappy. Franca succeeded in creating a comfortable, protected home for him, in which he could feel at ease and pursue his many interests, which reached far beyond physics.

He became very interested in various forms of mysticism, mainly through his connection with the Swiss psychologist Carl Gustav Jung. Later he developed a deep friendship with Gershon Scholem, the great scholar and world authority on Jewish mysticism, the *Kabalah*. (The *Kabalah* ascribes a number having a deep symbolic significance to each word of the Hebrew language. The number corresponding to the word Kabalah happens to be 137, which is almost exactly the ratio between the product of Planck's quantum of action, multiplied with the light velocity and the square of the charge of the electron, a number that plays a fundamental role in physics but whose value is completely unexplained.) Pauli and Scholem saw each other frequently and exchanged their views in letters. With a few notable exceptions, Pauli rarely spoke about this side of his interests to his physicist friends. He did not speak much about it with me, except that he urged me to visit Scholem when I went to Jerusalem. It was a unique experience to meet that great man and to be introduced to ideas that are so alien to those of our science.

Pauli's interest in these different avenues of human experience was in many respects a natural expansion of his involvement in modern physics. He was a disciple of Bohr—perhaps Bohr's closest disciple. Bohr often applied his concept of complementarity to human concerns beyond natural science. The rational scientific approach is only one way of dealing with the world around us. There are other, seemingly contradictory approaches—as contradictory as the particle and wave pictures within physics—that deal with aspects of our thoughts and emotions. A given concept seems fragile and senseless when analyzed within the framework of another approach, but is forceful and convincing within its own frame. Pauli was very much attracted by this generalization of complementarity.

Pauli created a style of theoretical thinking and research that influenced physics all over the world. It is a style that emphasizes the essential roots and the symmetries of the laws of nature in their mathematical form without much talk or hand waving. His clean way of thinking and working appears to all of us as an ideal to be emulated. We often ask ourselves, "What would Pauli say to this?" We often come to the conclusion, "Pauli would not accept it."

However, Pauli set his example through more than the character of his work. He personified the striving for utmost clarity and purity in science and human relations. We owe it, in part, to Pauli that in the community of physicists there is still a certain amount of healthy simplicity, honesty, and directness, in spite of all the politics, publicity, and ambition—attitudes that were so foreign to Pauli. He was not only a physicist, he was also a great personality, able to see deeper than others into scientific and human problems. The dark riddles of the human psyche were not unknown to him. He is an example to all of us of how to live a quiet and contemplative life of intellectual and moral integrity in these unruly times.

12

Werner Heisenberg

In the years between 1924 and 1927 some of the deepest riddles that nature posed to us were solved: how to understand and describe the structure of atoms and, therefore, the structure and behavior of matter, since all matter is made of atoms. It was a truly revolutionary step, because it required the abandonment of many old concepts and prejudices and the creation of new concepts and a new language called quantum mechanics in order to understand and describe what happens within and between the atoms. A new, subtle reality was discovered to exist in this realm on which the ordinary reality of our daily life is based. The new insights were achieved not by any single individual, but by a small group from different nations, with Niels Bohr in Copenhagen as the most powerful leader. Most of these people were very young, in their twenties, whereas Bohr was in his forties at that time. It was a little group of enthusiastic young spirits, well aware of being at the front line of knowledge, of shedding light on a previously murky and contradictory situation. Never before have so few contributed so much insight into the workings of nature in such a short time.

One of the young men in this group was Werner Heisenberg. He was perhaps the most active and creative among them, the one who provided the most important ideas and formulations. He and the others did their work mostly at their home universities, but they spent much time in Copenhagen or had a vivid correspondence with Niels

Bohr and among themselves. For many of them, especially for Heisenberg, Niels Bohr was a father figure; he provided encouragement, criticism, and the philosophical view that was necessary to understand, interpret, and accept those new ideas that, even today, are difficult to grasp.

Heisenberg had a special, intuitive way of getting to the essential point. This, together with an incredible force of persistence and determination, made him the most prolific and successful physicist of the recent past. Whenever important problems turned up in the subsequent development of quantum mechanics, more often than not, it was Heisenberg who found the solution. He pointed to the direction of further developments by inventing new ways of looking at the situation. Apart from his fundamental contributions to the formulation of the quantum mechanics of the atom, he was able to decipher the helium spectrum that had puzzled physicists for decades; he explained the magnetism of iron and similar metals; he paved the way to get a profound description of nuclear structure by considering the proton and the neutron as two states of the same basic particle. These are only a few of his outstanding contributions. All of them contained seminal ideas which led research into new directions and found their way into the foundations of physics.

The most quoted of his contributions is the Heisenberg uncertainty relation, which is the basis of the new understanding of atomic reality. It defines the limits to which the ordinary classical concepts, such as "particle" and "wave," are applicable. Beyond these limits the new, subtler reality of the quantum state emerges. Heisenberg's discovery and formulation of these fundamental limits is a typical product of the collaboration of Niels Bohr with his younger colleagues. It was largely the result of numerous discussions, extended over long periods, in the institute, in letters, on excursions along the Danish coast, or in the German Alps. Bohr, in his Socratic way, asked the relevant questions and pointed to the depths of the problems and the plenitude of the phenomena. Then in the minds of the best of his disciples, the new ideas grew and took shape. Obviously, such a relationship must bring along a deep personal friendship, a sharing of philosophy and of common outlook in many other human, artistic, and literary concerns. So it was between Bohr and Heisenberg until . . .

Heisenberg was a pleasant man who made friends easily. Everybody who came in touch with him liked and admired him. He was interested in all sides of human culture; he was an accomplished pianist and an enthusiastic mountaineer and skier. So one would have thought that he would have had a happy and fulfilled life as a leading scientist, in the midst of many students, a life devoted exclusively to a deeper understanding of physics and the enjoyment of art, music, and literature and the beauties of nature.

It did not come out that way. He and his contemporaries lived in times of political upheaval. Europe, and in particular his homeland, went through one of the worst periods in world history. The Nazi regime unleashed the most destructive side of human nature, antithetic and opposed to the cultural values cherished by Heisenberg and the group he belonged to.

The upheaval in Europe caused untold horror and destruction. Millions of people lost their lives, millions had to live under the cruelest oppression and humiliation; the minds of western civilization were perverted to such a degree that it still has its aftereffects forty years later, in having weakened our sensitivity toward human life and oppression. Those who survived the holocaust should consider themselves lucky; most of them do not think about it anymore. (Our present time has its own madness, the nuclear arms race and the threatening nuclear war.) They suffered in various degrees from the cruel acts of Nazi oppression, from the mild form of forced emigration to the cruelest form of corporal and mental torture and humiliation in the concentration camps. Heisenberg and his family were not exposed to any of these punishments. They did not suffer in this direct sense of the word. Compared to the fate of those victims of Nazism, their burden was light.

Elisabeth Heisenberg's book, *Inner Exile: Recollections of a Life with Werner Heisenberg* (Birkhaeuser, 1984), is important because it provides insight into some aspects of life under an oppressive regime that are not often recounted. Here was a man deeply rooted in the best of German cultural life. It was in the German intellectual tradition to devote oneself to the "higher" concerns and to leave the dirty games of politics to lesser spirits. One assumed that those political uproars would somehow go away and the better part of German conscience would win out. Heisenberg was looking for positive signs in the national movement, but he saw its true nature and was deeply repelled by its spirit, by its actions and excesses.

What then were his choices? He could emigrate, he could actively participate in the underground movement, or he could retire from public life and live as decently as possible with his family and his work. The last possibility existed for many other Germans but not for him. He was much too prominent and influential. Active participation in the underground movement required an amount of heroism that one cannot ask from any person. Heisenberg was the head of a family of five children. He was not the heroic type, but rather, a careful and prudent character. An active role in the underground could not have been his way.

Why did he not choose to emigrate? Many friends abroad strongly encouraged him to do so and offered him, of course, the best possible opportunities. His life and that of his family would have been much easier. But he thought it would be a cop-out. He was deeply attached to Germany and he felt a responsibility toward those who shared his feelings and whom he might be able to help because of his influence and reputation.

Was there another way? The answer to this question is the main concern of Elisabeth Heisenberg's book. It was a hard way, not in the sense of bodily suffering—he and his family were spared that— but in the daily struggles of conscience and the fear of being found out as a doubter, or even a traitor. It must have driven him to utter despair and depression that his beloved country had fallen so deeply into the abyss of crime, blood, and murder. He learned the truth of what Max Planck had told him: "In the ghastly situation in which Germany now finds itself, no one can act entirely decently." He "envied those of his friends whose lives in Germany had been made so impossible that they simply had to leave." He wanted to stay in Germany and to help create "islands of decency" where, within small groups, some of the cultural achievements might be saved to serve as the beginning of a new cultural life when the Nazi holocaust was over.

The question was raised whether Heisenberg believed in a German victory before the turn of events. There were people who had heard him say so. But he says definitely that he never did. This is not necessarily a contradiction. Heisenberg was very prudent and circumspect when he talked to others during the Nazi time. Those who never lived under a dictatorship may not comprehend the tremendous danger of being given away, the fear for their life and the lives of their family. A report back to the Nazis that he doubted victory could have been a death sentence. Even if he were a hero—he was not—he would not risk his life only to improve his reputation among his acquaintances.

Obviously, by remaining in Germany, he was soon involved in the efforts of the Nazi regime to exploit nuclear energy. The possibility of a bomb was evident. There was a vast difference between the position toward the bomb held by scientists on the allied side and the position held by those on the German side who were more or less opposed to the regime. Heisenberg was certainly one of the latter. The allied scientists were terrified by the idea of a bomb in the hands of Hitler; they trusted the policies of their leaders, Churchill and Roosevelt. Those German scientists would have been in a terrible situation in devising this awesome weapon, torn between distrust for Hitler and the pressure to collaborate with the Nazis. Fortunately for them and for the world, something happened that helped them out of this dilemma. The estimate Heisenberg and his collaborators made of the time and effort necessary to devise and construct the bomb was set at several years, and the effort was considered to be beyond the German industrial capacity during the war. So the Nazi government decided to give it up and concentrate only on the power production as a long-range project, of questionable use during the war but of promise for the future.

It is improbable that Heisenberg and his colleagues consciously exaggerated the time and the effort in order to avoid the possibility of giving the weapon to Hitler. They probably expressed their true opinion. But in such situations nobody knows how much he is influenced by his willingness to do it. Every great project can succeed only if its proponents support it with full conviction of its necessity. Indeed, such conviction usually leads to an underestimation of the time and effort; without such underestimations, few daring projects would ever have been begun and accomplished.

The negative bomb decision saved Heisenberg and his colleagues from many troubles; Nazi authorities would have breathed down their necks day and night; unavoidable setbacks would have been interpreted as treason and the responsible people persecuted. Furthermore, Heisenberg and his group would have been torn between the pangs of their conscience and their sense of duty to the nation. So a stroke of luck enabled them to retire to a reasonably well-supported government side effort, a haven for saving people from service at the crumbling front lines. They considered their work, not without justification, as a basis for the start of a nuclear industry in the postwar world.

One tragic point needs to be discussed. It is the unfortunate and abortive visit of Heisenberg with Niels Bohr during the war. A great friendship and a creative human bond was shattered. Certainly, an end to a friendship cannot be compared to the mass murders and the effects of mass bombings, but it is a symbol of the tragedies of war. Heisenberg went to Copenhagen, to his old friend, mentor, and father figure in order to talk to him about the great problems that nuclear explosives had created for mankind and in particular for the community of scientists. But he did not consider how deep and justified the feelings of hate and desperation were in a nation victimized by the Nazis. He expressed himself very vaguely, fearing that any direct statement about Germany's nuclear effort, or any doubt of a German victory, would put him and his family in mortal danger. Under these conditions, it was difficult for Niels Bohr to see in Heisenberg only the old disciple and friend and not a representative of the oppressors. Perhaps one could have expected that Heisenberg would have spoken openly and clearly with Bohr when they could not have been overheard. Here it was not a question of what others might think of him. He faced his fatherly friend who would have taken all precautions and would never have given him away in spite of his misgivings, knowing the consequences only too well. Perhaps such an open exchange would have been useful.

Whatever happened, nobody has the right to reproach anybody for having avoided a deadly risk. Who can stand up and say he would have taken the risk in the same situation with the same responsibilities? Those who have never been in such situations must be grateful to their fate of being spared such decisions.

In times of oppression and persecution, the general principles are less important than individual personal actions. We know that Heisenberg did what he could to protect the Bohr Institute after the German occupation. He saved the lives of a number of people. He never made much of it and did not mention it in his writings, but we hear about several such cases in *Inner Exile,* and there was a letter published in the magazine, *Science News* (Vol. 109, p. 179, 1976), by one of those whose life was saved by Heisenberg. Such acts weigh more than any statements.

Heisenberg believed in the importance and strength of the international community of scientists. He had become acquainted with it during the early years of quantum mechanics research in Copenhagen. He saw the great edifice of thought emerge from a group of human beings of very different national origin, but united by their common enthusiasm to lift a part of the veil behind which the secrets of nature were hidden. He was disappointed that this spirit of community did not withstand the divisive forces of the World War.

When he was free again, after the war, to devote part of his efforts to fundamental problems of physics, his intuition enabled him to contribute again some important seminal ideas about the structure of elementary particles. But in the postwar period two unsuccessful attempts cast a shadow over his life and robbed him of some of his optimism. One was his failure to establish an effective board of scientists to advise the government on essential questions; the second was his failure to convince the world of physicists of the power of his last attempt to formulate an all embracing theory of matter. He may have overextended himself in both attempts. His greatest source of success was always his ability to forget about details and aim directly at the essential points. Perhaps at the end of his life, the plenitude of events in physics as well as in public life had become too overwhelming. This may be one of the predicaments of today's world in general.

It is hoped that his doubts about the future of the scientific community were exaggerated. After all, the international spirit of science is not at all dead today. One of the most significant examples is CERN, the international laboratory in Geneva that he helped to bring about. Not only is it run by thirteen European nations, but under its roof, scientists of the whole world collaborate, irrespective of political differences. We find Americans, Russians, and Chinese working together on the same experiment. There exists a strong urge among physicists to establish better bonds and better understanding between the politically divided parts of humankind. Perhaps this urge comes to some extent from a feeling of guilt: that some of the great insights of their research have been exploited to serve as weapons of annihilation and as a threat to the future of mankind.

Elisabeth Heisenberg's book, *Inner Exile: Recollections of a Life with Werner Heisenberg*, is an important human document. In it she describes the difficulties, tribulations, and conflicts that people encounter under a regime of dictatorship and oppression even when they are not direct victims of the system. She describes the hardship and mental sufferings of a woman, wife, and mother, who accepted the decision of her husband to choose a thankless and difficult path and helped and supported him as much as she could. Great were the sorrows and fears, but great also were the moments of joy and gratitude when things worked out better than they had feared. Her book shows us how complex and how exasperating life can be when you are forced to compromise with, and adjust to, intolerable conditions in order to save what you consider to be more important. Such regimes still exist all over the world. That is why this book will also enhance our understanding of the predicaments of scientists in similar situations today. It will help to improve the bond between those who suffer and those who have been spared. In this sense, her book will contribute to the strenghthening of the international community of scientists.

V

Science and Society

13

————— ✺ —————

On Knowledge, Wonder, and World Peace

An Interview

W eisskopf is one of the world's most eminent physicists—a highly accomplished researcher, innovative administrator, scientific states-man, inspired teacher, and articulate spokesman for international arms control. He is also a warm, compassionate, and unpretentious human being: around MIT, and throughout the scientific community, Victor Frederick Weisskopf is known simply as "Viki."

Professor Weisskopf's career in physics has spanned a great variety of projects, institutions, and countries. To mention just two: he played a key role in the Manhattan Project at Los Alamos, New Mexico, from 1943 to 1945, which produced humanity's most awesome tech-nical achievement—the atomic bomb. He also served as director gen-eral from 1961 to 1965 of the European Center for Nuclear Research (CERN), a fruitful international collaboration for basic inquiry into the structure of matter.

In addition to his continuing activities in physics, Professor Weiss-kopf has devoted himself to stimulating public awareness of the range, depth, and beauty of science, as well as the dangers of its abuses. His book, *Knowledge and Wonder* (MIT Press, 1979), has been widely acclaimed. He has also been a tireless campaigner for reducing the magnitude and reversing the direction of the nuclear arms race.

Viennese by birth, he was educated in Germany (receiving his Ph.D. from the University of Göttingen in 1931), and worked with some of Europe's most distinguished physicists before coming to the United

States in 1937 to join the faculty of the University of Rochester. In 1945, he was appointed professor of physics at MIT, later became department head and Institute Professor, and is currently professor emeritus. He is also a member of the Soviet Academy of Science and of the Pontifical Academy of Sciences, a nondenominational body of advisors to the Vatican. Widely honored, his most recent are Israel's Wolf Prize and the U.S. National Medal of Science.

Professor Weisskopf met with *Technology Review*'s managing editor, Steven J. Marcus, to discuss the enlightened use of science and creativity in general. A revised transcript of their conversation follows.

MARCUS: The issue that dominates your popular writing—what you clearly consider to be "the number-one problem"—is the nuclear arms race. You've stated that "with the discovery of fission, mankind entrained cosmic forces with human irrationality," and you've labeled the situation "a mighty tinderbox," "a manmade volcano," "a Sword of Damocles," ultimately calling it "the triumph of craziness." And yet you often cite Robert Oppenheimer's observation that nuclear weapons are both a peril and a hope—the hope being that humanity may now be forced to make some basic changes. Do you truly feel that there is a good possibility we will be forced onto a different, more humane track?

WEISSKOPF: Sure. I am an optimistic character. I believe in the ability of humankind to save itself; otherwise I would stop working on arms control altogether. From its very beginning, the human race has had to rely upon its intelligence to survive. There is always hope, and as long as there is hope, we must persist. You can choose another quote from my writings: that "a miracle may be needed to avoid the holocaust, but this miracle must happen."

MARCUS: But "miracle" is a religious term. It's one thing for the president to say "let us pray" and leave it at that, but for a scientist to invoke the supernatural is a little surprising.

WEISSKOPF: What I mean is that we need not only the powers of intelligence but also the powers of morality, conviction, ethics, and all the things that religion has stood for. We cannot end the arms race by purely rational—scientific—means. We can solve it only by moral means.

In this connection, let me paraphrase the Pope's letter to President Reagan (1981). He says that he is very worried about public opinion, that people are becoming accustomed to the idea that the use of such murderous weaponry, previously quite unthinkable, is now possible, if not probable. The greatest danger, he says, is to believe it will happen. He is deeply convinced that our generation has the moral duty to spare no effort to exorcise the spectre of nuclear war.

MARCUS: It seems that your own activity, and that of many other scientists over recent years, has been to influence leaders—to help "exorcise the spectre"—indirectly through stimulating public awareness.

WEISSKOPF: I don't believe that the leaders we have now—and I'm not speaking only of our own country—will really take up new ways by themselves. That will come about only through public pressure, motivated by public awareness. And this public awareness must be twofold. People must first understand the tremendous danger, but that's not enough. On the contrary, that is almost self-defeating because if you know only about the danger and you don't know what to do about it, you become inured to it, or you repress it, as the Pope suggested. So in our public-education efforts we also have to show that there are possibilities for getting rid of the danger—at least in steps.

The first step, of course, is to stop building more weapons and to hold a moratorium, or "freeze." The usual argument against the freeze is that we are not equal, that the Russians are running ahead. But this is nonsense. If you really count, you'll find that in some ways we are ahead and in some ways they are ahead. All together we are just about on par. Indeed, I have the impression that overall the West is stronger than the East, not that numerical differences carry much importance for nuclear forces anyway.

But there must also be more steps—for example, a comprehensive test ban so that the development of new weapons is largely stopped because they can't be tried out. Then, further steps would involve a gradual decrease in the number of weapons, particularly the tactical nuclear warheads deployed in Europe. They represent a very special danger because the likelihood of their use would be rather high in the event of a Soviet invasion: commanders might be motivated by the pressure of the "use-them-or-lose-them" syndrome and the level of nuclear exchanges might then escalate out of control.

This is why I am so strongly in favor of a "no-first-use" pledge by all governments.

MARCUS: Assuming that the quest for immediate personal gain is not involved, what could be motivating people—particularly the leaders in Washington—who are moving to *increase* the number of nuclear weapons?

WEISSKOPF: It's a matter of interpretation. You could make a case, just like any lawyer can make a case: you could simply point out that here and here and here the Russians are ahead of us, without mentioning that there and there and there we are ahead of *them*. Why do they do this? I am not a psychoanalyst, but if I may guess, I would say first it is out of personal fear—individuals in charge of a particular type of armament are afraid that they will be blamed later on if the Russians have more of that weapon than we do. Second, it is out of political fear—that the Communists are out to snow us under and become the world leaders. And so, they say, we must be stronger. But the fact is that the Russians are just as afraid of us as we are of them.

We must not forget, however, that the Soviet regime persecutes and often arrests those who openly dissent, it violates the civil rights of Jews and other minorities, and it limits free speech, choice of profession, and travel both abroad and within the country, although some improvements happened recently under Gorbachev's regime. Most Western democracies are superior in these respects. The Soviets have also taken numerous repressive actions outside their country—in Czechoslovakia, Hungary, Afghanistan, and Poland, for example. But here, I am sorry to say, the Western record is not so spotless either. Think of Vietnam (our "Afghanistan"), the American support of oppressive military regimes in El Salvador and Guatemala, and our support of the rebels in Nicaragua. We and they keep acting out of fear, trying somehow—by *any* possible means—to gain political advantage.

So those people who believe that simply by being stronger we can force our will upon the Soviets are misguided. But let's also examine what it means to be "stronger." We're talking about nuclear weapons, where it doesn't make a damn bit of difference whether you have a thousand or ten thousand or fifty thousand bombs. Two hundred would be more than enough to destroy all major cities in the other country. So what does it mean to have more? Nothing. That is the madness of the arms race.

MARCUS: Personally, I wouldn't feel all that much calmer with two hundred weapons pointing this way than with ten thousand—any *one* would be devastating. Do you think it will ever be possible to achieve complete disarmament, to actually dismantle nuclear weapons down to zero?

WEISSKOPF: No, because then both sides would live in fear of the other having secretly accumulated a few hundred of them. But *reducing* the number is possible, and that could have a beneficial effect, not only numerically but psychologically. Our land-based missiles, for instance, which contain a quarter of our strategic weapons, are a tempting target for the Soviets and a haunting presence for everyone living east of the launching pads. (The radioactive plume of only a few hits, driven eastward by prevailing winds, could kill hundreds of thousands of people rather quickly and produce environmental contamination that would later kill thousands more.) Given our missiles on submarines and airborne bombers that are much more difficult for the Soviets to locate, the land-based leg of the "triad" is virtually useless and unnecessary. We should scrap it altogether—and soon.

Another important reduction could involve tactical nuclear weapons—for use, presumably, on the battlefield only. But if there is ever a war in Europe or the Middle East and people start to use them, there is probably no way of limiting the war—the losing side could keep upping the ante until we are in the midst of a holocaust. I say *probably*, of course. There is maybe a 10 percent chance that the war could be limited, which means there is a 90 percent chance that the world would come to an end. Is that any way of running the show? Some people maintain that tactical nuclear weapons deter any conventional aggression. But it would be far better to deter such aggression by conventional means.

MARCUS: Do you mean that a smaller power's nuclear actions could trigger all-out nuclear war? Despite "rational" decision-making in Washington and Moscow, could it really be in the hands of someone like Libya's Kadaffi?

WEISSKOPF: Not quite. If smaller nations acquire nuclear weapons—following the unfortunate example that the big powers set for them—they would still have only a few. And if these weapons were used, it would be a great catastrophe, but it would not necessarily bring on the holocaust. That would occur only where the superpowers were directly involved—say, in Europe. Now I am not arguing in favor of nuclear bombs for small powers. We should certainly do what we can to prevent that, and we really don't do enough to prevent the use of reactors for bomb making. But I don't see the main danger there.

MARCUS: What about an "accidental" attack—caused by technical malfunction or "human error"—among the superpowers?

WEISSKOPF: Pentagon people maintain—but I don't really believe it—that our launching pads are so safe, and our submarines are so safe, etcetera, etcetera, that this could never happen. Haven't computers gone wrong before? And what do we know about the Soviet launching procedures? Most probably, they are less safe than ours. I think there *is* a big danger of accident and that is one very good reason for decreasing the tension between the United States and the Soviet Union. As long as there is good communication between the two countries and a reasonable spirit of détente, an accidental launch might cause a catastrophe, but not the final catastrophe.

Despite the occasional talk of "winnable" nuclear war, most people realize that one superpower simply cannot destroy the other without being destroyed itself. An intentional first strike is really out of the question, but we cannot exclude the danger of a precipitating "accident." We can only *minimize* this danger by minimizing the number of nuclear weapons and by reducing the probability that they are used. This speaks for the elimination of tactical weapons as well. And all this is possible only by working toward détente. Successful negotiations are our only hope.

MARCUS: I'd like to look back a little by asking about your Los Alamos experience. The great incentive for the Manhattan Project, it seems, was the German threat—the fear that the Nazis would develop the atomic bomb first. Yet when it became clear that the Germans were not even close, and after they were defeated, the work continued. Most of the individuals at Los Alamos were hardly stereotypical cold-blooded scientists; they seem to have been, by and large, warm and sensitive people. Yet they just kept right on working, a group of "the best" creating "the worst." What motivated them after the threat was gone?

WEISSKOPF: Let's not forget that, even after the Germans were defeated, we were still not sure the bomb would work. There was still the possibility that neutrons would be absorbed too strongly to permit a chain reaction, and we all hoped that this would be the final result—that such a bomb could not be made at all. That hope, of course, was quashed. But then why did we go on? Maybe because it's a human kind of drive: when you're almost finished with something you keep on going until you finish it. There were other reasons too: we were told that the bomb would end the war with Japan— which it did. Tens of thousands of lives were lost almost daily in the fire raids on Japanese cities and an invasion of Japan would have cost millions of lives on both sides. We also believed that if such a weapon were possible, it would eventually be built by somebody else, and therefore let us better develop it here because we had such great confidence in the United States. But perhaps we were naive: many of us thought the weapon was so terrifying that it would have to be "internationalized," that it would compel all nations to get together. We proposed an international administration, and we thought that surely the Soviets would participate because it was the same threat to them as to us. But people who knew Stalin and the Soviet spirit at that time certainly could have told us that the Soviets would never have accepted such arrangements.

MARCUS: Even without a Stalin, have leaders ever been willing to abandon nationalism? Even with the sudden "millionfold increase in the power of technology," as you've called it, how likely was it that politics could change that quickly and drastically?

WEISSKOPF: Changes *have* occurred in human affairs, both slow and fast ones. Sure, one can easily take a pessimistic view: that we've always had wars, that the most effective weapons have always been used, and therefore that there is absolutely no hope of avoiding nuclear catastrophe. But we are now at a point where things are qualitatively different from all that has gone before, and this gives me reason to hope that there will be a fundamental change in attitude toward war.

Whenever I visit Europe, I think of this. When I go, for example, to Florence and then to Siena—they are just 50 kilometers apart— I recall that these Italian cities used to have terrible wars. Other neighboring cities in Europe have similar histories. But in time such conflicts ended and were replaced by wars between larger countries. And now, wars between European countries no longer seem likely. Instead, we think in terms of "intercontinental" wars. But given this progression, and the finite radius of the earth, and the terrible, long-range power of nuclear weapons, it's possible that the whole idea of war may become senseless. The question is: Will it become senseless before or after the Third World War?

MARCUS: Given its patterns of collaboration both domestic and international, do you see the scientific community serving as a model for better understanding among nations? In many ways, the Manhattan Project was a great, perhaps unprecedented, success in terms of its team spirit and technical accomplishments. And it has struck me that in many of your professional activities since then you've tried to recreate that spirit for more humane applications. You've described the work of CERN (European Center for Nuclear Research, in Geneva) for example, as participatory, cooperative, unselfish, exciting, rewarding, international. And it seems that you're almost uniformly in favor of nonmilitary scientific exchanges between East and West for the same reason.

WEISSKOPF: Absolutely. I don't want to imply that the scientific community is better or more advanced than any other group, but it does have a little more experience in international collaboration. However, I'm worried that present trends may curtail this. During the so-called détente, we had quite a few scientists from the Soviet Union and other Eastern countries working with us at CERN, and it went extremely well. Indeed, I consider this collaboration one of my important achievements there. But later the atmosphere was different. People were angry at the Soviet leadership for all kinds of things—from civil rights (such as anti-Semitism and the Sakharov oppression) to the invasion of Afghanistan and the Soviet influence in Poland. These are certainly serious political matters, but I find it completely wrong when physicists and other scientists react by declaring themselves no longer willing to work with their Soviet colleagues. And I've been trying to convince these people to continue their collaborations.

First of all, who are we to cast stones? The situations in Afghanistan and Poland, as bad as they are, are not unlike actions the United States has taken. The oppression within the Soviet Union and the infringement on human rights are, in my view, a reason to keep *up* our relations. Ironically, the scientific community in the Soviet Union is probably the "best" in the country—the most sympathetic from a moral and political point of view. It shares, in large measure, the Western value system. To cut off connections with them would be counterproductive. And if we stop collaborating with them, they will lose the little hope they have. The window to the West would be closed.

The only link we have for the future is *collaboration*—in science as well as in other areas—and to have broken this off, to my mind, was a very big mistake. Fortunately, scientific collaboration has again begun under the influence of the Gorbachev regime.

MARCUS: You've often referred to science as "supranational" or "supraideological." But do you really think that science is any more immune to outside political pressures, or its own internal political pressures, than other human activities?

WEISSKOPF: No, of course not. Scientists are just as subject to political trends and ideas as other people. But science, perhaps together with sports, can really be supranational because its aims, language, and style are the same for all nations. It is much easier for scientists or athletes from different cultures to understand one another than it is for lawyers or politicians, for example. And in fact, experience has shown that the scientific community has been a very good bridge between different ideologies.

MARCUS: Science may be a model for building bridges, but I worry about some of the great popular misconceptions: that science is supposedly apolitical and value-free; that all research and development is part of some inexorable progress; that if a scientist is involved it must be all right.

WEISSKOPF: Yes, people debate whether science and technology are dictated by human needs or whether they are expressions, as you say, of some inexorable progress that we cannot control and that may bring us to the abyss through the development of nuclear weapons and by the pollution of the environment. The danger, I think, is not in science per se but in its possible domination of other ways of thinking. This is a danger that humankind has always faced, and suffered from, and that scientists and technologists ought to be aware of: when one way of thinking is dominant, it leads to abuses. Think of the influence of religion during the Middle Ages—of the millions of deaths, and indifference to suffering, in its name. I'm not antireligious, but if religion is the dominant way of thinking, as with any other predominant view, we get exaggerations, abuses, and catastrophes.

The same is true of technological development. We certainly live in an age in which it is overvalued. And just as religion serves some purposes admirably and others poorly, so we should think about certain technical applications as reasonable and others as not reasonable at all.

Whenever one way of thinking has been developed strongly— even claiming to encompass all human experience—other ways of thinking have been suppressed. This has its roots in a strong human desire for clear-cut, universally valid principles containing answers to every question. But because human problems always have more than one aspect, universal answers do not exist. The aim should not be to choose which viewpoint is right or wrong but to know how to decide when one or another is appropriate.

And I'm not just talking about weapons. Look how commercial interests can produce serious pollution problems through one-sided thinking—the buildup of carbon dioxide in the earth's atmosphere, for example. An equilibrium among technical, scientific, and moral values is certainly necessary.

MARCUS: You've often referred to a second kind of pollution, what you call "spiritual pollution," of which the "triumph of insanity"—neither side knowing where to stop the nuclear arms race—is a notable example. Given its ideology-bridging property, can science play a useful role in helping to abate this "spiritual pollution"? Can science serve as a model for global-scale collaboration, in the spirit of CERN, involving all kinds of human knowledge and interests?

WEISSKOPF: I think that public opinion, not the activities of the scientific community, will be the critical factor. And I would take as a model not CERN or other international endeavors but the public reaction to the war in Vietnam. Logically, militarily, and politically, it would have gone on and on, but public opinion turned against it. People realized that what we were doing there was wrong and they eventually brought it to a stop. This was an instance where "superlogic" (which in fact was madness) was turned around by the public's reasonableness, and this is my hope for the nuclear case, too.

There's another reason why the scientific process should not be a model for combatting "spiritual pollution." Public opinion, as with the anti-Vietnam War movement, can never be purely rational. It is fundamentally emotional, and here rational thinking, moral thinking, religious thinking, and so on must all come together in a constructive way. I have always said—*preached* is more like it—that the scientific–technical way of thinking is only one approach to the problems of humankind and the human experience. There are other avenues to problem solving, such as art, poetry, morals, ethics, and religion. All these different approaches are necessary to have a mass movement that is really effective. It must be based on all these things, on the beauties of life itself, if the spiritual pollution we mentioned is to be eliminated.

But fundamentally, people must see some sense in life. I was very disappointed that my good friend Steven Weinberg, who wrote this excellent book, *The First Three Minutes,* made a terrible statement in its final pages: "The more the universe seems comprehensible, the more it also seems pointless." I believe strongly in exactly the other way. Science *does* give us a sense of purpose. When you look at the development of the universe, from the "big bang" to sentient beings, there is clearly a pattern. There is something that develops, something in nature that is creative. Science, of course, is not the only way of giving sense to our lives. Art does it; so does religion. But when this sense is missing, that's when spiritual pollution is present, when people don't know why they are here. We can have leisuretime diversions, of course. But until we learn to fill the vacuum in our minds with *content*—with meaning, with sense—we will never find solutions to our problems.

MARCUS: And how do you see that happening?

WEISSKOPF: By developing new creative outlets, not only for the scientist and the artist but for everybody. Here again I am relatively optimistic. When my wife and I came here fifty years ago, we didn't encounter very many people during our walks in the mountains of Vermont and New Hampshire, and the few we did meet had German accents. But now you'll find a great many people—young and not-so-young Americans—on the trails. For them, contact with nature has become one way of filling their souls. There are other ways, of course, some more intellectual and some more social in flavor (such as helping other people to cope with their problems). We have to find them and develop them. Where there is a need, there is usually a solution.

I often tell my students, when they are depressed by the world, that there are two things that make my life worth living: Mozart and quantum mechanics. What I mean is that the achievements of humankind—whether in art or in understanding nature—ought to impress and inspire people. There are so many great creations in the world that are readily appreciated. But a lot of education is necessary.

MARCUS: In dramatizing why inadequate public awareness of technical issues can distort priorities, you've often expressed dismay at public preoccupation with the risks of nuclear power and people's relative lack of concern with the risks of nuclear bombs. You've made some pretty strong statements about which system poses the greater risk—for example, that "in comparison to the overwhelming threat of nuclear war, the nuclear-power controversy dwindles to picayune dimensions." There's no doubt, of course, that this statement is true with regard to physical damage, but I worry that, even though the threat of nuclear war is humanity's number-one problem, such statements trivialize all the other problems. A serious reactor mishap (from accident or sabotage), a worrisome environmental trend, or just about any other conceivable catastrophe all would produce far less serious "impacts" than would global holocaust. But does that mean people shouldn't be concerned about them or try to take action to prevent them?

WEISSKOPF: You are touching on an important set of issues, and I fully agree with you about such problems as ocean pollution, river pollution, CO_2 pollution. . .

MARCUS: Or *any* problem. It doesn't have to be pollution.

WEISSKOPF: Yes, of course. Social problems such as poverty or the decay of urban centers are extremely important—they're a kind of "pollution," too. I fully agree that the danger of nuclear war should not make us blind to other dangers, but ironically, many people on the political right obviously disagree. They seem to argue that the Soviet military danger is so great that we must put all our money there and let the poor go hungry. I've said what I have about comparing nuclear risks because I believe many of the people who have been so much against nuclear power are actually repressing their fear of nuclear bombs. Possibly, because they did not see any solution to the bomb problem, they concentrated on reactors instead. Radioactivity, of course, is potentially dangerous. But people have gone to lengths that I really don't understand—and that I've criticized.

MARCUS: The concerns of the anti-nuclear-power movement, it seems to me, are not just the technological risks but the social and political aspects of nuclear power: it is highly centralized and therefore socially "unstable," highly sophisticated and therefore controlled by a technical priesthood.

WEISSKOPF: I don't quite agree with that. The only point on which I agree with the anti-nuclear-power people is the proliferation angle. The haste to sell as many reactors as possible to small countries has allowed them the possibility of cheating by making plutonium for bombs. That, to my mind, is the only really serious objection to nuclear power. But the point you raise is one we simply must face anyway—it doesn't apply only to nuclear power but to any electric power station of the same order of megawatts. And I don't really see the great advantage of dividing it into smaller parts.

MARCUS: But wouldn't you agree that decentralization has desirable implications for democratic control?

WEISSKOPF: You mean "small is beautiful"?

MARCUS: Not necessarily small, but "appropriate." You yourself have written about the great need for popularly controlled production units and the consequent "humanization" of technology—in language that could have come from E. F. Schumacher.

WEISSKOPF: "Appropriate" is the right word. You should make something big only if it is really an advantage. And you might even sacrifice some of that advantage to allow workers to participate in the administration. You may lose a little efficiency, but it will pay in the end. And the same is often true for smaller units—they may be less efficient but perhaps it is better that they are more "human-scaled." There are limits to this, however, and electric power stations, it seems to me, are more appropriately large and centralized. The one great advantage of nuclear power, by the way—and of fusion, if it ever comes to pass—is the alleviation of a very serious concern: the CO_2 problem.

MARCUS: You don't have comparable worries about disposal of nuclear waste?

WEISSKOPF: I worry, I worry. But at least some solutions are possible. The CO_2 problem is not comparable: if you burn coal, you cannot avoid making CO_2.

MARCUS: And if you operate a nuclear reactor, you're stuck with plutonium for many thousands of years.

WEISSKOPF: I don't want to minimize the waste problem—it is a big one that hasn't really been solved. But you can at least see a direction, and some possibilities, for solutions. There is no possibility of avoiding CO_2 emissions when you stick to the old-fashioned methods of energy production.

MARCUS: Turning to another kind of size phenomenon, what do you think is the power of the individual scientist or technologist who refuses to contribute to an enterprise—whether it's nuclear power, the nuclear arms race, whatever—that he or she considers objectionable? What do you think is the overall impact of such individual acts of conscience?

WEISSKOPF: Not much. Refusal at this point is not a way to solve these problems. Only a change in public awareness can do that. If the public is not aware of a problem, or is not motivated to solve it, you can always find people who will do the work that others refuse to do. A "strike" of scientists is a little bit like the Aristophanes play *Lysistrata,* where the women refuse to have sexual intercourse with the men unless they stop waging war. It's a sincere and colorful gesture, but it doesn't get to the heart of the problem and therefore has no lasting effect.

MARCUS: If you were given carte blanche by the president—essentially unlimited authority, time, and money—to get to the heart of the problems, right now, what would you start doing?

WEISSKOPF: In foreign affairs, I would try to change the relations between the superpowers from confrontation to cooperation, not only in nuclear matters but also in the other problems that threaten the world. Mutual fear could be reduced by mutual collaboration. In nuclear matters, I would scrap unnecessary and dangerous systems, with land-based nuclear bombs and tactical nuclear weapons the first ones to go. Then I would launch a massive public-awareness drive on the threat of nuclear war, emphasizing the many ways in which it could be reduced. My hope would be to replace the "triumph of craziness" with a more rational view. I would continue negotiating with the Soviets until we achieve a mutually acceptable sharp reduction of nuclear weapons on both sides. I do believe, however, that significant arms reductions are possible only if the attitudes of the superpowers change from fear and confrontation to mutual trust and cooperation.

In other matters, I would get the West and the East together to solve political and environmental problems in common efforts, beneficial to both sides. In domestic affairs, I would put much more effort and money into removing poverty from the richest country in the world, and into improving education. Not only do we not have enough education, but we have the wrong kind. Our high schools are in a deplorable state. Science teaching in high school is especially bad, and it is driving people away from science for life. It's the opposite of "knowledge and wonder": just cold figuring-out with no awe and no joy. I would train better teachers by investing heavily in teacher's colleges, and I'd pay them well. This would apply to every level of education, right down to the earliest stages of elementary school.

MARCUS: Do you see the microprocessor's inroads into education, with more and more children having "computer literacy," as a step in the right direction?

WEISSKOPF: Any one thing has both a good and a bad side. The advantage of the computer is that it allows gifted kids to widen their horizons. I see it in my grandson—he doesn't only buy computer games, he also *invents* them. But the opposite effect also occurs: computers can repress thinking in kids and stifle their creativity. For example, it's not really necessary, with computers available, for students to know the multiplication table. And because the computer gives an exact result, they cannot estimate anymore, either. Even digital watches, for all their convenience, are actually very bad for the mind; they don't have this quantity-quality aspect. I see by the old-fashioned clock on the wall, for example, that it's *roughly*—we are nearing—five o'clock right now. "Estimation" is a very important way of looking at the world. The computer, like all useful things, can be misused.

Reliance on any one technique or any one way of thinking, whether scientific, artistic, or religious, is unbalanced and subject to abuse. We need many different approaches to cope with the predicaments of humanity, to enable people to find a sense and a purpose, and to change the attitudes that threaten the very survival of our society. In the long run, it is all a matter of education.

14

The Double-Edged Sword Called Technology

During this century, there have been tremendous developments in science and technology. While these achievements were mostly created in Europe and America, they have now spread to all civilizations throughout the world. The values underlying this development have frequently been called into doubt. But during the last twenty years, these doubts have increased in intensity and fervor to such an extent that we now face a crisis. It is fashionable today to emphasize the shortcomings of scientific-industrial civilization and to de-emphasize its benefits. The industrialized world must therefore take stock of itself.

The question arises whether this crisis is a symptom of aging, presaging the end of Western civilization—either through annihilation by nuclear war or through internal disintegration—or whether it is in some way a manifestation of "growing pains." After the storm and stress of adolescence, in which a great deal was done without a thought to possible consequences, the present crisis could represent a transition to thoughtful maturity.

Technology, like science, sprang from an openness of mind toward individual phenomena, from a systematic study of the details of what is going on in nature. The first technical applications of such studies date back even further than the origins of the natural sciences. We find examples in the Greco-Roman period and in the early Middle

Ages. The necessary spur was provided by the growth of cities and their interest in better methods of production of metallic utensils. It was not until technology made it possible to build measuring instruments that science could develop properly. Initially, then, the natural sciences were a consequence of technology.

Later on, science and technology became much more closely linked. The steam engine was by no means invented on the basis of scientific research. Quite the contrary: it gave impetus to research into the theory of heat. Possibly the first great achievements in which science and technology worked side by side involved the invention of the electric dynamo and motor, based on the discoveries of electric and magnetic phenomena of Ampère, Neumann, Faraday, and Maxwell. It is interesting to note, moreover, how short a time these technical developments took. Electric dynamos were constructed a little more than twenty years after the discovery of the connection between electricity and magnetism. Nowadays, progress is not much faster. For instance, the time which elapsed between the discovery of the neutron and the practical application of nuclear power was of the same order. There are more scientists and engineers today but the problems become more complicated. On average, these two factors balance each other.

There is an important point to be recognized here. Very rarely are scientific discoveries made with a specific purpose in mind to which they are going to be applied. Faraday did not think of the motor when he studied the relations of electricity and magnetism. Hertz did not think of communication when he discovered radio waves, and certainly, Curie, Rutherford, and Chadwick did not contemplate nuclear energy or cancer treatment when they worked on radioactivity. After the famous lecture on electricity given by Faraday to the Royal Society, a British Member of Parliament asked: "What is the use of all your beautiful experiments?" and Faraday replied: "What use is a newborn baby?" The baby grew up to be the electrical industry.

Today, technology and science depend completely upon each other; they are in a symbiotic relationship. Technology cannot advance without science, nor science without technology.

Here is a brief outline of some essential steps of this symbiosis. Considering only the physical sciences, three great scientific discoveries were made during the nineteenth century: the existence of atoms and molecules, the nature of heat as a disordered motion of atoms, and the unity of electricity, magnetism, and optics. The theory of heat evolved from the steam engine; the development of electromagnetism and optics led to the electrical, optical, and communications industries; and, of course, the recognition of atoms and molecules brought the chemical industry into existence.

The twentieth century witnessed, in its first quarter, an ever growing insight into the structure of the atom by means of quantum mechanics. In parallel we saw the development of electronic industries based upon a better understanding of the interactions between electrons and atoms. When the nature of the chemical bond was revealed by further applications of quantum mechanics to atomic and molecular dynamics, a deeper understanding of the structure of metals, crystals, and other materials was achieved. This led to an expansion of chemical industries and to the production of new materials. It finally brought about the invention of transistors and semiconductors on which the computer industry thrives.

The next scientific step into the deeper layers of matter was the penetration into the structure of the atomic nucleus. Nuclear physics has brought about the exploration of nuclear power and the applications of artificial radioactivity to medical purposes and materials testing. Biology, with its revelations of the chemical nature of the life process, has found many fruitful applications in medicine and in the chemical industry.

On the other hand, none of these scientific steps could have been taken without the help of technology. This is most obvious in more recent developments, that would have been impossible without the help of the latest achievements of electronics and other precision technology. I remind you of the complicated and sophisticated technology that goes into the construction of a modern accelerator.

This tremendous development was much wider and greater than ever expected. It underwent an exponential growth that we still witness in the recent development of computers and lasers. The astounding success of science and technology had a deep influence on the entire social fabric. Our society, our philosophy, and our thinking have been shaken to the core.

We begin with the effects on the structure of society. Technological development has brought about a pervasive social regrouping. It produced the working class and it thoroughly changed the world of agriculture. Formerly, more than 80 percent of all people worked on the land. Now, in the developed countries, it is only 4 percent or less—brought about entirely through mechanization and by the so-called green revolution. Traffic and transport have been completely transformed: from classic times until the ninteenth century, transport was by horse-drawn wagons; Virgil and Mozart used essentially the same means of transportation. Now, we can span the globe in a day or two.

Cities have grown, and a population explosion has taken place because of the successes of medical science, amounting to what one may call "death control," through improved hygiene and the eradication of epidemic diseases. When I was young there were only two billion people on this earth. Now there are nearly five billion.

Furthermore, because of advances in technology, it would be possible to stamp out hunger, feed people adequately, abolish need, contain epidemics, render strenuous physical labor unnecessary, and above all enable people to lead a substantially more comfortable life. Of course, these possibilities have by no means been realized everywhere, but they have been achieved to a considerable extent in the developed countries—western Europe, Japan, and the United States—but only to a small extent, if at all, in the third world. Please note, however, that my enumeration consists of factors that make life easier, reduce need, and tear down obstacles that used to make life hard and difficult. Here we have a kind of double negative, the abolition of the burdens of life. I shall be returning to this particular point and its spiritual consequences.

This mighty upsurge had a major influence on thought and philosophy. The first manifestation was the spirit of enlightenment. Man makes his own world. He is capable of changing it to his advantage. This was the source of the dream to bring about a golden age of bliss in which nobody would have to suffer or go hungry any longer. The golden age, which earlier philosophies and religions set in the past or in heaven, was moved to the near future and on earth. This was the program for mankind in the age of enlightenment, during the nineteenth century, and in the early twentieth century. Progress in science and technology would abolish need, and moral progress, based on absence of need, would abolish evil.

How have things actually gone? Some parts of the dream came true, but vast and rapid progress and change in social and philosophical thinking have created (and are still creating) serious problems. Some of these problems have been solved. At this very time, it is important to stress this fact. Many are not yet solved, however.

Let me start with the positive side of the balance sheet of human development in the scientific-industrial age. In the middle of the nineteenth century and before—at the beginning of the industrial society—workers were ruthlessly exploited. There was child labor, a twelve-hour working day, and so forth. Today we have social legislation, trade unions, workers' rights, medical care, old-age care, all developed to varying degrees. In the West, and also in the East, we witness a certain humanization of the capitalistic industrial system. In the East, the private capitalist system has been dismantled in favor of state capitalism, but in both parts of our world industrial society has been humanized in essential ways. In my view, Europe is further advanced in this respect than the United States. In general, there are better social services, especially in the smaller countries such as the Netherlands, Austria, and Scandinavia. To some extent, social progress in these countries has come about because they have more homogeneous populations and because they are fairly small.

The situation in the third world, however, is considerably worse. The benefits of the industrial system are at a lower level and are not shared among different strata of the population. Although it is true that there are fewer countries under the domination of developed nations, the power has been transferred from foreign to indigenous "exploiters" without any major increase in general welfare. These countries must, in a few decades, catch up with what has taken the western world a century or more to achieve; this cannot be done without some crises and disasters. We observe a similar kind of nationalism, fanaticism, and jingoism pervading the developed world in previous periods. I do not wish to pursue these problems here, although they are extremely important to the future of our world.

We now come to the unsolved problems, the negative side of the balance. What is involved here is pollution. There are two categories—material pollution and spiritual pollution. Let us begin with material pollution.

The expansion of technology over the surface of the globe has produced effects on nature that can no longer be neglected. Earlier, the regions and areas where technology changed the natural world for the worse or for the better were small, compared with the regions that remained entirely unaffected. The chalky plateau of Dalmatia, for example, was ruined by the Romans when they chopped down the forests, but that was only a small part of the earth's surface. Today, the entire surface of the earth is involved. We constantly increase the content of carbon dioxide in the air, we reduce forest areas, we pollute rivers and oceans, and we use up raw materials. Lately, some people assert that the use of nuclear power stations could produce global damage.

I am convinced that these questions, in the foreground of discussion nowadays, can be solved technically. It will not be easy and it will increase the cost of industrial production, but this is nothing new. Social progress, to which I referred earlier, also increased the costs of industrial production, and rightly so. Humanization of the industrial system was also expensive. For costs should correspond not only to what is needed to produce goods, but also to what is needed to correct possible damage to nature or the social sphere. Efforts must no longer be exclusively directed toward innovations and new inventions; they must also go to avoiding undesirable consequences. How can pollution be prevented? How can the production of carbon dioxide be decreased? How can the safety of nuclear power stations be increased? How can radioactive waste be safely disposed? How can we produce energy from means other than combustion of fossil fuels? How can we reduce energy consumption?

These problems are solvable, but only under certain conditions. One of these conditions is a stable population. We need birth control in order to offset death control that was introduced by medical advances. Another condition is a reasonably stable political situation, without irrational outbursts and conflicts nurtured by emotions and fanaticism. This will be very difficult to maintain in the third world, where there are understandable pressures for fast industrial development, without considering environmental costs.

But the first and foremost condition is avoidance of nuclear war. It is not clear whether the danger of nuclear war should be regarded as material or as spiritual pollution; it stands somewhere in between. There has always been tension between nations, of course, and this has led, unfortunately too often, to wars. But earlier, war damage was repairable. The dead could not be raised again, but life could be resumed by those who survived. Today the situation is totally different. We can no longer recover from a nuclear war. If only a few of the modern bombs are used, it would cause a catastrophe of unfathomable severity; we are not even able to estimate the number of victims or the immense danger to lives, to the environment, and to agricultural soil by radioactive contamination and to the functioning of such important services as rescue operations, hospitals, and evacuation procedures. Compared to that, the effects of the worst reactor accident shrink to total insignificance.

The penetration of science into the atomic nucleus has revealed the existence of cosmic forces that, under ordinary conditions, are dormant on the surface of the earth. Their exploitation has increased the arm of technology by many millions. Humankind must be aware that this arm is not abused for purposes of destruction. Nuclear weapons are not weapons of war but the means of national and international suicide.

Every thinking person knows this. Yet, in spite of this knowledge, the solution and answer to the threat of war continues to include the proliferation and improvement of nuclear arms. The nuclear armament race goes on and on. Today, 50,000 nuclear bombs are ready to be launched. It is a triumph of insanity in a civilization that calls itself rational; it is the apotheosis of madness. Unfortunately, the public worries more about the dangers of nuclear power than about nuclear war. People do not trust the experts on nuclear-power production. Why do they trust the experts of nuclear weapons buildup? More public pressure against the suicidal nuclear armaments race is urgently needed.

We now come to spiritual pollution. We speak of progress. To be sure, the progress of scientific-technical culture has been immense. In the realm of science, we are on the threshold of entirely new, profound insights into what takes place in nature—the primeval big bang, or origin of the universe, the formation of the elements, the structure of matter. The fundamental forces that govern the world become known, and so do the molecular processes at the basis of life. The twentieth century will be known as the age in which humankind acquired its deepest insights into the workings and history of the natural world, if it will be able to avoid being remembered as the age of the great nuclear catastrophe.

On the technical side, as already mentioned, there exists the possibility of avoiding hunger, want, illness, and oppressive manual work. The world has become accessible to all through modern transport. The abolition of want has been reasonably successful in the developed countries. It is a double negative: it has freed humanity of burdens. Freed it for what? What does one do with one's life when one no longer has to fight for existence for twelve hours a day? The individual is thrown back upon himself and must find the meaning of his or her life. Work in the industrial complex is mechanical and secondary. It does not rest on the personal achievement of those working, but on that of the engineers who have invented and developed its methods. The average worker has little influence on the direction of the enterprise of which he is a part. What becomes of human dignity? Where is individual sense and purpose?

Earlier, religion provided sense and purpose, but religion has grown weaker nowadays. By "religion," we mean the feeling of deep commitment to a great cause beyond our own personal interest—a cause whose value is never put into question. We certainly find such commitment among many social workers and persons who have devoted their lives to the improvement of our society. We find it among many medical and technical researchers and practitioners. We also find it among scientists for whom the greatness of scientific ideas is a source of enthusiasm and inspiration.

By and large, nonscientists are not inspired by scientific insights. What they understand of science nowadays is roughly this: because everything follows the laws of nature, we do not need a god. Science is appreciated mainly because of its technical applications. In part, this is the fault of scientists themselves. They have achieved great things, but they have not made sufficient efforts to convey the greatness and wonder of these ideas to their fellow beings in a comprehensible way. I believe that conveying these insights is possible, but it is a difficult task that is tackled by far too few gifted people. The situation is equally bad in respect to the great achievements of technology. It is true that the proliferation of science fiction helps in some ways to excite a certain enthusiasm for the wonders of technology. (Science fiction is a misnomer; most examples of it should be called technology fiction.) Still, prevalent reaction to technology consists in a certain accommodation to present levels that have made life more comfortable. But it also expresses the fear that further innovations will lead to more deadly weapons and to the destruction of the environment.

Can art and literature provide a sense of purpose to our lives? When art was still in the service of religion, it was no doubt generally comprehensible and acknowledged by the majority. When religion lost its influence, art acquired independence. It continued to be the expression of the great ideas of its time. But it was accessible only to an upper stratum of society. Where is the art that concerns itself with the ideas of science and technology? Surely it is the task of artists to bring the great ideas of our time closer to the public. I believe that Sinclair Lewis's *Arrowsmith* is the last great novel that describes the excitement of scientific research.

True enough, contemporary art is full of new ideas and impressive examples of original creativity, but it does not get close enough to the positive ideas of our culture and mankind's need for sense and purpose.

For most people, however, neither art nor science is of deep significance. When the most important needs have been provided for, the content of life generally amounts only to a desire for passive entertainment such as viewing TV or driving a car, and the like. What is sorely lacking is a fulfilled, creative content of life for the population at large.

The disease of senselessness has unfortunately also penetrated science and technology to some extent. There is a lack of interest in visionary enterprise. Instead, we witness an excessive emphasis on material security and lack of risk. The greatest risk, however, is avoidance of all risk.

At the beginning of this essay, I raised the question whether the present crisis represents the end of the scientific-technical culture or whether it is merely a transitional crisis from a relentless drive to a more mature and calmer period. I cannot answer this question, but I know that the optimistic interpretation rests on the achievement of *three* basic aims. The first is the abolition of nuclear weapons, so that this terrible sword of Damocles no longer hangs over mankind.

The second is the prevention of environmental catastrophes. Technical creativity should be redirected away from commercial and military tasks and toward environmental problems, in order to arrive at a pollution-free technology.

The third aim is the provision of a creative and purposeful life for the majority, not only for the few.

The second and third aims would represent additional steps of humanization, this time by improving not only the relationship of industry to humans, but also its relationship to nature. The third step is the most difficult one. We must find a social and industrial organization where most people feel responsible for what is going on. The present forms of industrial organization are antidemocratic in many respects. They put a premium on highly specialized skills; they are based upon centrally controlled authoritarian leadership. What we need is a more popularly controlled technology, which we probably can achieve only by smaller units of production. In all probability, it would be less efficient and would increase costs. Small is beautiful, but expensive and less efficient. In order to overcome these difficulties, we need inventiveness not only in technical innovations but also in social management.

Apart from the problem of participation in the production process, we also face the task of finding creative outlets or activities outside the workplace that are accessible to all. There are already promising beginnings in this respect, such as the "do it yourself" trend, increasing interest in the enjoyment of nature, and other free-time occupations.

We are facing one great danger. The search for sense and meaning may turn toward ideologies such as militant religion or fanaticisms of various kinds. Unfortunately, trends toward such fundamentalisms are visible all over the world. The absence of a dominant ideology in western culture is an advantage for the creative minority. Can we maintain this advantage and supply sense and meaning to the majority?

What we need is a broader sense of complementary attitudes. Scientific, ethical, artistic, and religious approaches are not contradictory, they complement each other. Here, today's educational system faces an important task. It needs reform in many ways. Regarding the problems raised in this essay, it should include teaching tolerance and enthusiasm for the variety of human endeavors. This is not ethical relativism or the denial of values. On the contrary, it would derive ethical principles and a system of values from many sources. Education on all levels, from elementary school to college, should foster an attitude of openness and understanding for different complementary approaches to the realities of life. Such an attitude is one of the preconditions for the survival of our civilization.

15

Thoughts of a Hitler Refugee

More than fifty years ago, the rise of Nazism brought horror, humiliation, death, and torture to so many free-thinking people, to Jews, and to other minorities. There were some lucky ones, like myself, who were able to escape, thanks to the help of many organizations, particularly those here in the United States, such as the University in Exile in New York.

I was born and brought up in Austria in the spirit of German culture. I consider my transfer from Europe to the United States as an invaluable source of intellectual enrichment. Our forced emigration, in which we passed through French, British, Scandinavian, and other European cultures and finally landed here in America, was for us an opening of new worlds in many senses. I often think of how narrow my thinking would have been had I lived as a German or Austrian professor all my life, as I had expected to do. This breadth of experience—quite apart from having escaped Nazi persecution and later gotten the means to earn a livelihood—is a point we too often forget and for which we must be grateful to our fate.

Before coming to the United States, my family and I went first to France, England, Switzerland, and Denmark. We were treated extremely well. I am especially grateful to Denmark and to Professor Niels Bohr, who supported us and a number of other refugees from Nazism with money from the Rockefeller Foundation and from Danish funds, such as the Carlsberg Foundation. There were great names among them, such as James Franck, Georg von Hevesy, and Otto Frisch. Bohr traveled every year to the United States "to sell his Jews to American universities," as we called it. But we always felt like foreigners or at best as guests, not truly part of the community.

When we came to this country, we were accepted as equals. The United States is the only place where an accent is an asset; it is a country that actively assimilates different world cultures. We were considered special people and given the best opportunities for work and intellectual contact. It is often said that we refugees have widened American cultural perspectives. I don't think this is quite true. Actually, the United States was then ready to accept a broader outlook. It was the period of the New Deal, with all its cultural effects, that created a new intellectual atmosphere in the country. It was an environment most suitable for us and for our American colleagues to produce and to develop a spirit of international culture. I wish that more of this spirit survived in the present. We immigrants did not reform the intellectual life in this country. Americans put us in positions where we could exert some influence, with the help and support of kindred spirits among our U.S. colleagues.

Here is one personal experience showing how we were treated as equals: just a little more than five years after I came to this country—when I was working at Los Alamos—I was elected chairman of the town council, the mayor of the city, as it were. It was a relatively unimportant event, but it made a tremendous impression on me, as a newcomer, to receive the confidence and trust of the community.

Today Nazism is over, and there is a very different, and far better, spirit in Germany and Austria. I have had many opportunities to observe life in those countries during the time when I was director of CERN, the cooperative European basic physics laboratory. Western Europe has changed for the better, but humanity is still threatened by very similar dangers, by totalitarianism from the left and right. I do not want to equate communism with Nazism. There are a number of reasons why the communist system is not as totally negative as the Nazi system was. Yet with respect to repression of intellectual freedom, there are some similarities (a situation that fortunately has changed for the better since Secretary General Gorbachev's policy of *glasnost*, which has alleviated some of the worst pressures on intellectual freedom in the Soviet Union.) There are all too many examples of repressive regimes on the other side of the political spectrum, which is like a circle that meets at the two radical ends.

Today we face a problem that did not exist fifty years ago: the existence of nuclear weapons. It was quite clear then what the free world should do: save as many refugees as possible, confront and attack the Nazi regime with every possible means, ostracize them, create an intellectual isolation (which was not difficult, as they didn't want any contact), shun appeasement, use military force, and go to war to defeat them.

But it was the last occasion in history, I believe, where you could get rid of an objectionable regime by using military force. Today we face a much greater dilemma, which poses grave problems for intellectuals. A war employing nuclear weapons means not only the annihilation of hundreds of millions of people, but also the complete destruction of our civilization, of everything that makes life worth living.

What can we do then to fight persecution and oppression without increasing the danger of nuclear war? How can we help oppressed people? Naturally, there are different opinions about this situation, but I would like to offer my own. What shall we do? We certainly should never cease to publicly condemn, anywhere we find it, the denial of freedom of expression and of civil liberties. And we should continue to welcome those who succeed in escaping from oppressive regimes. These new immigrants will contribute to our culture, just as earlier refugees from Nazism have done.

But in contrast to my thoughts regarding the Nazis fifty years ago, I now believe strongly that we must seek all possible contact with the intellectuals who live under oppressive regimes. We should promote collaboration. We should go to congresses. We should visit their universities and our colleagues there, officially and privately. I very much opposed the decision of the National Academy of Sciences to break off official relations with the Soviets which, fortunately, has been rescinded recently. Most Soviet scientists are fundamentally in agreement with us: they seek more freedom and condemn oppressive acts. Therefore they need encouragement and contact and must not lose the feeling of being part of the world community of intellectuals. It will help them to consolidate and enlarge the freedom of expression that has been introduced by the "glasnost" regime.

When we go over there, we must express our opposition to the remaining repressions and travel inhibitions, and try to meet and talk to those who suffer under them. Furthermore, we should not let the Soviet regime's remaining oppressive acts prevent us from inviting Soviet scientists to visit and collaborate with us. Sometimes the Soviet regime did not permit those who were invited to go abroad. Today it happens less frequently but it remains an impediment to the free exchange of scientific knowledge. Science is international and cannot tolerate such inhibitions. Full scientific collaboration will help to change the present confrontational posture of the superpowers to a more cooperative attitude, and thus help to achieve a more peaceful world.

But there is another factor that makes the current situation worse: our government's foreign policy. It fosters a cold-war mentality, aiming at military confrontation and superiority to rid the world of evil communism. Yet, at the same time, we support repressive regimes that happen to be anticommunist. But let us not forget that in the days of nuclear weapons, it is impossible to rid the world of "evil communism" by military means. Using force was probably the right policy in 1940 against Hitler; it exacted terrible costs in lives and destruction, but, after all, it succeeded. Today military solutions cannot succeed. They will only increase the fear of Western ideas in the Soviet Union and therefore increase oppression and persecution of dissidents. A military response will not offer a solution, but it may very well lead to Armageddon.

In my view, intellectuals must denounce infractions against human rights, yet they must also build bridges. We must live and let live— an attitude that can be called appeasement. We have no other choice today. We cannot force any regime to grant civil rights to its people by using threats and cold-war methods. As recent events have shown, an improvement of human rights can only be achieved from within. Further consolidation and extension of these improvements requires a period of political détente, after the abatement of fear of aggression between the superpowers.

We are beginning to observe the decay of ideologies. We see movements against oppression all over the Eastern world. Once fear of war and obstruction recede, technocrats may come to power for whom the ideological questions are of less importance. (Gorbachev's influence is the first indication that the process has begun.)

The oppression of intellectual freedom from the right and the left is one of our most critical problems. The life and creativity of dissidents and free thinkers and racial minorities are threatened. But one of the greatest dangers today is a nuclear confrontation. Such an event would destroy us all, free and oppressed, and everything for which we care and live.

16

~

Forty Years After: Thoughts of a Nuclear Witness

Forty years ago in the early morning hours of July 16, 1945, a truck driver in New Mexico reported that he saw the sun about to rise at 4 A.M. The sun decided it was too early, he said, so it went down again and came up an hour later.

A historic event had taken place at that time in a desert of New Mexico: the first man-made nuclear explosion. It was a test of the atomic bomb, designed and assembled at Los Alamos. As one of its designers, I witnessed the event from a distance of 10 miles. It was an awesome experience, hardly describable in words. The landscape was lit up twenty times stronger than midday sunlight. Even at that distance, we felt a blast of intense heat on our faces. A roaring thunder reverberated in the adjacent mountains. We saw the fireball steadily ascend, changing its shape from a bright hemisphere on the ground to an expanding full sphere in midair and finally assuming the well-known mushroom shape. We saw the change of color, from dazzling white to yellow and pink, surrounded by a blue halo caused by the radioactive glow of the atmosphere. Finally, we saw the red light of the rising sun illuminate the giant mushroom that quietly dominated the sky—all unforgettable impressions that filled my colleagues and me with awe, with pride of a unique achievement, and with misgivings about the future of mankind.

Three weeks after the test in the New Mexico desert, two bombs were dropped over two cities in Japan. A group of scientists under the leadership of James Franck in Chicago proposed, in a letter to the authorities, that the bomb be exploded over an uninhabited territory in Japan as a demonstration. It might have persuaded the Japanese leaders to sue for peace. We, in Los Alamos, did not know much about this initiative. Had I known it, I would certainly have signed it. Whatever one may think about the wisdom of America's use of the bomb, in particular about the necessity of destroying a second city, it did end a murderous war and, most probably, saved more lives than it destroyed. We meant so well. We served our country, and we thought that such powerful weapons would make wars between great powers unthinkable. Some of us thought that the existence of these dangerous power sources would lead to international administration of military and peaceful applications of nuclear power. We hoped that it would end the age-old human custom of organized mutual mass murder.

It did not turn out that way. The political scene was not yet ready for such an undertaking. It is true that the fear of the bomb has prevented war between the superpowers for forty years. During the same time, however, the great powers found no other way to maintain this state of affairs but to indulge themselves in an ever-increasing arms race. At this moment in history, forty years after that fateful event in New Mexico, the two superpowers are on a collision course. The nuclear armaments race continues at an accelerated pace, more warheads are deployed, missiles become more efficient, and new types of weapons are introduced. Technical innovations, such as cruise missiles, get in the way of arms-control agreements because they make it harder to verify compliance. As a result, our own security and the security of the whole world declines. The consequences of a potential military conflict become more terrible with every new turn of the arms-race spiral. The growing number of weapons increases the probability of an outbreak of nuclear war, intended or unintended. At this moment, more than 50,000 nuclear warheads are deployed on both sides, with a total power of 6000 times the amount of explosives used in World War II. Only a few hundred of these warheads are needed to destroy Western or Eastern civilization. The present arms race represents a dangerous case of collective mental disease that has gripped humanity—all the result of our work at Los Alamos and at other nuclear laboratories. The bomb was our brainchild, our achievement.

Most statesmen, and much of the public, are aware that the actual use of even a small part of the presently deployed nuclear weapons would plunge mankind into an unparalleled catastrophe. What then drives the superpowers to go on producing and improving nuclear weapons? Why is it that we go on increasing the probability and the dimensions of the potential catastrophe every day? True enough, the existence of a nuclear threat has prevented the outbreak of war between the superpowers. But why must the threat be multiplied by a steadily increasing factor that today is more than 50 times what is sufficient to incapacitate the other side? Why can't people and governments understand the basic point that enough is enough and recognize the deadly risk of the present escalation?

One of the main reasons is fear and there are many kinds of fear. First, there is the fear that a first strike by the opponent may destroy most of one's own land-based missiles before retaliation—a fear that is completely irrational, because the United States has more than half and the Soviet Union about a quarter of their strategic missiles on submarines, which cannot be destroyed by a first strike. So far, no reliable means exist to locate submerged submarines. Given the destructive power that resides even in a single submarine, it is plain that a first strike could not disarm either adversary.

Second, there is the fear of being weaker than the other side. Until the mid-seventies, the United States had considerably more nuclear weapons than the Soviet Union, although the Soviets had enough to destroy the United States, even in a second strike. Since then the Soviet Union has reached approximate equality, after accelerated production, following a large increase in U.S. warheads in the early seventies. The Soviet build-up jolted U.S. authorities and contributed increasingly to feelings of insecurity. Ironically, present approximate parity adds to the pressure for a continuing arms race because it is difficult for one side to estimate the efficiency and accuracy of warheads deployed by the other, especially in the Soviet Union, because of its exaggerated secrecy measures. Each side feels obliged to assume the worst about the other and tries to catch up with its most pessimistic estimates. This is one of the driving forces of the arms race, in spite of the obvious fact that any real or perceived difference in numbers is irrelevant, in view of the immense overkill capacities on both sides.

Third, there is the fear of being outdistanced in developing or stockpiling a specific type of weapon. For example, the Soviet Union has more land-based intercontinental missiles than the United States, some with greater explosive power than those in the U.S. arsenal. But that is by no means an advantage as land-based missiles are easy targets and therefore exposed to a first strike. Furthermore, excessively large power is not necessarily an asset as the destructive effects are less than proportional to the explosive power. Still, the United States feels that it has to overcome that apparent deficiency, for example, by adding MX missiles. The Soviets are behind in submarine-based missiles, so they feel they must construct more of them. These are only two examples of the strategic asymmetries that fuel the arms race, without adding strength to deterrence, because each side has far more than enough to destroy the other.

Both sides perceive the other as bent on world domination. In Western eyes the Soviet Union wants to spread communism all over the world, in Eastern eyes the West wants to convert the whole world to capitalist democracy. This may be so in wishful dreams but it is patently impossible in the age of nuclear weapons. We will have to learn how to peacefully coexist with different social and political systems.

Another fear comes from the perceived, or actual, aggressive policy of the opponent. Both sides believe that the other is bent on aggression, whereas they themselves act purely defensively. This is a destabilizing condition. What the United States sees as an aggression by the Soviets in Afghanistan and in Southeast Asia may be seen by the Soviets themselves as "defensive" acts to insure the security of their borders or to counterbalance Western, or noncommunist, power. Conversely, U.S. "defensive" actions to prevent the spread of communist influence in Central America or in the Middle East may be perceived in the Soviet Union as attempts to build Western influence wherever possible. The belief that the United States wants to spread "democracy" to Nicaragua or that all the Soviets want is to maintain a communist system in Afghanistan is only partly correct. Both sides want to prevent the other from achieving a military foothold in those regions. The United States is not very eager to spread democracy in countries such as Chile, where there is no danger of Soviet influence, and the Soviets are friendly with countries whose political systems are far from communist.

Recent U.S. Administration plans to establish an effective defense against missiles ("star wars") are perceived by the Soviets as a preparation for a first strike since it would, if successful, prevent second-strike retaliation. Such plans would induce the other side to build more missiles in order to penetrate the defense. It leads to increased fears, heightened tensions, and would make it more difficult to reach an agreement on reduction of nuclear missiles. Furthermore such defenses are technically extremely difficult, very costly, and probably unreliable. Each military and political action abroad can be interpreted as aggressive or defensive by one side or the other. During a political crisis, such misrepresentation of acts by an opponent—when a defensive move is interpreted as offensive—can lead to escalating conflict or war.

Failure to understand the motivations of the other side is caused by a deep distrust between the superpowers. Differences in political systems are major obstacles to understanding. The authoritarian regime, the ideology of world communism, lack of certain human rights, treatment of minorities in the Soviet Union, and suppression of freedom by its satellites arouse fears in the United States. The capitalist ideology of free enterprise, virulent anticommunism, support of right-wing dictators, along with the call for human rights that are denied by left-wing dictators and the talk of liberating the world from the evils of communism, arouse fears in the U.S.S.R., not only in leading circles.

I have had many opportunities to speak with Soviet scientists during my frequent trips to the USSR and during meetings outside the Soviet Union. I have reason to believe that some expressed their honest opinions—some even being critical of certain measures taken by their own government. These conversations have convinced me that Soviet fears of Western aggression and of Western attempts to blackmail the USSR by developing superior weapon systems are genuine, justified or not.

To understand how anxiety on the Soviet side may influence some of the acts the Soviets have taken, we must consider their present situation. Today, four large power complexes dominate the globe: the United States, Western Europe and Japan, the Soviet Union, and China. Three have one potential enemy: the USSR One has four: the other three and the population of its East European "allies." One reason for the existence of large, conventional Soviet forces is fear of an Eastern European revolt. While the West has not intervened in East European revolts so far, the USSR still fears that it might yet happen, especially if help were requested by a provisional anti-Soviet government.

These anxieties are not the only causes of an escalating nuclear arms race. Another cause of increasing importance is the momentum of the military machine. Years of intense development and build-up of weapons, of the means of their delivery, and of methods to improve their accuracy have established an interwoven system of vested interests. These ambitious and dedicated groups are unwilling to give up their activities not only because of financial interests, but also because of a commitment to pursue a difficult task when it is about to yield more and more results. No doubt, most of the participants believe that what they do will enhance the security of their country. This is true in the East as well as in the West.

I remember a similar situation at Los Alamos. The main reason why I and many others joined the effort to build the bomb was the fear that the Nazis would acquire the bomb first. After all, the fission process was discovered in Germany and we know there were excellent physicists and engineers able to carry out the job there. In April 1945, Germany was defeated, but there was practically no one at Los Alamos who thought of quitting then. We were too deeply committed to a promising technical development. Of course, there were a number of good reasons to justify continuing our work, but most of us never mentioned quitting. So strong was the attraction of a "technically sweet" project, an uncanny term coined by J. Robert Oppenheimer. Today, the same motivation compels others to remain working on weapons developments. The inexorable growth of manpower and financial support for the military establishment on both sides is one of the most dangerous factors preventing a cessation of the arms race.

Another dangerous cause of the escalating arms race is the ongoing preparation for waging nuclear war. Strategies and tactics are developed and an escalating search goes on for military targets to be hit "in case." The more such targets are found, the more bombs have to be deployed on both sides. Should deterrence fail, so goes the argument, nuclear war may come and we must be prepared to "prevail" in a limited nuclear war. But can nuclear war be limited when the losing side has no choice but escalation? Such preparations would only worsen the catastrophe they are designed to prevent. Two archers face each other, saying, "The tighter I draw the bow, the safer I become."

Unfortunately, preparations for the eventuality of a nuclear war are also driven by their own momentum. The more such development is pursued, the more possibilities for attack are found and the more pressure develops for deployment. Such preparation made sense in the past, when war was an acceptable last resort for which we needed to be well prepared. "*Si vis pacem para bellum*" is written on a war memorial in my home town, Vienna: "When you wish for peace, prepare for war." Today this slogan is no longer valid. To prepare for nuclear war is to prepare for mutual suicide. It contributes to fears on both sides and increases the chances of irresponsible response in a crisis.

The arms race is the product of irrational fears felt by the contending superpowers. It is a self-perpetuating mechanism that creates its own momentum by increasing fears on which it was based and by drawing more and more efforts, projects, and dedicated people into the whirl-pool. This is why the present confrontation between the superpowers is so dangerous in all its forms. It exacerbates antagonistic feelings and attitudes which may provoke military actions in a crisis. Then it would be hard to avoid a nuclear conflagration.

Forty years after the birth of the atomic age is an appropriate mo-ment to recall some of the efforts made to avoid the impending ca-tastrophe. Some scientists who worked on building the bomb felt an obligation to inform the public about the awesome consequences of a nuclear war. We made public speeches about the bomb and about our hopes for international understanding. I remember quoting John Donne: "No man is an island entirely for itself, every man is a piece of the continent, a part of the main . . . Never send to know for whom the bell tolls, it tolls for thee." We talked to civic groups, we wrote articles, we tried to create committees of well-known people, such as the Emergency Committee of Atomic Scientists, headed by Albert Ein-stein. Was it a feeling of guilt for having participated in devising this new weapon that drove us on? Maybe it was, but the most important reason was our nightmarish vision of an actual nuclear conflict, based on our particular understanding of the power of the weapon we had made.

Just after the end of the war, a group of us created the Federation of Atomic Scientists, an organization that still exists, but "Atomic," has been replaced by "American." One of the purposes of the Fed-eration was to alert the public to the dangers of nuclear war. We were not overly successful. Only when women's groups, physicians, and bishops joined our campaign did grass-root movements, such as the nuclear-freeze campaign, against the nuclear danger begin to develop. Only then did the public become aware of the problems.

The purpose of the Federation of Atomic Scientists was not only to alert the public. Under the able leadership of William Higginbot-tom, an electronic engineer in Los Alamos, the Federation waged a political fight for a civilian administration over nuclear energy for military and peaceful purposes. Two bills were proposed at that time: the McMahon bill, which intended to put nuclear matters under ci-vilian control, and the May-Johnson bill, which would put them under military control. We supported the McMahon bill; at that time, we did not recognize how little difference it would make. The Atomic Energy Commission and the subsequent Department of Energy are under civilian control, yet they did not prevent the arms race or the vast overproduction of nuclear weapons.

To avoid an arms race, the Federation also strongly supported the creation of an international agency to keep nuclear weapons and energy production under international control—a plan that failed, despite its support by many idealistic people. It was resisted not only by Stalin's regime in the East, but also by nationalists in the West.

In the late summer of 1949, four years after the first American bomb, the Soviets succeeded in exploding one themselves. As soon as they learned the only important secret—that it was possible—it was not hard for them. In reaction against the Soviet success, there were lively discussions within leading U.S. circles as to whether a much stronger weapon—the hydrogen bomb—should be developed. Oppenheimer and other scientists opposed it, proposing instead some kind of agreement with the Soviets not to build such a devastating weapon, but that approach wasn't even tried. Work on the H-bomb was taken up intensely. Still, twelve scientists (I was one of them) spoke out against it early in 1950: "This bomb is no longer a weapon of war but a means of extermination of whole populations." The first H-bomb was tested by the United States in 1951, and as expected, the Soviets developed theirs quickly and tested it less than two years later.

Then the arms race began in earnest. Until five years ago, the United States definitely held the edge. Actually, in the first half of the seventies, the United States increased its strategic warheads from 4000 to more than 8000, when the Soviets then had about 2000. But in the second half of the decade, the USSR caught up, reaching almost 8000 by 1981.

In the past, negotiations between the superpowers to stop or reduce this monstrous stockpiling have been rare and quixotic. The recent successful negotiations about the removal of intermediate missiles in Europe are an encouraging sign that reason has begun to enter arms negotiations. Although it deals with only a few percent of the available nuclear forces, it is the first time that a class of nuclear weapons is going to disappear by mutual consent.

To be sure, we also have made some progress in the past, such as the ban on nuclear testing above ground, the limitations imposed by SALT I, and the nonratified, but more or less adhered to, SALT II treaty. A treaty restricting nuclear testing to below ground was, to a great extent, the result of a one-man campaign launched by Linus Pauling. He was able to arouse worldwide concern about radioactive contamination from above-ground tests. Unfortunately, the ban did not help to reduce efforts to improve nuclear weapons, because underground tests are relatively easy to perform.

SALT I and II treaties did not halt the arms race, but they had a restraining effect. The agreements placed a limit on the number of missiles each side could have, and they also limited to ten the number of warheads permitted on each missile. For example, if the United States wants to adhere to the SALT II treaty, it will have to scrap some of its older submarines when it deploys the newer, more efficient Trident II submarine.

One of the most important restrictions of SALT I is the so-called antiballistic missile (ABM) treaty. It bans defenses against ballistic missiles, while it allows each side limited defenses for two sites only. The Soviet Union chose to build some defenses around Moscow, whereas the United States built one defensive system but later dismantled it. The history of the ABM treaty is of interest in view of the present excitement about antimissile defenses because it restricts severely the deployment of defensive measures against strategic missiles. Moreover, the scientific community played an important role in shaping this treaty on two accounts. First, under the intellectual leadership of Jerome Wiesner, the President's Science adviser under John F. Kennedy, a group of scientists emphasized the technical shortcomings of the then planned defense measures, which consisted of nuclear or conventional explosives directed at missiles entering the atmosphere on their last leg to their targets. Second, scientists and certain statesmen pointed out that defensive measures, if they are effective, would merely induce the opponent to increase the number and efficiency of its offensive missiles. Indeed, when it seemed probable that the U.S.S.R., before the treaty was concluded, would defend its launching sites and its cities, the United States put several warheads on its missiles—"multiple independent re-entry vehicles," or MIRVs. The purpose was to overcome defensive measures by making missiles that did penetrate defenses more effective. The Soviets then followed suit after a few years, inevitably after the United States introduced that new type of weapon. The result was less security for both sides.

It was difficult at that time to convince the Soviets that defensive measures are something that should be avoided. Starting as early as 1964, we held conferences with Soviet scientists on that topic at several "Pugwash" meetings. Pugwash is a village in Canada where scientists from the East and West met to discuss East-West relations for the first time in 1957 at the invitation of the late Canadian industrialist, Cyrus Eaton. The initiative came from the physicist and biologist Leo Szilard. Pugwash meetings became a regular institution. They now have taken place several times a year at different localities, organized by an international Pugwash committee with seats in London and Geneva.

We tried very hard to convince the Soviets that antimissile defenses would only serve to increase the number of missiles. For a long time, Soviet scientists insisted that defensive measures cannot have negative effects. They argued very much along the lines of today's defenders of President Reagan's Strategic Defense Initiative (SDI), or "star wars." It took a number of years before we could convince them that defenses against missiles would accelerate the arms race since it would force the opponent to increase the number of its warheads. Soviet scientists transmitted these arguments to their government, and they were instrumental in getting the Soviet government to accept the ABM treaty.

Today, the roles seem inverted. The Soviets now adhere to their acquired position: Defensive measures against missiles would induce the other side to raise its offensive potential. Moreover, a highly successful defensive system, that is deployed by one side before the other has reached the same stage, may even encourage a first strike by the former, with little danger of retaliation. The U.S. government argues that defensive measures cannot be harmful and that they are morally justified.

The same group of U.S. scientists that was able to convince the Soviets fifteen years ago is now not able to convince its own government of the futility of most defensive measures and of the dangers inherent in an abrogation or reinterpretation of the ABM treaty, which would be necessary for testing and deploying a defensive system.

It is not easy to argue against defense. Obviously, it is an attractive thought to protect the nation from the ravages of a nuclear war by building a leakproof defense against all nuclear bombs. In spite of the technological advances since the conclusion of the ABM treaty, this aim is still an illusion and will remain impossible in the foreseeable future. With the present number of missiles deployed, even a small leak in the defenses would be devastating. Arguments against a partial defense are the same today as they were twenty years ago: It can be overcome by increasing the offensive strength and by other countermeasures. The effect would be an accelerated arms race, not only in offensive weapons, but also in measures to attack the defenses and in countermeasures to render defenses ineffective. To insist on those defenses is a tragic example of shortsighted and dangerous planning, driven by fear and irrational arguments.

Nevertheless, a certain amount of research into new defense methods is called for in order to be alert to all possibilities. Such research should be—indeed is—carried out by the superpowers, but announcing an intention of going ahead with deployment, if it turns out to be feasible, is harmful to any negotiated reduction of offensive arms. How could one party agree to reduce its missiles if the other says it plans to shoot down as many as possible?

The SDI efforts are also an obstacle to concluding a treaty banning the development and testing of devices to destroy satellites (ASATs) because of the possibility of using similar weapons against missiles in flight. Such a treaty would be highly desirable, since satellites are a most important means to find out what military movements and preparations take place on the other side. If they are destroyed in a crisis, each side would be left guessing and would assume the worst. Two blind men would face each other with deadly weapons in their hands. The safety of satellites is a critically stabilizing factor. They are an important means of verification in any arms control agreement. Moreover, the testing of antisatellite systems can be easily verified, and no system can be used with any confidence that is not tested.

It is often said that the Soviets have already tested an ASAT system whereas the United States has not. But the present Soviet ASAT system is very clumsy and does not reach the more important satellites at high altitudes. It is not even a serious threat to low-orbit satellites. Furthermore, increased antisatellite capabilities are more dangerous to the United States, with its dependence on highly developed satellite systems. The difficulty in getting a treaty banning ASATs is another example of how the Strategic Defense Initiative is counterproductive to effective arms control measures, quite apart from the fact that it is a most questionable project from technical and political points of view. What sense does it make to jeopardize immediate steps to improve the situation for doubtful long-term advantages?

There is a school of thought that pretends that the ultimate catastrophe can be avoided by establishing military superiority. It says to forget about arms control and make use of technological advances that the other side may not be able to duplicate. Not an easy task. In the past, the Soviet Union has been able to match every move made by the United States. Every new step in weapon refinements invented in the United States has been turned against it within a few years. However, in the future, it may become more difficult for the Soviet Union to emulate American developments, because their high technology is not as advanced. Frequently in the past, they have had to replace quality with quantity or size.

The drive toward military superiority is based on the notion that we will be safer if we have more and better weapons than our opponent. This is an illusory and dangerous dream, stemming from the prenuclear era. What does superiority mean when the other side already has many times the means of destroying its opponent? Furthermore, if the United States is perceived to be on the way to becoming superior, either offensively or defensively, even if it is not actually so, the danger of a nuclear war is much greater. Soviet leaders would then feel driven to the wall, fearing being subject to future blackmail. They would be forced to go to the limit and beyond to forestall prospective inferiority.

Of course, such actions by the Soviets would be irrational and suicidal. But we cannot rely upon rational planning under such conditions. In the Cuban missile crisis, the Soviets acted irrationally, even in the face of an obviously unfavorable geographical situation. Governments have taken irrational steps many times in the past, especially when they feel in terror of a perceived possibility of superiority before it is achieved. What we must realize is that what counts is the *perception* of such an attempt, not necessarily the reality.

The most positive aspect of nuclear developments in the last forty years is the success of mutual deterrence. No serious military conflict has occurred between the superpowers, but in most other respects, developments have been disappointing. The arms race goes on, with little hope for a turnaround as more and more nations produce nuclear bombs. One hopeful aspect is greater public awareness and the knowledge of some statesmen that nuclear war is unacceptable and that an ever-increasing arms race is not going to prevent a catastrophe.*

These last four decades have taught us one important lesson: negotiations to reduce the level of nuclear weapons have little chance of success in a prevailing atmosphere of fear, distrust, confrontation, and increasingly offensive and defensive weapons development. On the contrary, there is a danger that some treaties, which helped to slow down the speed of the arms race in the past, will now be eroded. Is there a chance to change that course in the coming decades and arrive at a mutual understanding that would effectively reduce the threat of a military conflict between the superpowers?

There are compelling reasons for a change. Each superpower has an interest in the other's security, since insecurity breeds distrust and leads to an increased level of armaments. A significant reduction of

---

* This essay was written in 1985. In the meantime, things have turned to the better. The advent of a new leader in the Soviet Union and an increasing awareness among Western statesmen have brought about the first turnaround of the arms race—the abolishment of nuclear intermediate-range weapons.

nuclear weapons is in the interest of both sides. Nuclear weapons are not weapons of war. Their only purpose is to deter the opponents from using them. The present level of deployment is many times greater than needed.

The events of the past four decades revealed two important causes of the arms race: mutual fear and the driving forces behind increasing arms efforts. What can be done against them? In the past, it was sometimes advantageous for a power to make an opponent fearful in order to extract political concessions. Today, in the present super-power confrontation, inducing fear in the opponent is against a nation's self-interest, leading to an escalation of the arms race and an increase in the probability of dangerous, irrational acts. The difference comes from the fact that today, in the event of war, the weaker power can also inflict unacceptable damage on the stronger.

Fear is not an objective fact, like the number of warheads; it arises from the interpretations and misinterpretations of statements and actions by the other side. From any rational point of view, neither side would ever start a war or initiate a destructive first strike. Starting a war would almost certainly lead to a nuclear exchange and holocaust. A totally effective first strike is technically unachievable for a variety of reasons (one of which is the impossibility of destroying your opponent's submarines). But politics is not always rational. Fear originates because one side is afraid of irrational acts by the other. There is no point in claiming that all actions of the West have always been purely defensive and that the West will never start a war against the Soviet Union under the present circumstances. This is not the way the Soviet Union sees it. In times of distrust, each opponent feels compelled to interpret the other's intentions in the worst possible way.

There are ways to reduce mutual fear and distrust. An indispensable first step is an awareness of the problem. Every statement and every action of both governments should be examined with a view as to how it will be interpreted by the other side. Will it increase or reduce fear and distrust? If it increases fear, that ought to be regarded as an important argument against the measure. There are a number of currently relevant examples, such as the deployment of the superpowerful SS18 by the Soviets and the deployment of MX missiles and the Trident II submarines by the United States. Such measures are perceived by the other side as steps toward first-strike capabilities.

How can we deal with anxiety over the superiority of the other side? Today, East and West maintain that the opponent is militarily stronger. As remarked before, it is not so much reality, but perception, that counts. Therefore, we must not only strive to maintain offensive and defensive parity, but also nourish the perception on both sides that parity exists and can be maintained. This is a difficult task because the two powers do not put the same value on different weapon systems. It will be necessary to compare conditions of equivalence of one system with another. We rarely put ourselves into the position of the adversary in order to understand his attitudes.

The problem of parity ought to be studied intensely in bilateral discussions. If the two sides cannot agree, at least approximately, on what is parity, there is not much hope for a negotiated reduction of arms. The allied countries of both superpowers should actively participate in these studies. They may have a more objective point of view on the situation and should be most interested in a mutual understanding, as unprotected victims in a defensive build-up or as launching pads in an offensive one.

To reduce the fear of aggression and expansion, a better understanding of the motivations and actions of the opponent must be reached. One way to accomplish this would be to create an international body for crisis management to discuss actual and expected political or military events. There already exists a bilateral body—the Standing Consultative Commission—to deal with supposed or real infractions of present treaties. It has been useful in the past to avoid serious conflicts about compliance. Today, the Commission is less effective because perceived infractions are widely publicized before bilateral discussions have a chance to deal with them. Certainly, a body for crisis management would face more difficult problems. This is one of the reasons why it ought to be organized. It should also include other nations, but it may start as a bilateral effort.

The United States should seriously consider a declaration never to use nuclear weapons first or at least to use them first only in situations of utmost emergency, after intense negotiations to stop the conflagration. Such a no-first-use announcement is an almost obvious statement, since a first use would be tantamount to suicide and no sane government would ever take that step. Still, such a declaration would have a great moral and ethical impact since it clearly indicates that nuclear weapons were regarded solely as deterrence against their use by the opponent. A no-first-use statement by the United States has been criticized as weakening the present nuclear deterrence of a conventional attack on Western Europe. This reasoning is based on the questionable assumption that a suicide threat is an effective deterrent. In any case, the declaration ought to be connected with improvements in the defensive efficiency of NATO's conventional forces. An immediate no-early-first-use declaration would pave the way for a more sensible policy of deterring conventional war.

On each side there are about 8000 "small" nuclear weapons deployed in Europe to be used as battlefield weapons if a war breaks out. They are called "tactical" weapons and are small compared with "strategic" bombs aimed at the military installations and cities in the heart of the adversary. Still, some of these tactical bombs are as big as the Hiroshima bomb. There is a chance that successful negotiations will be concluded covering these weapons. Their number has already been reduced unilaterally by the United States. It must be obvious to both sides that these weapons present too low a barrier against a transition from a conventional to a nuclear war.

One could establish a nuclear-free zone along the East-West frontier to reduce the probability of an early use of nuclear weapons. As things are presently set up, military authorities might be presented with the alternative of "use it or lose it," in case of small intrusions across a border.

A most desirable, and easily verifiable, aim for negotiations would be a comprehensive ban on bomb testing, including underground tests. This would slow down developments toward more effective nuclear weapons. The present ones are efficient enough.

A special responsibility falls on Europe in these matters. The two superpowers are locked in a struggle of military and political competition. Their efforts toward arms control and cooperation are hampered by political considerations, by face-saving tendencies, by attempts to outsmart the other side, and by efforts to place blame on the opponent. But the future existence of Europe and of the world, for that matter, must not depend on the whims of superpowers, on whether they decide to bargain or to fight or to give in or not give in on some secondary item.

Europe is much less stuck in previous policies and propaganda. So far, it has played a bystander's role, leaving the initiatives to the superpowers. Why does Europe leave proposals, counting, and decisions to the United States and to the Soviet Union? True enough, some influential Europeans have come forward with proposals for treaties and measures for the reduction of tensions (such as the Palme commission's proposal of a nuclear-free zone in Europe). But by and large European governments have been passive. They could orbit their own observation satellites and install their own evaluation centers, independent of the superpowers and less subject to political bias. Unfortunately, the present mood in Europe is not conducive to taking an active role in world affairs, yet there has seldom been a time when it would be more important.

The last forty years have shown that attempts to reduce tensions by independent or negotiated military measures have not been very successful. What is needed is a deeper change of attitude from paranoic distrust to mutual understanding. How can it be done? The United States and the Soviet Union must think of themselves not as enemies but as adversaries. They have a common enemy: nuclear war. They have many common interests, apart from escaping mutual nuclear destruction. Richard von Weizsäcker, President of the Federal Republic of Germany, said: "We must find other than military concerns in order to establish peace."

The world is threatened not only by nuclear war. For example, we face a steady increase in carbon dioxide in the atmosphere, causing a rise in the earth's surface temperature, possibly leading to an increased melting of the polar ice caps, with tragic consequences after several decades. Coastal cities may disappear from the map because of the rising level of the seas. We are not certain about these consequences because much is still unknown about the fate of carbon dioxide produced by combustion of fossil fuel and by deforestation.

Chemical pollution of the atmosphere threatens animals and vegetation. This phenomenon is usually referred to as "acid rain," but there are many other partly unknown components and processes that play an important role. In Germany, half the trees in the forests are sick. In the United States and the Soviet Union, the effects are only beginning to show because of lower population density. But there is no question that these regions will be gravely affected in the future. The extent of the expected damage is not widely recognized. The demise of forests can change the climate. It could make mountain regions uninhabitable because forests protect human habitation against avalanches and inundations. During the next century, Florida could disappear along with many U.S. coastal cities because of the rising sea level, and Switzerland could become uninhabitable because of the death of its forests.

These two possible catastrophes may be more dangerous than nuclear war, since we know what to do to avoid it: Do not use nuclear weapons! We do not yet know what to do to guard against other catastrophes. In spite of this, the superpowers spend billions on the perfection of offensive or defensive weapons and exploit a large part of our scientific personnel for that purpose. Not much money or brainpower is left for averting other dangers.

We have mentioned only two possible dangers. Of course, there are many others: ocean pollution, overpopulation, atmospheric ozone depletion, and the exhaustion of agricultural soil, to name a few. These dangers require scientific, technical, and social innovations for which our societies provide little manpower and financial means.

All these dangers threaten the superpowers directly and indirectly. They therefore provide great opportunities for cooperation between East and West. The recognition of common interest and active collaboration to solve common problems is a way of reducing fear and distrust. The transfer of scientific and technical interest to aims other than weaponeering would help to counteract the self-propelling momentum of ever-increasing armament efforts.

Great opportunities for collaboration are also found in basic scientific research. Exchanges of results, meetings of scientists at international conferences, extended visits in the West and East of teams from the other side have taken place in recent decades and still go on, now at a reduced scale. (However, because of an improved political atmosphere in 1987, a new upswing of scientific collaboration seems to be in the making.) Such contacts are excellent ways of increasing mutual understanding. Basic science is far enough from technical or military application, and offers little occasion for confrontation or distrust. There is only one common aim: a better understanding of how nature works.

Commerce is another important means of contact and mutual understanding. In times of distrust, commerce is hampered by the fear in the United States that exchanges of high-technology products would support the Soviet military effort—another instance where fear plays a negative role. While some restriction over certain types of military merchandise is necessary, highly developed commercial interdependence reduces the danger of military conflicts because both sides are interested in keeping things going. In this respect, Western European nations have shown a higher degree of realism when they constructed a gas pipeline to supply Western Europe with fuel from the Soviet Union. The United States should follow the European lead.

Unfortunately, past experience in major collaborative efforts has not been very encouraging. But there exist examples of successful collaboration, in spite of political tensions: Fusion energy research and the use of large arrays of antennas for radioastronomy are examples. The development of cooperation on a larger scale will be a slow process and will require continuous effort and patience. Nevertheless, it must remain an important item in superpower dealings.

One of the main obstacles to collaboration is the different attitudes of the two powers over the question of human rights. The West puts great emphasis on freedom of dissent and on free travel everywhere; communist regimes consider the right to work and free medical care as part of basic human rights. Whenever a collaboration begins, it is often disrupted by incidents of persecution of individuals or by other episodes, such as the Soviet occupation of Afghanistan and the exiling of Andrei Sakharov. Such disruptions have occurred not only because of Soviet actions: the Soviets reduced collaboration during U.S. involvement in the Vietnam War.

Here we face a difficult dilemma. Obviously, the citizens of the Western world cannot sit idly by and ignore persecutions and abuses of power perpetrated in communist as well as in right-wing dictatorships. Certainly, public protests against violations of human rights are useful; indeed, they have helped in some cases to mitigate such abuses. But criticism and protest should not disrupt cooperation with the Soviet Union. Breaking off collaboration on such grounds is counterproductive. It isolates those segments of the Soviet population who privately condemn infractions against civil liberties. Protests are more effective when they occur during direct contacts established by collaboration. When large numbers of Soviet citizens visit the West, it influences their thinking. In the past, cessation of collaboration and a harder attitude have not improved Soviet civil liberties. On the contrary, they have become worse. Real improvement will be a very slow process and will probably take a long time. If fear, confrontation, and distrust subside, technocrats, for whom ideological questions would be of less importance, may come to power.

Developments over the past forty years did not inspire much confidence in our ability to arrive at a world without the threat of annihilation. But there is still hope for the next forty years. The fear of nuclear war has kept an uneasy peace between the superpowers and has given us time to understand that the continuing arms race is only a metastable solution: it will not last forever. We still have time to learn the lesson and to change the present course, which in the long run is a collision course. It will require political and military insight, an understanding of the psychology of our adversary, a great deal of wisdom, and a readiness to compromise—none of which has been much in evidence in these times. Progress must be based on an absolute, pragmatic, ethical, and moral dedication to the aim that nuclear war should not, cannot, and must not occur. Time is running out. The longer we wait, the harder it will be to get off the present collision course.

My colleagues and I constructed the atomic bomb. If we hadn't, others would have done it sooner or later. What nature has made possible cannot be avoided. Yet the lessons we draw from it and what we do with it depend on us, not on nature.

Remarks Added in 1988

Since 1985, when this essay was written, efforts to improve understanding between East and West have come from a side few would have expected: General Secretary Gorbachev challenged the West to reconsider long-held positions that have stood in the way of mutual understanding. Gorbachev has also introduced some measures to improve civil liberties in his country. Who would have expected that Sakharov would be released from exile and the Soviets would agree to intrusive verification measures on their soil? It was encouraging that the superpowers agreed, as a first step, to reduce nuclear arms by eliminating missiles of intermediate range and that serious negotiations are underway, aiming at a 50 percent reduction of strategic nuclear weapons.

All this is still a long way from reducing 50,000 nuclear warheads to a reasonable number, sufficient for keeping the peace. The apparent changes in the Soviet Union toward more openness and the change of attitude on both sides toward effective reductions of nuclear weapons should give us hope. Openness in world politics was urged by Niels Bohr in his open letter to the United Nations in 1950. Bohr did not necessarily mean full democracy; after all, the traditions and the histories of the Soviet Union and other countries may not always be compatible with the Western ideas of democracy. What Bohr meant was an openness to face relevant questions and attitudes and to discuss them openly to reach an understanding of different points of view.

Today, we are in a more favorable position than ever since World War II to gain a better insight into the aims, fears, and actions of the other side. It is a propitious moment to replace confrontation with understanding and cooperation and to reach a stage in East-West relations in which the peaceful intentions of both sides emerge. Such an opportunity may not come again if the present improvements in our relations are not fully exploited and extended. In the future, it will be more difficult to turn from madness to reason.

Acknowledgments

THE PRIVILEGE OF BEING A PHYSICIST was originally published in *Physics Today*, August 1969. The essay was adapted from an address given at the joint annual meeting of the American Physical Society and the American Association of Physics Teachers. I am grateful to Isidor I. Rabi for drawing my attention to Henry Rowland's address.

THREATS AND PROMISES was delivered as a commencement address at Brandeis University on May 22, 1983.

IS PHYSICS HUMAN? was originally published in *Physics Today*, June 1976. This essay was based on my response as recipient of the Oerstad Medal of the American Association of Physics Teachers at the 1976 joint annual meeting of the AAPT and the American Physical Society and on a similar paper which I presented at the International Conference on Physics Education held in Edinburgh from July 31–August 6, 1975. The paper was published in *Physics Education*, 11, 75 (1976).

TEACHING SCIENCE was delivered as a keynote speech at the Annual Symposium for Science and Mathematics Teachers, held by the Illinois Science Lecture Association on May 14, 1984.

ART AND SCIENCE is an expanded version of an article that appeared in *The American Scholar*, volume 48, number 4 (Autumn 1979). It also appeared in a shortened version in *Daedalus*, volume 115, number 3 (Summer 1986).

THE FRONTIERS AND LIMITS OF SCIENCE was originally published in *Daedaleus*, volume 113, number 3 (Summer 1984). The essay was based in part on a paper with a similar title, which appeared in *American Scientist, 65,* 405 (1977). It was presented in part as an address at the Bicentennial of the American Academy of Arts and Sciences in May 1981.

WHAT IS QUANTUM MECHANICS? was written for this collection.

WHAT IS AN ELEMENTARY PARTICLE? was originally published in *Physics 50 Years Later,* edited by Sanborn C. Brown, National Academy of Sciences, Washington, D.C., 1973. It was expanded to include recent results.

CONTEMPORARY FRONTIERS IN PHYSICS was originally published in *Science,* volume 203, January 19, 1979. It was updated for this collection.

THE ORIGIN OF THE UNIVERSE was originally published in *American Scientist,* volume 71, September–October 1983. The parts describing the inflationary universe have been expanded.

WOLFGANG PAULI was originally published in *Physics Today,* December 1985.

WERNER HEISENBERG was originally published in the Introduction of *Inner Exile: Recollections of a Life with Werner Heisenberg,* by Elisabeth Heisenberg, Birkhaeuser, 1984.

OF KNOWLEDGE, WONDER, AND WORLD PEACE was originally published in *Technology Review,* volume 85, number 4, May–June 1982.

THE DOUBLE-EDGED SWORD CALLED TECHNOLOGY is an expanded version of an article originally published in the *Bulletin of the Atomic Scientists,* April 1980.

THOUGHTS OF A HITLER REFUGEE was originally delivered as a speech for the Fiftieth Anniversary Convocation of the University in Exile, New York, 1984.

FORTY YEARS AFTER: THOUGHTS OF A NUCLEAR WITNESS was written for this collection. A shortened version appeared in the *Miami Herald,* August 4, 1985.

Index

About the Author

Dr. Victor F. Weisskopf, Institute Professor Emeritus and Professor of Physics Emeritus at the Massachusetts Institute of Technology, is regarded as one of the great men of physics.

Widely noted for his theoretical work in quantum electrodynamics, the structure of the atomic nucleus, and elementary particle physics; he has also taken a leading role in explaining science and its role in society to the public. In the years since World War II, he has been an outspoken advocate of arms control and has warned repeatedly of the growing danger of nuclear war.

Dr. Weisskopf was director-general from 1961 to 1966 of the European Center for Nuclear Research (CERN) in Geneva, Switzerland. From 1967 to 1973 he was head of the department of physics at MIT, where he was a major force in the development of physics research. Dr. Weisskopf formally retired from MIT in 1974, but remained active as senior lecturer in the department of physics.

Dr. Weisskopf once told an interviewer that he had come out of the "golden age" of physics, when European scientists in the 1920s created a new picture of how the world behaved at the atomic level. In 1943 he joined the Manhattan Project at Los Alamos, where he worked on the atom bomb project. He was first appointed to the physics department at MIT in 1945.

Dr. Weisskopf has written hundreds of scientific articles and several books. His text, *Theoretical Nuclear Physics* (co-authored with John M. Blatt) is probably the most widely-used book on that subject. He is also author of *Knowledge and Wonder: The Natural World as Man Knows It; Physics in the Twentieth Century;* and *Concepts of Particle Physics.* He is also the recipient of many international awards and honorary degrees including the National Medal of Science.